THE COMPLETE GUIDE TO
KITCHENS

Design, Plan & Install
a Dream Kitchen

CREATIVE
PUBLISHING
international

CHANHASSEN, MINNESOTA

www.creativepub.com

Contents

Copyright © 2004
Creative Publishing international, Inc.
18705 Lake Drive East
Chanhassen, Minnesota 55317
1-800-328-3895
www.creativepub.com
All rights reserved

Printed on American paper by: R. R. Donnelley

10 9 8 7 6 5 4 3 2

President/CEO: Ken Fund
Vice President/Publisher: Linda Ball
Vice President/Retail Sales & Marketing: Kevin Haas

Executive Editor: Bryan Trandem
Creative Director: Tim Himsel
Managing Editor: Michelle Skudlarek
Editorial Director: Jerri Farris

Lead Editor: Karen Ruth
Copy Editor: Barbara Harold
Art Directors: Tim Himsel, Kari Johnston
Mac Designers: Dave Schelitzche, Jon Simpson
Technical Illustrator: Earl Slack
Project Manager: Tracy Stanley
Photo Researcher: Julie Caruso
Studio Services Manager: Jeanette Moss McCurdy
Photographer: Tate Carlson
Scene Shop Carpenter: Randy Austin
Director of Production Services: Kim Gerber
Production Manager: Stasia Dorn

THE COMPLETE GUIDE TO KITCHENS
Created by: The Editors of Creative Publishing international, Inc.,
in cooperation with Black & Decker. Black & Decker is a trademark
of The Black & Decker Corporation and is used under license.

Library of Congress
Cataloging-in-Publication Data
on file

ISBN 1-58923-138-4 (soft cover)

Portions of *The Complete Guide to Kitchens*
are taken from the Black & Decker® books
*Advanced Home Wiring; Advanced Home
Plumbing; Remodeling Kitchens; Customizing
Your Home.* Other titles from Creative Publishing
international include:
*The New Everyday Home Repairs; Basic Wiring
& Electrical Repairs; Carpentry: Remodeling;
Building Decks; Home Masonry Projects &
Repairs; Workshop Tips & Techniques; Home
Plumbing Projects & Repairs; Exterior Home
Repair & Projects; Advanced Deck Building;
Bathroom Remodeling; Built-in Projects for
the Home; Landscape Design & Construction;
Refinishing & Finishing Wood; Building
Porches & Patios; Flooring Projects & Tech-
niques; Finishing Basements & Attics;
Stonework & Masonry Projects; Sheds,*

*Gazebos & Outbuildings; Building & Finishing
Walls & Ceilings; The Complete Guide to
Home Plumbing; The Complete Guide to
Home Wiring; The Complete Guide to Build-
ing Decks; The Complete Guide to Painting &
Decorating; The Complete Guide to Creative
Landscapes; The Complete Guide to Home
Masonry; The Complete Guide to Home
Carpentry; The Complete Guide to Home
Storage; The Complete Guide to Bathrooms;
The Complete Guide to Easy Woodworking
Projects; The Complete Guide to Flooring;
The Complete Guide to Ceramic & Stone
Tile; The Complete Guide to Roofing & Siding;
The Complete Photo Guide to Home Repair;
The Complete Photo Guide to Home Im-
provement; The Complete Photo Guide to
Outdoor Home Improvement.*

INTRODUCTION

The kitchen is so often referred to as the heart of the home that it seems trite to repeat that notion one more time. However, there is a great deal of truth behind it. We all spend a sizable chunk of time in the kitchen—not just cooking and eating, but also entertaining, socializing and running our households.

The ideal kitchen serves all these needs well. It is spacious, well organized and well lit. Unfortunately, many real kitchens are cramped, poorly designed and badly lit—which is probably why you are reading this book.

Kitchens in older homes reflect a time when built-in cabinets were not standard, pantries, larders and ice chests stored foods, and tables did double duty as work surfaces and eating and gathering places. Mid-century kitchens feature built-in cabinets and spaces for modern appliances, but often lack proper task lighting and a place for casual meals. Along the way, most kitchens have been remodeled to fit the current owners' needs, and even contemporary kitchens need makeovers and upgrades.

This is exactly where this book enters the picture. You like your kitchen, but wish it weren't so dark. You love your kitchen, but with the kids it is getting cramped. You like the charm of your old house, but hate the tiny galley kitchen. All these and a million more factors give you reason for sprucing up, fixing up, reconfiguring, or tearing out and starting over.

The Complete Guide to Kitchens is the place to start regardless of where you are on the kitchen frustration continuum. In this book we cover a multitude of basic ways to make your kitchen brighter and easier to use—from painting the walls, refacing the cabinets and updating the lighting to raising the dishwasher, installing pop-up shelves and building booth seating.

We also cover more advanced kitchen makeovers, such as installing cabinets and countertops, removing and installing floor surfaces, and wiring new light fixtures. These are all projects that can be done by do-it-yourselfers with moderate skills.

If that is not enough, we have included an overview section on tearing your kitchen down to the studs, plumbing a kitchen island, creating new electrical circuits and adding windows and doors. These projects are for the serious home remodeler. But the information given will also be important if you decide to pay someone else to do the work. If you understand the steps involved, you will be better informed when it comes time to make decisions or evaluate costs.

Throughout the book, information boxes give you pointers on universal design, which makes space more usable, and green design, which is more environmentally friendly. Shopping tips clue you in on features to look for. Photographs from manufacturers, designers and builders show you what is new and trendy as well as what is tried and true.

NOTICE TO READERS

For safety, use caution, care and good judgment when following the procedures described in this book. The Publisher and Black & Decker cannot assume responsibility for any damage to property or injury to persons as a result of misuse of the information provided.

The techniques shown in this book are general techniques for various applications. In some instances, additional techniques not shown in this book may be required. Always follow manufacturers' instructions included with products, since deviating from the directions may void warranties. The projects in this book vary widely as to skill levels required: some may not be appropriate for all do-it-yourselfers, and some may require professional help.

Consult your local Building Department for information on building permits, codes and other laws as they apply to your project.

This large, rustic kitchen is full of texture from the stone fireplace and aged beams to the turned wood sink supports. Painted designs make the otherwise flat fridge panels appear textured as well.

(above) **Sleek, smooth** and polished surfaces were chosen for this moderate-sized contemporary kitchen.

(left) **This galley** kitchen, though small, hosts a professional-grade stove and refrigerator. The beautifully stained cabinets lend a feeling of warmth to this cozy space.

Photo courtesy of Mill's Pride

Photo courtesy of Armstrong World Industries, Inc.

(above) **This classic** carries on the long-standing tradition of using white in the kitchen. Darker walls and floors soften the white so it is not stark or blinding. Matching appliances blend in for a uniform look.

(right) **Bright colors** add warmth to a space that might otherwise appear industrial with its stainless steel appliances and concrete floor.

Blues and grays keep this kitchen looking cool and soften the contrast between stainless steel and black granite.

(left) **A kitchen island** can be as simple as this worktable with shelves and drawers.

(right) **This multi-purpose** island holds the sink, cutting board and cabinets as well as providing seating.

(below) **Islands styled to look like furniture** are very popular. Here, the island houses the sink. Bar stools make this fixed island into a great place to sit and watch the chef.

DESIGNING & PLANNING

Where to start? That's a key question in any remodeling project, but with kitchens you are confronted with extra layers of decision making. This is because the kitchen is such a condensed working space with so many surface, fixture and appliance options to consider. Because of the longevity and expense of most kitchen items, making well-informed decisions can save an expensive heartache later.

All these layers may make a kitchen update or remodeling project seem a daunting task. But if you break it down into individual parts, it becomes much easier. This chapter introduces you to some of the aspects of kitchen remodeling, such as how to assess what your old kitchen has and what to consider for your updated kitchen.

Your dream kitchen may involve removing walls and adding an addition. This remodeling project opened the kitchen into a newly added family room, resulting in a large, airy space perfect for family time.

Getting Started

A crucial first step toward your future satisfaction is to carefully evaluate your present kitchen and determine what problems it has and what features are lacking. Creating a new kitchen that simply puts a new face on old problems may make you feel better for the moment, but it's ultimately a waste of time. If you take the time now to determine what features are necessary and appropriate for your new kitchen, this effort will pay big dividends in the end.

Your motives for remodeling your kitchen probably fall into one of two categories: efficiency or appearance. In other words, either your kitchen is inconvenient for your family to use, or you just don't like the way it looks. Or maybe it's both dysfunctional and ugly. A logical place to start, then, is by documenting the elements that need improvement.

Begin by simply taking the time to observe how you now use your kitchen. Keep a notepad handy and jot down any major or minor problems and annoyances that prevent you from being as efficient or comfortable as you'd like to be when cooking or eating. Also consider how your kitchen is used for special occasions and what issues arise at those times. Don't forget to make note of the positives. If you love having that window over your kitchen sink or the skinny cabinet next to the stove, jot those observations down as well.

(above) A corner pantry cabinet may be the answer to storage problems in a smaller kitchen. It provides plenty of storage without using up too much floor space.

(left) **New flooring** can add color and style to an older kitchen.

Once you have documented the problems with your kitchen, give your imagination permission to roam. Don't worry about money yet. This is your dream kitchen, after all, and there will be plenty of time to bring your fantasies down to earth as you begin the planning stages. Now is the time to consider every possibility. Look at friends' kitchens, at magazine kitchens and at model kitchens. When looking at photographs like the ones included in this book, or those in magazines, look at both the overall effect and the individual components. Don't let an odd color scheme scare you away from a faucet that you love. Use a file folder to collect pictures of kitchens or items you like.

If you've lived with a small kitchen for many

years, you may think of it as simply a work space in which to prepare meals, clean up dishes and store foods and utensils. As you brainstorm for kitchen ideas, remember that this room can serve many more functions, as well. If your kitchen has no eating area, consider changing the layout to add a cozy breakfast nook. If your home doesn't have a den or study, think about including a home office and study desk in your new kitchen.

Finally, consider how your kitchen will be used over the next five to twenty years. The needs of a family with young children are much different than the needs of a mature family whose children are about to leave the nest for college.

Looking at the Layout

Kitchen remodeling projects can be grouped into five levels, based on how much the room's layout will be changed. To determine the amount of change you need, ask yourself a few questions. Do you have enough space to prepare meals? How far apart are the refrigerator, range and sink from one another? Are there efficient and convenient pathways through the kitchen—or are other people always crossing your path as you work? Is there an adequate eating area or does the eating area block the flow of traffic through the room?

If you've identified problems with your layout or floor plan, ask yourself if they can be corrected simply by rearranging your existing kitchen. If not, explore how you might address them, perhaps by adding or moving doors, redirecting traffic or expanding the kitchen.

If your current needs are few, or you simply want a new look in your kitchen, you'll probably plan a Level 1 project—a relatively inexpensive cosmetic makeover, in which you simply redo the surfaces and make only minor changes to the layout and floor plan. This level is popular because the cost is relatively low and many homeowners can complete most of the work themselves.

On the other hand, if you would like to move the refrigerator over a few feet or put the sink closer to the range, you're thinking of a Level 2 project. Rearranging the whole kitchen? That's a Level 3. Level 4 often means knocking out an interior wall to expand the kitchen into an adjacent room, while Level 5 involves an expansion that requires a room addition. With each higher level, you're likely to need more professional help, but even a Level 5 job offers several tasks you might choose to do yourself, including managing the job.

Five Levels of Kitchen Remodeling

Level 1: The cosmetic makeover. Though relatively inexpensive, this option can be enormously rewarding. While retaining the same basic layout of the kitchen, you replace the flooring and, in some cases, the countertops. You'll also be repainting or installing new wallpaper, and may want to install new storage features in your cabinets. Appliances and fixtures are usually retained, unless their age and condition make replacement necessary. DIY cost: $2,000 to $10,000.

Level 2: Changing the layout.

With this option, you'll retain the same basic floor space as the existing kitchen, but will change the positions of the appliances, fixtures and eating areas to create a more efficient floor plan. This level of remodeling includes most elements of the cosmetic makeover, but may also require the work of a carpenter, electrician and plumber. Homeowners with ample do-it-yourself experience might choose to do most of this work themselves. DIY cost: $7,500 to $20,000.

Level 3: Redirecting traffic.

In a slightly more complicated scenario, you might find it necessary to change the layout more radically in order to redirect traffic moving through the kitchen. Often this means adding or moving a doorway in a partition wall, as well as redesigning the basic kitchen layout. Unless you are a very experienced do-it-yourselfer, much of this work will require the help of a carpenter and other subcontractors. At this fairly extensive level of remodeling, many homeowners also take the opportunity to add new windows, patio doors and skylights. DIY cost: $15,000 to $40,000.

Level 4: Expanding inward.

If your present kitchen just isn't large enough to accommodate your needs, one option is to extend the space by borrowing space from adjacent rooms. This generally means that interior partition walls will need to be removed or moved, which is work for an experienced home construction carpenter. This level of remodeling often includes significant rearrangement of the appliances and cabinets, as well as the installation of new windows, doors or skylights. In a major remodeling project of this kind, some homeowners may want to hire professional contractors for some of the work. DIY cost: $30,000 to $50,000.

Level 5: Expanding outward.

This is the Cadillac of kitchen remodeling possibilities, as big as it gets. If you find more space essential and can't expand inward into adjoining rooms, then the last option is to build an addition onto your home. This ambitious undertaking requires the aid of virtually the same collection of professionals it takes to build a home from scratch: architects and engineers, excavation and concrete contractors, construction and finish carpenters, plumbers and electricians. At this level, some homeowners choose to hire a general contractor to manage the project. Typical cost: $50,000 and up.

Kitchen Elements

The following overview of kitchen elements will help you assess your needs and desires for each area.

Floor, Walls & Ceiling

Your kitchen walls, floor and ceiling provide the backdrop for all the other elements of the room. Sometimes all a kitchen needs is a fresh coat of paint or a new wallcovering to give it an updated appearance. Installing new flooring is also an excellent way to transform a kitchen, since the floor is usually the largest surface in the room.

If you plan to add beautiful new appliances, counters or cabinets, it's almost always worthwhile to make sure the old surfaces won't look dull in comparison. You may want to replace the

old surface coverings, or simply renew them.

Kitchen ceilings are generally given a fresh coat of paint whenever the walls are refinished, but you may also want to add a bead-board, paneled or tin ceiling.

Countertops & Work Areas

Countertops are one of the most important visual elements of a kitchen, and replacing an outdated, worn or unattractive surface is a common kitchen remodeling project.

Increasing available countertop space is a top priority, since a kitchen's primary function is meal preparation. Evaluate your countertops and work areas by asking yourself the following questions: Is there enough space to perform kitchen tasks? Are two or more people able to work at the same time without bumping into one another? Is there enough countertop work space

(left) **Raising an existing cabinet** provides more usable counter space. Or, if you are replacing cabinets, consider varying the heights and sizes to maximize features.

(below) **Mounting a microwave** below the counter frees up valuable counter space.

Photo courtesy of Asko

Photo (left) courtesy of Mill's Pride

Photo courtesy of Mill's Pride

(above) **Distinctive hardware** gives your kitchen a unique flair. New hardware can be a quick pick-me-up for older cabinets.

(left) **Slide-out shelves** can solve kitchen storage problems by making a greater portion of a cabinet accessible.

around the sink, cooktop, oven and refrigerator? Is there at least one long, uninterrupted countertop where you can assemble meals and prepare recipes? Or, do you have the rarer problem of too much counter space, so that the sink, stove and refrigerator are too far apart to use efficiently?

In some cases, the problem isn't really a lack of counter space; it's a lack of storage space that results in cluttered counters. If small appliances are taking up too much work space on your countertops, consider installing a cabinet that's specially designed to store these items.

If you determine that you don't have enough counter space in the right locations, ask yourself if the problem can be remedied by rearrangement. If not, or if you clearly don't have enough room to work, consider adding to the size of your kitchen with a room expansion.

Cabinets & Storage

Resurfacing or replacing kitchen cabinets is another relatively simple way to make a kitchen look brand new. If the problem with your existing cabinets is more than cosmetic, determine if you can solve it by organizing the cabinets more efficiently or by adding shelves. If not, you may need to completely redesign your cabinetry or expand your kitchen to add more storage space. If you have more cabinet space than you need, consider replacing some cabinets with a countertop desk area or a built-in appliance, such as a microwave oven.

To assess the changes your cabinets might need, ask yourself: Does the kitchen have adequate storage space for all the food, dishes and utensils? Are the food, tools and equipment stored near their points of first use? Are the frequently used items stored within easy reach, 2½ to 5 feet above the floor? Also, is all of the space, including the corners and the spaces above appliances, being used well?

Appliances & Fixtures

Replacing sinks and faucets can give your kitchen's appearance an upgrade as well as improve convenience and efficiency. Newer faucets and sinks have easy-clean finishes and many advanced features.

Think about your major appliances. Are any of them more than fifteen years old? If so, they're probably at the end of their useful lives and should be replaced during your remodeling project. Even if your appliances are not old, it may still be worthwhile to upgrade them. During your planning process, research current models to determine if an investment in more energy-efficient appliances would save you money in the long run.

In addition to upgrading larger appliances, consider adding smaller appliances such as a water purifier or on-demand water heater, warming drawers, a cabinet-mounted microwave, and built-in stereo, computer or television units.

Lighting, Electrical & Ventilation

Simply replacing outdated fixtures with new ones is a lighting project that can dramatically improve the appearance of a kitchen. In most cases, this is a small job that doesn't require rewiring.

Insufficient lighting is a common problem in kitchens, especially task lighting for work areas. WIthout it, you're typically working in your own shadow. Poor task lighting can be improved by adding recessed ceiling lights, track lighting or under-cabinet light fixtures. Poor ambient lighting can be remedied by adding light fixtures, skylights or windows.

Do you blow a fuse or trip a circuit breaker every time you turn on the toaster and the coffee maker at the same time? If you have a typical older kitchen, you probably don't have enough amperage or electrical circuits to power all your appliances. The time to address this problem is during remodeling.

Many kitchens have inadequate ventilation. Older kitchens may have no vent hood at all, while some kitchens have a recirculating vent hood rather than the preferred outdoor venting. With today's houses being more airtight, venting kitchen odors and moisture is an important consideration.

A colorful border in this white kitchen draws the eye upward and balances the weight of the dark-colored floor.

Photo courtesy of Progressive Lighting, opposite photo courtesy of Wolf Appliance Company, LLC.

Above- and under-cabinet lighting can dramatically improve the appearance and usefulness of your kitchen.

Professional-grade appliances and marble or granite work surfaces may be the dream kitchen for a serious home chef.

CABINETS

*Y*ears ago the built-in kitchen cabinet was rare. Food was stored in pantries and freestanding cupboards such as Hoosiers, and plates and silver resided in chests or on shelves. Today you rarely see a kitchen without built-in cabinets.

If your cabinets are dated, marred or too dark, you might want to paint or reface them. This chapter has information on how to perform these updates. These relatively inexpensive measures can have dramatic results in changing the look and feel of a kitchen.

You may decide that you need new cabinets. Though installing cabinets yourself may seem like a daunting task, it actually is made up of easy to moderately difficult do-it-yourself steps. We cover each step with clear directions and photographs in this chapter.

You may want to modify the cabinets you have to be more usable or accessible. The section on pull-down and pop-up shelves shows you how to install these convenient amenities.

Also covered in this chapter is information on cabinet styles and features, factors to consider for design and layout of new cabinet installations, and issues of universal design and green design.

Photo courtesy of SieMatic Corporation

Cabinet Options

When purchasing cabinets, you have a number of decisions to make. First you need to decide if you want to go with stock, semi-custom or custom cabinets. Then you need to choose between face frame or frameless styles. Materials, door and drawer styles, and finishes must also be decided upon. And finally, you'll need to consider the wide range of specialty features, add-ons and hardware available.

Cabinets are generally divided into three categories: stock, semi-custom and custom. Stock cabinets and some semi-custom cabinets are available for homeowners to install themselves; custom cabinets are invariably installed by the fabricator or designated installer.

Stock

Stock cabinets are available as either ready-to-assemble (RTA) or ready-to-install. Ready-to-assemble cabinets, also referred to as knock-down or flat-pack, are shipped as flat components that the consumer puts together using connecting hardware.

In other words, in addition to installing the cabinets, you have to assemble them. Your options will be limited if you chose RTA cabinets, but because many of them are created by European designers, you will be able to achieve a slightly different look than the standard American stock cabinet. Be aware that some RTA cabinets are made with low-quality materials—½" particleboard and plastic veneer for example. But, just because a cabinet is shipped flat, that does not necessarily mean it is poorly constructed. It certainly pays to carefully inspect samples of assembled cabinets to check material quality and engineering quality. If possible, also look at assembly directions to check for clarity.

Ready-to-install cabinets are available in a number of quality levels, from utility units suitable for workshop or weekend home use, to good-quality, long-lasting kitchen classics. Standard stock cabinets range from 6" to 42" wide, in 3" increments. Most sizes are readily available, though they may need to be shipped from a warehouse. Also available with stock cabinets are filler strips and trim moldings.

Semi-custom

Semi-custom cabinets are also factory-made to standard sizes, but they offer far more options in

Face-frame cabinets with overlay doors have a slightly more traditional look than frameless cabinets.

finish, size, features and materials than stock cabinets. These are typically sold in showrooms, and are priced between stock and custom cabinets. Semi-custom is the best choice for homeowners who want better-quality cabinets with some special features but don't want to pay the high prices for a custom product. You should allow three to eight weeks lead time when ordering semi-custom cabinets.

Custom

Custom cabinets offer the most in terms of options. These cabinets are designed, built and installed to fit a unique space. It is wise to shop around before settling on a custom cabinetmaker, as price, quality and availability will vary widely. The minimum lead time for custom cabinet construction is six weeks in most markets. When you get bids, find out if the lead time is from acceptance of the bid, or from when the condition of the kitchen allows the cabinetmaker to take accurate measurements. Remember that exotic or difficult-to-machine materials and radically different styles will end up costing you more.

Framed & Frameless

Once you have decided whether you will be purchasing factory-made or custom cabinets, you (above) **Modular, furniture-style cabinetry** is popular in European kitchens. Most items are available as ready-to-assemble kits.

(right) **Face-frame cabinets** with flush-fitting drawers and doors require precise craftsmanship and are available only on custom cabinets.

need to decide which type of cabinet: face-frame or frameless.

Face-frame cabinets have frames made of solid wood around the front of the cabinet box, or carcass. Because the frame extends into cabinet space, the doors openings will be reduced and a certain amount of "dead" space exists within the cabinet behind the frames. The hinges for doors on face-frame cabinets mount on the frame. The door itself may be flush within the frame or raised above it. Flush-fitting doors were common on older cabinets, but because they require a precise fit, which means more time and craftsmanship, they will be more expensive and more difficult to find.

Frameless cabinets are often referred to as "Eurostyle." These cabinets do not have a face frame and the doors and drawers span the entire width of the carcass, which allows for easier access and somewhat more storage space. The doors are mounted using cup hinges, which are invisible when the doors are closed. Frameless cabinets have a somewhat "cleaner" look, which makes them a more contemporary style. One drawback of frameless cabinets is that they do not have the added strength of the face frame, so it is critical that they are solidly constructed and installed properly.

Materials

Most cabinet carcasses are now made using engineered wood products such as plywood, particleboard and medium-density fiberboard (MDF), and are veneered or laminated. These products are more dimensionally stable than solid wood, use fewer resources and are less expensive. Doors, drawer fronts and drawer bodies may be made from solid wood or engineered wood.

Plywood carcasses should be ⅜" to ½" thick and particleboard should be ⅝" to ¾" thick. The thicker the material, the stiffer and more sturdy the cabinet. A drawback of particleboard and fiberboard is that the cabinets can be quite heavy, which makes do-it-yourself installation a bit trickier.

Ideally, drawers should have solid wood or plywood sides (½" to ¾" thick) and plywood bottoms (¼" to ⅜" thick), with rabbeted, doweled or dovetailed joints. Beware of any drawer joints that are fastened only with staples or nails—these joints will not hold up to the constant pulling and pushing a drawer receives. Drawers or pull-out shelves for heavy appliances, cast-iron pots, or pottery will need to be sturdier.

Drawer glides can be side-mounted or under-mounted and extend either three-quarters, seven-eighths, or the full length of the drawer. Over-extending glides are also available and are handy for drawers located under counters with a deep overhang or drawers that store larger items. Drawer glides at minimum should be steel ball bearings, with a 75-pound rating.

Shelves should be made of plywood, with both faces and sides veneered. Particleboard shelves are more common, but particleboard, MDF and solid wood shelves will bow under the weight of dishes and appliances. Appropriate thicknesses of particleboard shelves for heavy use can be cumbersome and cut into available storage space. If you have glass-fronted cabinets, glass shelves are required.

Photo courtesy of Dura Supreme, right photo courtesy of Mill's Pride

(above) **Engineered wood products** can easily be molded into rounded forms like these end cabinets. The corner cabinet with tambour door is a great space saver.

(right, above) **Stainless steel cabinets** give a sleek, industrial look to a kitchen. Metal kitchen cabinets used to be inexpensive and common, but are now a high-end option.

(right, below) **Cabinet sizes and shapes** are available to fit any kitchen configuration. This kitchen uses flanking pantry cabinets to create the look of a built-in buffet.

A cabinet door cannot be a solid slab of wood because of wood's susceptibility to humidity. The slab doors common with frameless cabinets are actually plywood or fiberboard covered with veneer, laminate or melamine. High-pressure laminate is preferred to melamine. Most other door styles consist of a frame and panel. The frame is usually solid wood, and the panel will either be veneered plywood, if it is flat style, or solid wood if it is raised style. Though veneering technology can now apply veneer to raised panels, any raised-panel door will be more expensive than a flat-panel door. Doors can have glass or a variety of other materials from fabric, to wire mesh, to decorative metal fronts instead of wood panels.

Photo courtesy of SieMatic Corporation

Doors and drawer fronts are available in many styles made from a variety of woods with many finish options. If you are not a fan of woodgrain, another option is the "foil" clad door. These have the look of a raised-panel door, but are made of medium-density fiberboard coated with a durable vinyl material.

The door style, material and finish will be a major factor in determining the cost of your cabinets. The least expensive cabinets are the frameless style with a flat-slab door or a flat-panel door. Picture frame, cathedral, raised-panel, slatted and glass with individual panes all are more expensive door options.

Hardware

Your cabinet hardware—the door and drawer pulls and hinges—is another way to customize the look of your kitchen. With eclectic styling becoming more and more acceptable, it is fine to have a few decorative pulls mixed in with basic, less-expensive versions. Many cast-metal or handmade ceramic pulls are available. Though not having drawer and door pulls is common, it can mean that cabinets get dirtier.

Hinges may be fully concealed or semi-concealed on face-frame cabinets, but frameless cabinets always have concealed hinges. One

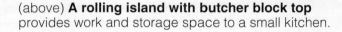

(above) **A rolling island with butcher block top** provides work and storage space to a small kitchen.

(left) **Glass-front cabinets add display space** for these face-frame cabinets.

(right) **Full-length, roll-out shelving** is available in many widths and can be used as pantry or cabinet space.

area not to skimp on with concealed hinges is their adjustability. Ideally they should have side, height and depth adjustments. No-mortise hinges for semi-concealed hinges reduce labor because they mount on top of the cabinet and door surface with no need for cutting mortises.

UNIVERSAL DESIGN

Making kitchen cabinets accessible to wheel-chair users involves incorporating open, roll-in space in the base cabinets so that sink, cooktop and countertops are accessible. Roll-in cabinets have no bottom or toe kick. The roll-in space can be concealed with a fold-away door. All other base cabinets should be modified to have an 8" toe kick. If upper cabinets are used, they need to have pull-down shelving. Base cabinets with pull-out shelves and pantries with lazy Susans are the best storage options.

Above photo courtesy of Mill's Pride

GREEN DESIGN

Kitchen cabinet cases are usually constructed of engineered wood. Many of these products are manufactured using urea formaldehyde resin. To lower levels of formaldehyde in your home, look for low-emission or formaldehyde-free medium-density fiberboard (MDF) or exterior-grade plywood. To eliminate formaldehyde, order custom cabinets made of solid wood from sustainable sources or install metal cabinets. Water-based finishes, wax or hand-rubbed oil finishes produce fewer air pollutants at the factory and in your home.

Look for cabinet manufacturers using suppliers who adhere to the Forestry Stewardship Council or the Sustainable Forestry Initiative's protocols for timber supply. This is especially important if you are choosing tropical woods for your cabinets.

Check your local salvage company for cabinets—and donate your old ones to a reuse center.

Stock cabinets are available in a wide range of sizes. Door, drawer front and finish options allow you to create the look you desire while still being budget conscious.

Standard Stock Cabinet Sizes

Base cabinets (without countertop)
Height   34½"
Depth   24"
Width   6" to 42", in 3" increments

Wall cabinets
Height   12", 15", 18", 24", 30", 36"
Depth   12"
Width   6" to 36", in 3" increments

Oven cabinets
Height   83", 95"
Depth   24"
Width   30", 33"

Pantry cabinets
Height   83", 95"
Depth   24"
Width   18", 24"

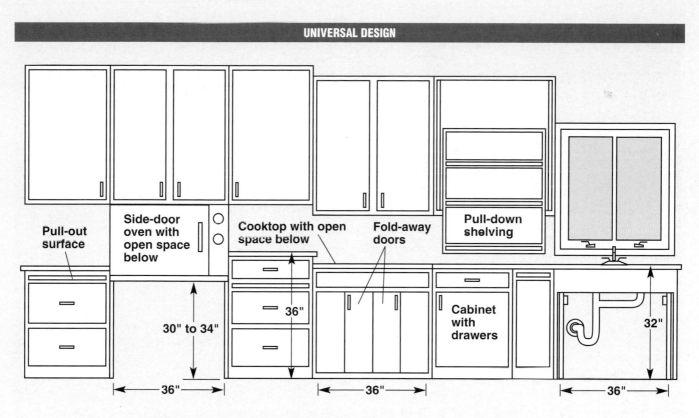

Pull-out surface

Side-door oven with open space below

Cooktop with open space below

Fold-away doors

Pull-down shelving

30" to 34"

36"

36"

Cabinet with drawers

32"

36"

36"

36"

Note: the arrangement of elements does not reflect an actual layout.

Universal design for kitchen cabinets puts the majority of items in the comfortable reach zone between 2 and 5 feet above the floor. Using pop-up and pull-down shelves can extend this area.

Full-extension hardware on drawers and pull-out shelves eliminates reaching and fumbling for unseen items at the back of drawers and cabinets. Base cabinets installed at various heights serve users of different heights.

Hanging some sections of upper cabinets at 12" to 15" above the countertop, rather than 18", makes it easier to see and access items. A full-length pantry also increases the amount of stor-

age space in the comfortable reach zone.

A pull-out pantry allows for easier viewing of the contents. Make sure the hardware is top quality and operates easily and smoothly.

An appliance garage, a cabinet with a tambour door that sits on the countertop, is an excellent way to efficiently use corner space and store heavy or frequently used appliances out of sight. Make sure an electrical outlet or two are inside the garage.

Magnetic touch latches or C-shaped handles are the easiest to open.

Avoid gloss cabinet finishes to reduce glare.

Framed cabinets have openings that are completely surrounded by face frames made of vertical stiles and horizontal rails. They give kitchens a traditional look.

Frameless cabinets, sometimes called "European-style," are more contemporary. Because they have no face frames, frameless cabinets offer slightly more storage space than framed cabinets. The doors and drawers on frameless cabinets cover the entire unit.

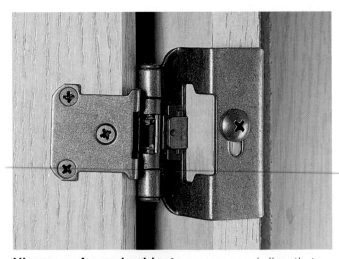

Hinges on framed cabinets are screwed directly to the face frames. Better cabinets have adjustable hinges that allow door realignment.

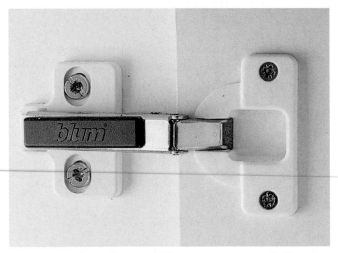

Hinges on frameless cabinets are screwed directly to the inside of the cabinet, eliminating the need for face frames. Hinges are hidden, providing a cleaner look.

Selecting New Cabinets

You can buy cabinets at home centers, cabinet showrooms and through custom cabinet shops. If you are working with a kitchen designer, she or he will help you with every step of your cabinet purchase. Home centers and showrooms have designers on staff who will take your kitchen dimensions and create a computer-generated plan and shopping list based on your requests. If you want to do this step yourself, create a kitchen floor plan and use the manufacturer's specification booklet, which lists all available cabinets and dimensions, to create your layout.

All cabinet manufacturers offer a selection of specialty cabinets, storage accessories and decorative trim. Check manufacturers' product-line catalogs for complete listings of available cabinets and accessories.

Cabinets can be purchased as "ready to assemble" or RTA. These cabinets must be assembled before installation. They are available in a number of styles and quality levels.

SHOPPING TIPS

- *Cabinet depth for uppers is typically 12"; make sure that your dinner plates will fit.*

- *Glass-doored cabinets should have glass shelves and cabinet interiors finished in the same way as the exteriors.*

- *Cabinets with thinner walls are easier to rack (twist) when they are shimmed, making installation more difficult.*

- *Avoid cabinets made with particleboard, staples and hot glue.*

- *Separate end and back panels with matching finishes are available for base cabinets, pantry cabinets and built-in refrigerators.*

- *Look for varnish rather than lacquer finishes. It is more durable for kitchen use.*

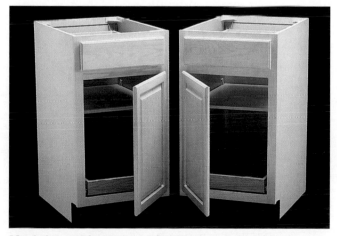

Modular cabinets have finished panels on both sides. Doors can be reversed to open from either left or right. Modular cabinets can be arranged to fit any kitchen layout. These cabinets are easy for do-it-yourself installation because no additional end panels are needed.

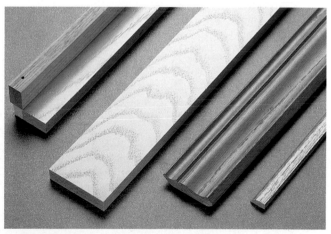

Prefinished trim pieces match the finish of stock and semi-custom cabinets. Filler strips are used in spaces between cabinets, or between a cabinet and wall or appliance. Small trim moldings cover gaps between cabinet edges and walls.

Painting Cabinets

If your current cabinets are in good shape and you are happy with their configuration but not their appearance, a coat of paint can dramatically change their looks. You can brighten dark wood, freshen up already painted surfaces or create a new look with faux finish techniques. Any wood, metal and previously painted cabinets can be painted.

As with any painting project, your final results depend on careful and thorough preparation and use of high-quality products. Removing doors, drawers and all hardware, and painting doors and drawer fronts as horizontal flat surfaces will eliminate many drips and sags.

Choose a high-quality enamel paint in either satin, low-luster or semi-gloss finish. A high gloss finish will highlight surface defects and create glare. Latex paint is suitable for this project. Using an alkyd (oil-based) paint may result in a smoother finish with fewer brush marks,

but the cleanup is more involved and the fumes make it necessary to use a respirator.

Previously painted and varnished cabinets need to be washed with trisodium phosphate or other degreaser, sanded or chemically deglossed, before painting. Varnished cabinets need an undercoat of primer to ensure good adhesion of the top coat. If the previous paint was dark or a highly saturated color, or bare wood has been exposed, an undercoat is also necessary. Do not spot-prime because the top coat will not cover evenly in those areas. Avoid applying two layers of top coat, but if you do, make sure to sand or degloss the first coat to get good adhesion of the second coat.

If you are also changing hardware, determine whether you will be using the same screw holes. If not, fill the existing holes with wood putty before sanding.

• *Always buy the highest quality brush.*

• *Use synthetic-bristle brushes for latex paint. Look for soft, flagged tips.*

• *Natural-bristle brushes should only be used for oil-based paints.*

• *Use a nylon brush for fine work.*

• *An angled, or sash, brush gives you more control.*

Tools and Materials

Tools: screwdriver, hand sander, brushes.

Materials: TSP or other degreaser, sandpaper, masking tape, primer, enamel paint.

1 Remove doors and drawers. Wash all surfaces to be painted with TSP or other degreaser. Scrape off any loose paint. Sand or chemically degloss all surfaces. Wipe away sanding dust and prime varnished surfaces, dark colors or bare wood with undercoat.

2 Remove shelves if possible and paint interiors first, in this order: 1) back walls, 2) tops, 3) sides, 4) bottoms. Paint bottoms, tops and edges of shelves last.

3 Paint both sides of doors beginning with inner surfaces. With panel doors, paint in this order: 1) recessed panels, 2) horizontal rails, 3) vertical stiles.

Refacing cabinet boxes and replacing doors and drawer fronts can dramatically change the look of your kitchen.

Refacing Cabinets

Refacing involves new veneer for resurfacing face frames and sides, plus new doors and drawer fronts for a dramatic change in style. Replacing hinges and hardware completes the update. Flat panel doors on contemporary frameless cabinets can be reveneered as well.

SHOPPING TIPS

• *Find refacing kits on the Internet or at woodworking stores.*

• *Refacing kits, doors and drawers are available in a wide range of styles and quality levels.*

Tools and Materials

Tools: utility knife, straightedge, combination square, handsaw, drill, cordless screwdriver, wallcovering roller, paint scraper.

Materials: refacing kit, stain and polyurethane finish (for unfinished refacing materials), cabinet hardware, 100- and 150-grit sandpaper.

How to Reface Cabinets

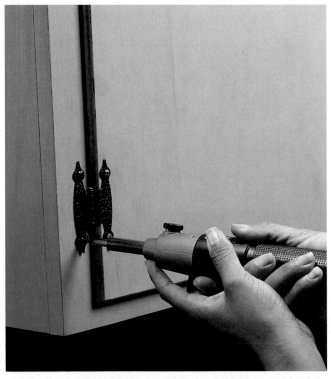

1 Remove the old doors, hinges, catches, and other hardware. Paint interior of cabinets, if desired (pages 34 to 35).

2 Scrape any loose or peeling finish. Fill any holes and chips with latex wood patch. Let dry, then lightly sand cabinet sides, faces and edges with 150-grit sandpaper.

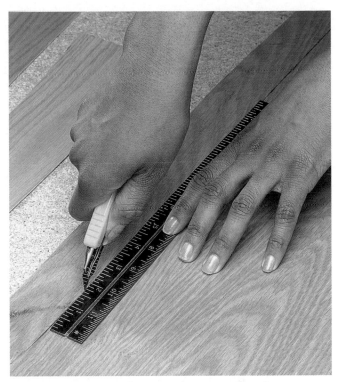

3 Remove veneer from package and lay flat on a smooth surface. Measure each surface to be covered, and add ¼" for overlap. Cut veneer pieces with utility knife and straightedge.

4 Apply veneer to vertical frame members first. Peel veneer backing off to reveal one corner of adhesive. Align veneer and press lightly to adhere corner. Gradually remove the backing, and smooth out air bubbles with fingertips. Trim excess veneer with a utility knife.

5 Apply veneer to horizontal frame members, overlapping vertical frame member. Trim excess with utility knife, using a straightedge as a guide. Apply veneer to cabinet sides, and trim excess with a utility knife.

(continued next page)

6 Bond veneer by rolling entire surface with a wall-covering roller.

7 Stain the new doors and drawer fronts, if they are unfinished. Stain unfinished veneer to match. Apply three coats of polyurethane finish, sanding lightly with 150-grit sandpaper between coats.

8 Lock a combination square at 2" mark. Use square to position hinges an equal distance from top and bottom of door. Use a finish nail or awl to mark screw locations.

9 Drill pilot holes and attach the hinges with screws. Mount knobs, handles and catches. A cordless screwdriver speeds up this job.

10 Attach cabinet doors to frames. Make sure doors overlap openings by an equal amount on all sides. Allow ⅛" gap between doors that cover a single opening.

11 Saw off all overhanging edges of existing solid (one-piece) drawer fronts. If drawer fronts are two-piece, remove screws and discard decorative face panel.

12 Attach new fronts by drilling pilot holes and driving screws through inside of drawers into new drawer fronts. Make sure drawer fronts overlap drawers by an equal margin on all sides.

13 Attach false drawer fronts on sink and cooktop cabinets by cutting wood blocks to span the drawer openings. Place blocks across openings on inside of cabinets. Fasten by driving screws through wood blocks into false fronts.

Swing-up, Glide-out & Pull-down Shelves

Customize your kitchen storage with swing-up, glide-out and pull-down shelves.

Incorporate heavy-duty, swing-up shelves to bring base-cabinet items like stand mixers to the counter-top. Build your own full-extension, glide-out shelves to divide larger spaces into two or more shelves and reduce bending and reaching for wheelchair users and people with back problems. Choose pull-down shelf accessories to bring upper-cabinet items like spices within reach. When purchasing specialized hardware accessories, check load ratings, locking mechanisms, arc swings and clearance heights to be sure they can support the items you want to store and they will fit in the intended location.

Installing Swing-up Shelves

Swing-up shelves are perfect for storing heavy appliances under the counter. Most swing arms are sold without the shelf surface, which must be purchased separately and cut to fit.

Take accurate measurements of your cabinet's interior dimensions, note any objects that protrude into the interior, and purchase the swing-up unit that is compatible with your cabinetry. Frameless cabinets often have fully concealed hinges that can interfere with swing mechanisms. Framed cabinets have a front perimeter face frame and may have hinges that interfere with lifting hardware.

Refer to the manufacturer's recommendations for the proper length of the shelf to ensure it will fit into the cabinet when the assembly is locked down and the door is closed. Cut the shelf from ¾"-thick plywood, MDF or melamine-coated particleboard. If the shelf is bare wood, finish all sides with a washable paint or varnish. For melamine-coated board, cover the cut edges with melamine tape to prevent water from damaging the wood core.

Tools and Materials

Tools: circular saw, tape measure, screwdriver.
Materials: shelving, 1 × 3 lumber, #8 machine screws.

How to Install a Swing-up Shelf

1 Carefully trigger the locking mechanism on each swing arm and set the arm in its fully extended position. Hold each arm against the inside face of the cabinet side and make sure the arm will clear the door hinge and/or the cabinet face frame. If the arms do not clear, you'll need to use wood spacers to allow the arms to clear the hinges or frames by at least ½". In most cases, one 1 × 3 spacer for each arm will provide enough clearance. Cut the spacers so they match the length of the mounting plate on the swing arms.

2 Mark the locations of the swing arm mounting plates onto the inside cabinet faces. Mount the swing arms with screws.

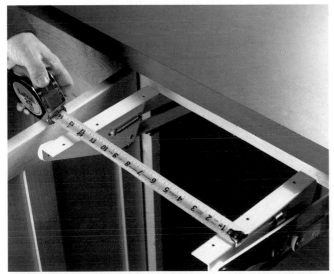

3 Unlock and rotate both swing arms so they are fully extended. Determine the width of the shelf by measuring across the swing arms, parallel to the countertop, and finding the distance between the outer edges of the shelf-mounting flanges (on the ends of the swing arms). Attach the shelf to the shelf-mounting flanges using #8 machine screws. Follow the manufacturer's instructions for shelf placement.

4 Fasten each locking bar to the bottom shelf face with the provided screws and plastic spacers to ensure the bars will slide smoothly. Test the locking bars' operation with the shelf in the extended and retracted positions, and make any necessary adjustments.

Installing Glide-out Shelves

Glide-out shelves make getting to the back of a base cabinet much easier. This project gives you directions for building the shelves and installing them. Before installing the shelves, carefully measure the items to be stored to truly customize your storage space.

To determine the proper size for the glide-out shelves, measure the inside dimensions of the cabinet and subtract the distance that hinges and face frames protrude into the interior of the cabinet. Then subtract 1" from the width for the two slides and tracks (½" each).

Tools and Materials

Tools: jig saw, router, hammer, clamps, drill, nail set, circular saw, straightedge, sander, level, screwdriver.

Materials: 4d finish nails, drawer guides (2), finishing materials, 1¼" utility screws, wood glue.

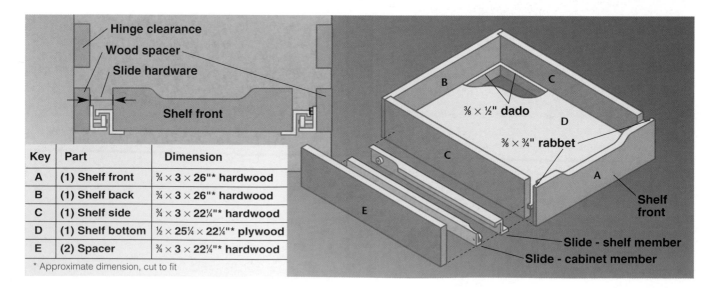

Key	Part	Dimension
A	(1) Shelf front	¾ × 3 × 26"* hardwood
B	(1) Shelf back	¾ × 3 × 26"* hardwood
C	(1) Shelf side	¾ × 3 × 22¼"* hardwood
D	(1) Shelf bottom	½ × 25¼ × 22¼"* plywood
E	(2) Spacer	¾ × 3 × 22¼"* hardwood

* Approximate dimension, cut to fit

How to Build & Install a Glide-out Shelf

½" dado

1 Rout a ⅜"-deep × ½"-wide dado groove into the front, back and side panels, ½" from the bottom edges, using a straightedge guide. Cut a ⅜"-deep × ¾"-wide rabbet groove across the inside faces of each end of the front and back pieces.

2 Spread glue onto the rabbets of the shelf fronts and attach the sides using three 4d finish nails to hold each joint. Countersink the nails with a nail set. Slide the bottom panels into the dado grooves, then glue and nail the back pieces in place. Clamp the shelves square, and allow the glue to dry.

3 Mount the glide-out rails to the bottom edges of the spacer strips. Then attach the spacers to the interior walls of the cabinet with 1¼" utility screws. Use a level to ensure the rails are installed properly. Screw a sliding rail to each side of the shelves, making sure that the bottom edges of the glides are flush against the bottom edges of the shelves. Install each shelf by aligning its sliding rails with the glides inside the cabinet and pushing it in completely. The rails will automatically lock into place.

Installing Pull-down Shelves

A pull-down shelf makes wall cabinets more user friendly by bringing all the contents down to eye level. Because of the space taken up by the mechanism and the shelf boxes, this is not a good project for a narrow cabinet.

Before you begin this project, hold each swing arm assembly against the inside face of the cabinet side and make sure both arms will clear the door hinge and the cabinet face frame. If the arms do not clear, add custom wood spacers of plywood or solid lumber that are at least as large as the swing arm mounting plates

Follow the manufacturer's specifications for the box dimensions, which will be based on the size of your cabinet. If the boxes are bare wood, lightly sand the edges and finish all sides with a highly washable paint or a clear varnish, such as polyurethane. For melamine-coated board, cover the cut edges with melamine tape, to keep water from damaging the wood core.

Note: The springs that help raise the arms are strong and may make it difficult to lower empty shelves. When the shelves are loaded, the weight of the items makes it easier move the shelf.

SHOPPING TIPS

• *Specialty hardware catalogs carry pull-down shelf hardware.*

• *Check that the capacity of the mechanism you are purchasing matches the items you will be storing on the shelf.*

Tools and Materials

Tools: tape measure, pencil, circular saw, drill, awl, hacksaw, Allen wrench.

Materials: swing-up shelf kit & hardware, ½" MDF, fasteners & finishing materials for shelf boxes, #8 pan-head screws, coarse-thread drywall screws, lumber for custom spacers.

How to Install a Pull-down Shelf

1 Using the manufacturer's paper template to determine the general positions of the swing arms, fasten the spacers to the inside faces of the cabinet sides with coarse-thread drywall screws. The screws should not go completely through the cabinet side.

2 Use the template to mark location of the swing arm mounting plates. Drill a small pilot hole at each awl mark. Fasten the swing arms to the custom spacers or cabinet sides with #8 pan-head screws (inset). The screws should not go completely through the cabinet side.

3 Build two shelf boxes from ½" MDF. Install the boxes between the sides of the shelf unit, using the predrilled holes in the side pieces. Secure the boxes with #8 pan-head screws. Because the lower box can be installed in only one position, install it first. Then, find the desired position for the upper box, and secure it in place. Slide the lower handle through the holes in the side pieces.

4 Cut the upper handle to length. With the assistance of a helper, position the box unit in front of the cabinet, rotate the lower arms down, and secure them to the side pieces using the bolts, washers and nuts provided. Insert the top handle. With a helper, lower the upper arms one at a time, and insert the handle end into the arm. Secure the handle with the two setscrews in each arm, using an Allen wrench.

Removing Trim & Old Cabinets

Old cabinets can be salvaged if they are modular units that were installed with screws. Some custom built-in cabinets can be removed in one piece. Otherwise they should be cut into pieces and discarded.

Tools and Materials

Tools : pry bar, putty knife, cordless screwdriver, reciprocating saw, hammer.

Materials: eye protection.

Remove trim moldings at edges and tops of cabinets with a flat pry bar or putty knife.

Remove vinyl base trim. Work a pry bar or putty knife underneath and peel off the vinyl.

Remove baseboards and base shoe moldings with a pry bar. Protect wall surfaces with scraps of wood.

Remove valances. Some are attached to cabinets or soffits with screws. Others are nailed and must be pried loose.

How to Remove Cabinets

1 Remove doors and drawers to make it easier to get at interior spaces. You may need to scrape away old paint to expose hinge screws.

2 At back of cabinets, remove any screws holding cabinet to wall. Cabinets can be removed as a group, or can be disassembled.

3 Detach individual cabinets by removing screws that hold face frames together.

Built-in cabinets are usually not salvageable. Cut them into manageable pieces with a reciprocating saw, or take them apart piece by piece with a hammer and pry bar.

Preparing for New Cabinets

Sanded high area

Stud finder

Filled-in low area

Installing new cabinets is easiest if the kitchen is completely empty. Disconnect the plumbing and wiring, and temporarily remove the appliances. To remove old countertops, see pages 72 to 73. To remove old cabinets, see pages 46 to 47. If the new kitchen requires plumbing or electrical changes, now is the time to have this work done. If the kitchen flooring is to be replaced, finish it before beginning layout and installation of cabinets.

Cabinets must be installed plumb and level. Using a level as a guide, draw reference lines on the walls to indicate cabinet location. If the kitchen floor is uneven, find the highest point of the floor area that will be covered by base cabinets. Measure up from this point to draw reference lines.

Tools and Materials

Tools: stud finder, pry bar, trowel, putty knife, screwdriver, straightedge, level, marking pencil, tape measure.

Materials: 1 × 3 boards, straight 6- to 8-ft.-long 2 × 4, wallboard compound, 2½" wallboard screws.

Stud locations

1 × 3
ledger

Reference
line

How to Prepare Walls

1 Find high and low spots on wall surfaces, using a long, straight 2 × 4. Sand down any high spots.

2 Fill in low spots of wall by applying wallboard taping compound with a trowel. Let dry, and sand lightly.

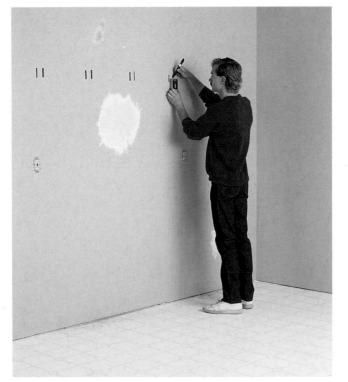

3 Locate and mark wall studs, using an electronic stud finder. Cabinets will be hung by driving screws into the studs through the back of the cabinets.

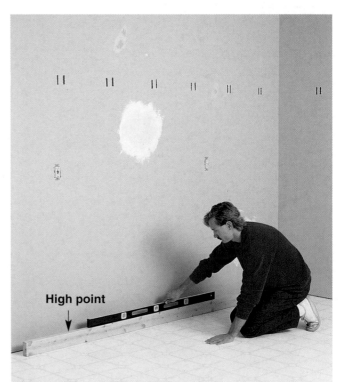

High point

4 FInd high point along the floor that will be covered by base cabinets. Place a level on a long, straight 2 × 4, and move board across floor to determine if floor is uneven. Mark wall at the hight point.

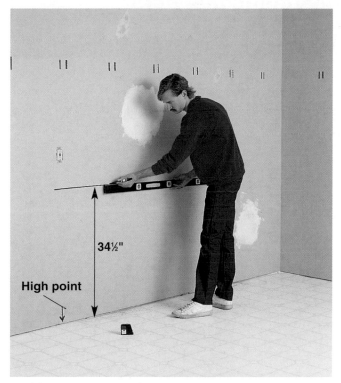

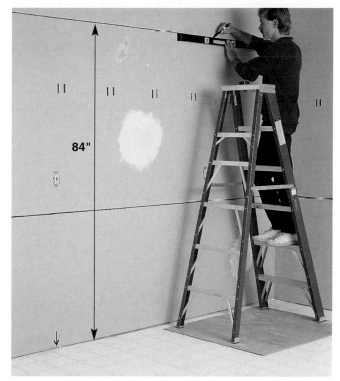

5 Measure up 34½" from the high-point mark. Use a level to mark a reference line on walls. Base cabinets will be installed with top edges flush against this line.

6 Measure up 84" from the high-point mark and draw a second reference line. Wall cabinets will be installed with top edges flush against this line.

7 Measure down 30" from wall-cabinet reference line and draw another level line where bottom of cabinets will be. Temporary ledgers will be installed against this line.

8 Install 1 × 3 temporary ledgers with top edge flush against the reference line. Attach ledgers with 2½" wallboard screws driven into every other wall stud. Mark stud locations on ledgers. Cabinets will rest temporarily on ledgers during installation.

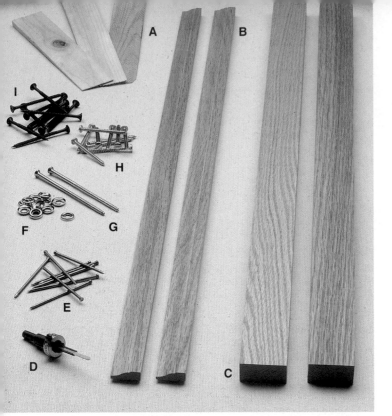

Tools and materials for installing cabinets include: wood shims (A), trim moldings (B), filler strips (C), #9 counterbore drill bit (D), 6d finish nails (E), finish washers (F), #10 gauge 4" wood screws (G), #8 2½" sheet-metal screws (H), 3" wallboard screws (I).

Installing Cabinets

Cabinets must be firmly anchored to wall studs, and must be exactly plumb and level, so that the doors and drawers operate smoothly. Number each cabinet and mark its position on the wall. Remove the cabinet doors and drawers, and number them so they can be easily replaced after the cabinets are installed.

Begin with the corner cabinets, making sure they are installed plumb and level. Adjacent cabinets are easily aligned once the corner cabinets have been correctly positioned.

Tools and Materials

Tools: handscrew clamps, level, hammer, utility knife, nail set, stepladder, drill, #9 counterbore drill bit, cordless screwdriver, jig saw.

Materials: cabinets, trim molding, toe-kick molding, filler strips, valance, 6d finish nails, finish washers, #10 4" wood screws, #8 2½" sheet-metal screws, 3" drywall screws.

How to Fit a Blind Corner Cabinet

Before installation, test-fit corner and adjoining cabinets to make sure doors and handles do not interfere with each other. If necessary, increase the clearance by pulling the blind cabinet away from side wall by no more than 4". To maintain even spacing between edges of doors and cabinet corner (A, B), cut a filler strip and attach it to the adjoining cabinet. Measure distance (C) as a reference when positioning blind cabinet against wall.

How to Install Wall Cabinets

1 Position corner cabinet on ledger. Drill ³⁄₁₆" pilot holes into studs through hanging strips at rear of cabinet. Attach to wall with 2½" sheet-metal screws. Do not tighten fully until all cabinets are hung.

2 Attach filler strip to adjoining cabinet, if needed (see page 52). Clamp filler in place, and drill pilot holes through cabinet face frame near hinge locations, using a counterbore bit. Attach filler to cabinet with 2½" sheet-metal screws.

3 Position adjoining cabinet on ledger, tight against blind corner cabinet. Check face frame for plumb. Drill ³⁄₁₆" pilot holes into wall studs through hanging strips in rear of cabinet. Attach cabinet with 2½" sheet-metal screws. Do not tighten wall screws fully until all cabinets are hung.

4 Clamp corner cabinet and adjoining cabinet together at the top and bottom. Handscrew clamps will not damage wood face frames.

(continued next page)

How to Install Wall Cabinets (continued)

5 Attach blind corner cabinet to adjoining cabinet. From inside corner cabinet, drill pilot holes through face frame. Join cabinets with sheet-metal screws.

6 Position and attach each additional cabinet. Clamp frames together, and drill counterbored pilot holes through side of face frame. Join cabinets with sheet-metal screws. Drill 3/16" pilot holes in hanging strips, and attach cabinet to studs with sheet-metal screws.

Join frameless cabinets with #8 1¼" wood screws and finish washers. Each pair of cabinets should be joined by at least four screws.

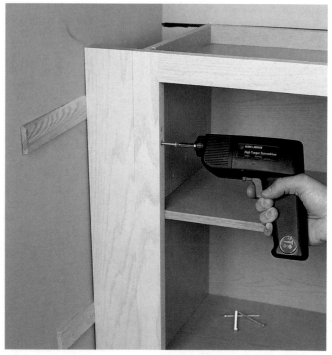

7 Fill small spaces between a cabinet and a wall or appliance with a filler strip. Cut filler to fit space, then wedge filler into place with wood shims. Drill counterbored pilot holes through side of cabinet face frame, and attach filler with sheet-metal screws.

8 Remove temporary ledger. Check cabinet run for plumb, and adjust if necessary by placing wood shims behind cabinet, near stud locations. Tighten wall screws completely. Cut off shims with utility knife.

9 Use trim moldings to cover any gaps between cabinets and walls. Stain moldings to match cabinet finish.

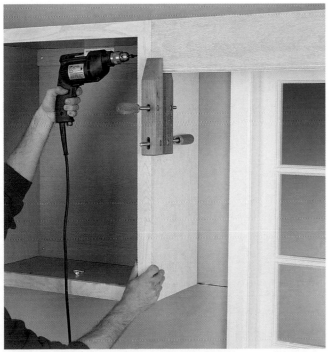

10 Attach decorative valance above sink. Clamp valance to edge of cabinet frames, and drill counterbored pilot holes through cabinet frames into end of valance. Attach with sheet-metal screws.

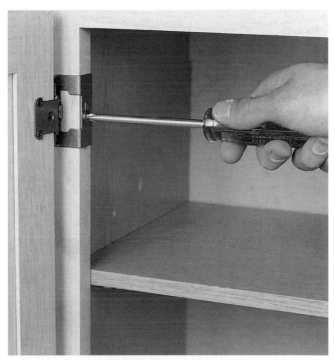

11 Install the cabinet doors. If necessary, adjust the hinges so that the doors are straight and plumb.

How to Install Base Cabinets

1 Begin installation with corner cabinet. Position cabinet so that top is flush with reference line. Make sure cabinet is plumb and level. If necessary, adjust by driving wood shims under cabinet base. Be careful not to damage flooring. Drill ³⁄₁₆" pilot holes through hanging strip into wall studs. Attach cabinets loosely to wall with sheet-metal screws.

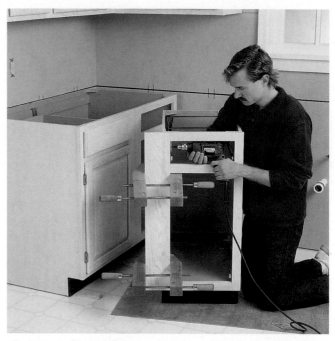

2 Attach filler strip to adjoining cabinet, if necessary (page 52). Clamp filler in place, and drill counterbored pilot holes through side of face frame. Attach filler with sheet-metal screws.

3 Clamp adjoining cabinet to corner cabinet. Make sure cabinet is plumb, then drill counterbored pilot holes through corner-cabinet face frame into filler strip (page 54, step 5). Join cabinets with sheet-metal screws. Drill ³⁄₁₆" pilot holes through hanging strips into wall studs. Attach cabinets loosely with sheet-metal screws.

4 Use a jig saw to cut any cabinet openings needed for plumbing, wiring or heating ducts.

5 Position and attach additional cabinets, making sure frames are aligned. Clamp cabinets together, then drill counterbored pilot holes through side of face frame. Join cabinets with sheet-metal screws. Frameless cabinets are joined with #8 gauge 1¼" wood screws and finish washers.

6 Make sure all cabinets are level. If necessary, adjust by driving wood shims underneath cabinets. Place wood shims behind cabinets near stud locations wherever there is a gap. Tighten wall screws. Cut off shims with utility knife.

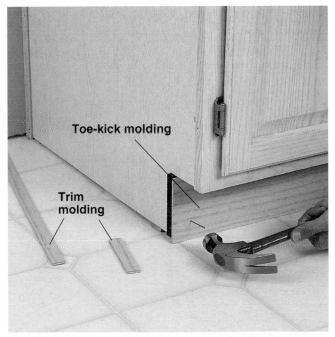

7 Use trim moldings to cover gaps between the cabinets and the wall or floor. Toe-kick area is often covered with a strip of hardwood finished to match the cabinets.

8 If corner has void area not covered by cabinets, screw 1 × 3 cleats to wall, flush with reference line. Cleats will help support countertop.

How to Install a Ceiling-hung Cabinet to Joists

1 Cut a cardboard template to same size as top of wall cabinet. Use template to outline position of cabinet on ceiling. Mark position of the cabinet face frame on the outline.

2 Locate joists with stud finder. If joists run parallel to cabinet, install blocking between joists to hang cabinet (below). Measure joist positions and mark cabinet frame to indicate where to drive screws.

3 Have one or more helpers position cabinet against ceiling. Drill ³⁄₁₆" pilot holes through top rails into ceiling joists. Attach cabinets with 4" wood screws and finish washers.

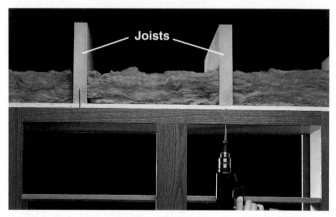

Shown in cutaway: Cabinet is attached to joists with wood screws and finish washers.

How to Attach a Ceiling-hung Cabinet to Blocking (joists must be accessible)

1 Drill reference holes through the ceiling at each corner of cabinet outline. From above ceiling, install 2 × 4 blocks between joists. Blocking can be toe-nailed, or end-nailed through joists.

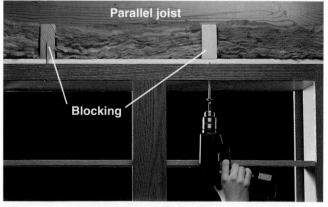

2 Measure distance between each block and the drilled reference holes. Mark cabinet frame to indicate where to drive anchoring screws. Drill pilot holes and attach cabinet to blocking with 4" wood screws and finish washers, as shown in cutaway (above).

How to Install a Base Island Cabinet

1 Set the base cabinet in the correct position, and lightly trace the cabinet outline on the flooring. Remove cabinet.

2 Attach L-shaped 2 × 4 cleats to floor at opposite corners of cabinet outline. Allow for thickness of cabinet walls by positioning cleats ¾" inside cabinet outline. Attach cleat to floor with 3" wallboard screws.

3 Lower the base cabinet over the cleats. Check cabinet for level, and shim under the base if necessary.

4 Attach the cabinet to the floor cleats using 6d finish nails. Drill pilot holes for nails, and recess nail heads with a nail set.

Building Banquette Seating

Almost everyone loves sitting in a booth at a restaurant—why not have one at home? Aside from providing an intimate, cozy setting for eating, games or homework, a banquette or booth solves a critical space issue. An L-shaped booth eliminates the space needed to pull out chairs on two sides, plus, it allows children to sit closer together. Three kids can occupy booth space that is smaller than that required for two kids on two chairs. This project can add even more usable space by creating a roll-out storage unit under the booth seats.

This project creates an L-shaped, built-in booth in a kitchen corner. It does not show you how to redirect air vents or electrical outlets.

Make sure you take into account the thickness of cushion foam if you plan on upholstering the backs. The plans assume you'll use 2" foam for seat cushions and back cushions. Thicker cushions will make the bench too shallow. Booth seating is most comfortable if the seats are 16" to 19" deep. The total height for the seat should be 18" to 19" to fit a standard 29"-tall table.

This project is designed to be painted, but if you wish to match your wood kitchen cabinets, you can use veneer plywood.

Before beginning to build the booth, carefully remove the base shoe or molding along both walls, using a pry bar. Using a stud finder, mark the stud locations along both walls. Use masking tape to mark the stud locations to avoid marking on the wall surface.

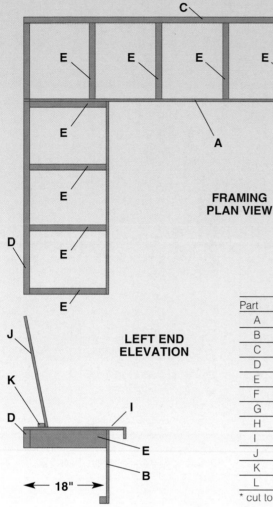

FRAMING PLAN VIEW

(Framing plan labels: C, E, E, E, E, A, D, E, E, E, E)

LEFT END ELEVATION

(Labels: J, K, D, I, E, B, 18")

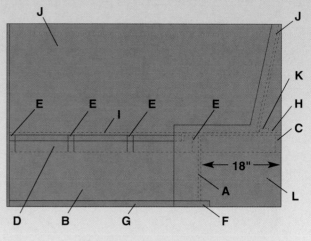

LEFT SIDE ELEVATION

(Labels: J, J, K, H, C, E, E, I, E, E, L, A, F, D, B, G, 18")

Cutting List				
Part	Name	Measurements	Material	Number
A	Kickboard, long	15½" × 60"	¾" plywood	1
B	Kickboard, short	15½" × 42"	¾" plywood	1
C	Ledger, long	60"	2 × 4	1
D	Ledger, short	42"	2 × 4	1
E	Braces	16½"	2 × 4	8
F	Cleat, long	60"	2 × 2	1
G	Cleat, short	42"	2 × 2	1
H	Seat, long	22" × 60"	¾" plywood	1
I	Seat, short	22" × 38"*	¾" plywood	1
J	Seat backs	60" × 24"	¾" plywood	2
K	Seat cleats	60"*	1 × 2	2
L	End pieces	20" × 40"*	¾" plywood	2

* cut to fit

How to Build a Banquette

Tools and Materials

Tools: tape measure, stud finder, pry bar, circular saw, cordless screwdriver, carpenter's square, level, bevel gauge, compass, jig saw, hammer.

Materials: masking tape, ¾" paintable interior plywood, 2 × 4 lumber, 1 × 2 lumber, #8 screws (1⅝", 2", 2½", 3"), 1½" finish head screws, finish nails, edge banding, trim molding, painter's caulk, wood putty, paint.

1 Cut the kickboards, ledgers and braces to length. Attach braces at each end of a ledger using two 2½" screws. Evenly space the other braces and attach. Attach the kickboard to the braces, using 1⅝" screws. Use a carpenter's or combination square to make sure all joints are squared.

2 Cut the long cleat to length. Measure 18" out from the wall and draw a line parallel to the wall. Align the cleat with the inside edge of the line and attach to the floor using 2½" screws.

(continued next page)

3 Turn the brace and kickboard assembly right side up and place against the wall and cleat. Check for level and make sure that the kickboard butts firmly against the cleat. Attach the ledger to studs using two 3" screws per stud. Attach the kickboard to the cleat using 1⅝" screws.

4 Assemble the short bench and attach to the studs and cleat following steps 1 through 3. Make sure the second bench butts firmly against the first bench.

5 Attach the long bench top using 1⅝" screws. Center the screws over the braces and not the kickboard. Measure from the edge of the long bench to the outside edge of the brace for the exact length of the short bench. Cut and attach the short bench top.

6 Lean one seat back against the wall so the bottom edge is 6" from the wall. Slide the long back cleat behind the back and mark its location. Use a bevel gauge to determine the edge bevel for the back. Remove the back and bevel the edge with a circular saw or table saw.

7 Attach the cleat to the seat top, using 1⅝" screws. Make sure the cleat is parallel to the wall. Apply edge banding to the top edge of the back. Replace the back and attach it to the cleat using 1⅝" screws. Attach it to the wall studs using 2" screws.

8 Lean the second back against the wall with its base 6" from the wall. Slide the short back cleat behind the back and mark its location. Use a compass to scribe the angle of the long back onto the short back. Cut along this mark using a circular saw. Attach the cleat and seat back as in step 7.

9 Place the end blanks against each end and trace the bench profile. Create a rounded or angular bench end that extends at least 1½" beyond the bench profile. This "lip" will prevent the cushions from slipping off the end. Cut the bench ends, using a jig saw.

10 Before attaching the ends, use the jig saw to radius the pointed bench ends to prevent bruises. Apply wood glue to the ends of the bench backs, kickboard and bench tops. Attach the ends to the braces and bench using finish head screws every 6" to 8". Apply edge banding to the bench ends.

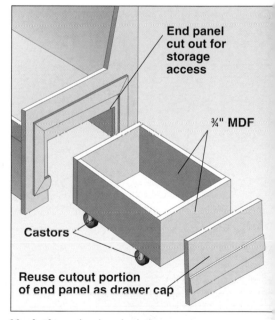

End panel cut out for storage access

¾" MDF

Castors

Reuse cutout portion of end panel as drawer cap

11 Attach the molding of your choice to the front edges of the bench with finish nails. Reattach the base molding if desired, or use trim molding to create panels, as pictured here. Fill all screw holes with wood putty, and sand smooth. Run a bead of painter's caulk along the joint between the bench top and back, the joint where the two bench backs meet, and between the bench back and wall. Smooth with a wet finger. Paint with a high-quality wood primer and satin, semi-gloss or gloss paint. Make cushions, if desired.

Variation: A wheeled drawer can add some storage space to your banquette. Before attaching the bench end, cut out an opening. Create a box with wheels and a drawer front to fit the opening.

COUNTERTOPS

*M*ore than simply a work surface, a kitchen countertop can dazzle with the look-at-me pizzazz of granite, or bring together a country theme with soapstone and butcher block. There are many choices in countertops, from the less-expensive laminate and linoleum, through ceramic and stone tile, to high-end stainless, granite and marble.

Countertop options for your kitchen depend on how much you are willing to spend, whether you will be doing it yourself or contracting out, and what look you want to achieve. In this chapter we will cover available countertop options, their pluses and minuses, and give directions for those you can install yourself.

Step-by-step instructions with photographs are included for three countertop projects: post-form laminate, custom laminate and tile. Also included in this chapter is a section on metallic laminates, and how to create a tiled backsplash.

Shopping tips, universal design tips, and environmental information are also included.

Countertop Options

When choosing countertops, remember that you do not need to have a 100% uniform countertop. Many people choose to use more expensive countertop materials as accents or for islands rather than for the entire kitchen. From least expensive to most expensive, these are countertop options currently available:

Laminate

Laminate countertops are formed from layers of resin-saturated paper and plastic that are bonded under pressure, then given a protective coating of clear melamine. The laminate is glued to particleboard to create the countertop. Also available is through-color laminate in which the surface color runs all the way through. This product doesn't have the dark edge of standard laminate and does not show surface damage as easily, but is two to three times more expensive.

The least expensive laminate countertop is ready-made post-formed. Post-formed countertop is backsplash, counter and rounded front apron formed in a seamless piece. Home centers have post-formed countertop available in various lengths and a few stock colors. You can have a custom post-formed countertop made, which will be slightly more expensive. You can install this yourself, or often have it delivered and installed by the fabricator.

(above) **Quartz surfaces** are available in a wide range of colors from muted naturals to dazzling reds, blues and blacks.

(left) **A custom laminate countertop** allows for numerous edging and backsplash options.

(right) **A tiled countertop** is a heat-resistant surface that is perfect for surrounding a cooktop.

A custom laminate countertop is discernable from a post-formed countertop by the square backsplash and seam between the backsplash and the countertop. Because the laminate used for custom surfaces is slightly thicker than that used for post-formed, it is a little bit sturdier. You can order custom laminate countertops to be fabricated for you, or you can make your own (see page 78).

Custom laminate countertops can be dressed up in a number of ways. A custom laminate can use constrasting or complementary colors for nosings and backsplashes. Hardwood trim or coved edgings are also an option. Mixing laminate countertops with tile or stainless steel backsplashes also adds to the list of possibilities.

A limitation of the laminate countertops is that sinks must be drop-in, not undermounted. Though the laminate itself is waterproof, the particleboard it is attached to will swell if it gets wet.

To get the most out of your laminate countertop, do not use scouring pads or abrasive cleaners, always use a cutting board, and never place hot pots and pans directly on the surface.

Ceramic & Stone Tile

Ceramic tile and stone tile countertops are popular, mid-priced options. If you like the look of granite, but don't want to pay the price, granite tiles can give you a similar look for substantially less, especially if you do the installation yourself (see pages 92 to 97). When selecting tiles for countertops, make sure they are floor tiles—wall tiles will not stand up to the wear and tear of countertop use.

Two major drawbacks of ceramic or stone tile are its hardness and the grout lines. Glassware and pottery will break and chip readily when knocked or dropped against this surface. Grout lines make the surface uneven and grout needs to be sealed on an annual basis to prevent it from staining. Using tiles for a backsplash is an excellent way to get the look of tile near the countertop.

Butcher Block & Wood

New adhesives and finishes have made wood more amenable to wet kitchen applications. Though best reserved for non-sink surrounds in the opinion of many, you will see undermount sinks in butcher block countertops. In most cases, wood needs to be reoiled frequently. Most people think a butcher block countertop is convenient because you no longer need cutting boards, but it's a poor idea to use them as direct cutting surfaces. Every nick and cut will collect dirt and will darken differently when reoiled. For basic hygiene, surfaces used to cut meat and fish need to be removable so they can be thoroughly washed in hot soapy water.

Concrete

Concrete is becoming a popular countertop choice. It can be cast in place or off site, dyed or stained in many different colors, and treated to have a number of finishes. It is a custom option, but is not as expensive as granite. Concrete needs to be sealed regularly, and it will

permanently stain if not. Acidic foods will etch the surface. Like ceramic tile and stone surfaces, it has no give, so expect a greater number of broken glasses and plates. Custom matched concrete sinks are also available.

Solid Surface

Solid surface countertops, also known by the brand names Corian and Surrell, are popular but more expensive options. As the name implies, these countertops are solid color from top to bottom. Pieces are joined with a bonding compound that leaves no visible seam line. Solid surface countertop can be shaped and inlaid, it comes in many colors and patterns, it is durable and it can be repaired.

An advantage of solid surface materials is that a sink basin of the same material can be used with the same seamless bonding. Sinks are available in three or four basic color options.

Solid surface should not be used as a cutting board and hot pans cannot be place directly on the surface. Most spills are easily cleaned with soap and water. If staining, etching or scorching occurs, they can be rubbed out with fine abrasives, though gloss surfaces will need to be buffed to regain their shine.

Though solid surface materials are easily worked with standard hand tools, do-it-yourselfers may have difficulty purchasing the material and bonding agents. If a non-licensed installer installs one of these countertops, the manufacturer will not honor any product warranties.

Edging options with solid surface are many. Because the material is easily cut with a router, the edges can be formed in a number of profiles, though there are two or three standard edges. Also possible are edgings with contrasting colors or patterns.

Quartz Surfaces

Quartz surfaces are manufactured from 93% quartz and 7% pigments, resins and binders. Regardless of the manufacturer, all quartz surfaces are manufactured using equipment and formulas developed by Breton Stone. The differences in appearance among products is due to the type of quartz used.

This surface is unscratchable, non-porous, non-staining, does not need to be sealed, and will not scorch or mar from high heat. Though as hard as granite, it has more inherent flexibility, so

(left) **Solid surface countertops** can be edged with color and a wide variety of edge treatments. Large as this countertop is, it is entirely seamless.

(below) **Wood countertops** may be highly polished, as this one is, or oiled for a matte look. Either way, wood is a versitile and beautiful countertop.

surface cracking does not occur. The surface is cool to the touch, like granite and marble. Installation is the same as granite. Because it is a pigmented product, color choices are numerous.

Stone

Soapstone, slate, marble and granite are all used for countertops. Though they are all quarried stone, and are all fairly expensive, they have numerous differences.

Soapstone has been used for kitchen countertops and sinks for hundreds of years. Though the stone itself is easily workable with non-specialized tools, its surface is non-absorbent and unaffected by either acids or alkalis. The surface will age to a glossy patina, or it can be oiled to achieve this finish. Surface stains are just that—limited to the surface and easily rubbed or sanded out.

Slate for countertops is durable, hard and dense. Scratches can be easily rubbed out if necessary. Like soapstone, its surface is non-absorbing and does not require sealing. Slate comes in shades of green, purple, gray and black, with a rare red available at higher cost.

Marble has long been popular for rolling pins and surfaces for pastry and candy making because it is cool to the touch. The advantage of a small movable marble surface is it can be placed in the refrigerator to provide an even cooler surface. The beauty of marble comes from its veining patterns—unfortunately these are mini faultlines along which the stone will easily break, especially if improperly installed. Some marbles are as hard as granite, but most are fairly soft and scratch or chip easily, and all are susceptible to staining and will be etched by acid.

Granite is the hardest of the stone countertops. It comes in an ever-increasing array of colors—ranging from whites and blacks to pinks, reds, yellows and greens—as more and more countries begin exporting their local granites. No two pieces of stone will be identical, so if your countertop is large, it should be cut from the same piece or adjoining pieces to get the best possible match. The main drawback of granite is that it must be sealed to prevent staining. Sealing is usually needed once or twice a year.

For all stone countertops, a honed or matte surface is recommended—a polished surface is a mirror gloss finish which creates unnecessary glare and reveals surface scratches and spotting more easily. These countertops are also

UNIVERSAL DESIGN

Kitchen countertops are usually installed at a single level. Because people are different heights and different tasks have different height requirements, varied countertop height is now becoming more common. To determine the proper counter height, stand by a table and add layers of wood until your elbows are slightly bent when your hands are flat on the raised surface. Practice chopping at this level, and raise or lower it until it feels comfortable. Make sure at least a portion of your counter is at this height. Other tasks, like kneading and rolling, may be more comfortable at lower levels.

very heavy, and except for soapstone, require specialized cutting and shaping tools.

Stainless Steel

Stainless steel is an impervious material that doesn't stain, can handle hot pots, and can be fabricated into seamless countertops and sinks. Stainless steel countertops for residential use are usually bonded to plywood or particleboard to deaden noise and prevent denting. Sinks can either be fabricated as part of the countertop, or, more likely, welded in. Either way, it is a seamless application. Stainless shows fingerprints and water marks, especially on a polished surface. It is best to get a matte or satin surface.

(left) **Countertops at varying heights** make it easier for multiple users to perform a variety of tasks more easily.

(above) **Soapstone countertops** with a soapstone sink create a one-of-a-kind rustic look.

(right) **The beauty and elegance of granite** is also available as stone tiles. These tiles are installed in the same manner as ceramic tiles.

Installing Countertops

Custom laminate

Post-form

Ceramic tile

The three countertop installations covered here, post-form, laminate and tile, are the most common do-it-yourself countertops. Post-form countertops are the easiest to install because the laminate has already been glued to the substrate and you can request left- or right-mitered pieces to create corners. Custom laminate gives you the opportunity to build your countertop from scratch, creating just the look you want with varied widths, edge treatments and backsplashes. Tile countertops also give you a chance to express your creativity with the hundreds of available ceramic and stone tile shapes, sizes and colors.

Custom laminate countertops are built by gluing sheet laminates to particleboard. Laminates are available in hundreds of colors and patterns to match any kitchen decorating scheme. Special edge treatments can be added to customize a laminate countertop.

Post-form countertops are made of sheet laminates glued to particleboard, and come from the factory ready to install. Post-form countertops have pre-attached backsplashes and front edge treatments. They are manufactured in a variety of colors and styles.

Ceramic tile is especially durable and creates a beautiful surface that resists spills and stains. Tile is available in a wide range of styles and prices, and creating a ceramic tile countertop is an excellent do-it-yourself project.

Tools and Materials

Tools: channel-type pliers, reciprocating saw, pry bar, utility knife, masonry chisel, circular saw, ball peen hammer.

Materials: gloves, eye protection.

How to Remove an Old Countertop

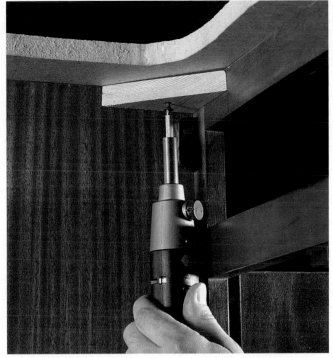

1 Turn off the water at shutoff valves. Disconnect and remove plumbing fixtures and appliances. Remove any brackets or screws holding the countertop to the cabinets. Unscrew the take-up bolts on mitered countertops.

2 Use a utility knife to cut caulk beads along the backsplash and edge of countertop. Remove any trim. Using a flat pry bar, try to lift the countertop away from base cabinets.

3 If the countertop cannot be pried up, use a reciprocating saw or jig saw with coarse wood-cutting blade to cut the countertop into pieces for removal. Be careful not to cut into base cabinets.

Ceramic tile: Wear eye protection. Chisel tile away from the base with a masonry chisel and ball peen hammer. Or, use a circular saw and abrasive masonry-cutting blade to cut the countertop and substrate into pieces for removal.

Installing a Post-form Countertop

Post-form laminate countertops are available in stock and custom colors. Pre-mitered sections are available for two- or three-piece countertops that continue around corners. If the countertop has an exposed end, you will need an endcap kit that contains a preshaped strip of matching laminate. Post-form countertops have either a waterfall edge or a no-drip edge.

SHOPPING TIPS

• *Stock colors are typically available in 4-, 6-, 8-, 10- and 12-foot straight lengths and 6- and 8-foot mitered lengths.*

• *Order custom post-form countertops in nearly any color and many configurations.*

Tools and Materials

Tools: tape measure, framing square, pencil, straightedge, C-clamps, hammer, level, caulking gun, jig saw, compass, adjustable wrench, belt sander, drill and spade bit, cordless screwdriver.

Materials: post-form countertop, wood shims, take-up bolts, drywall screws, wire brads, end-cap laminate, silicone caulk, wood glue.

How to Install a Post-form Countertop

1 Measure the span of the base cabinets, from the corner to the outside edge of the cabinet. Add 1" for overhang if end will be exposed. If an end will butt against an appliance, subtract 1⁄16" to prevent scratches.

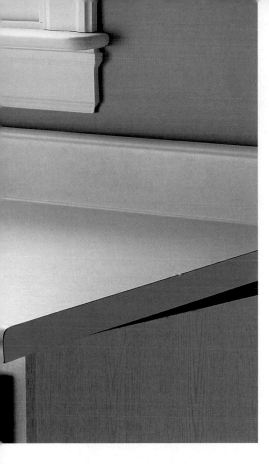

Countertop installation needs include: wood shims (A), take-up bolts (B), wallboard screws (C), wire brads (D), household iron (E), endcap laminate (F), endcap battens (G), silicone caulk (H), file (I), adjustable wrench (J), wood glue (K), buildup blocks (L), scribing compass (M).

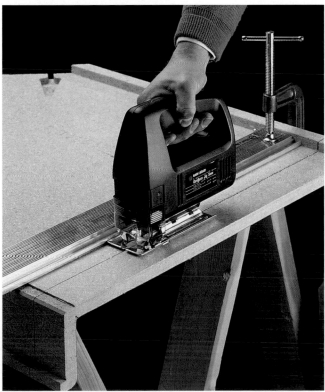

2 Use a framing square to mark a cutting line on the bottom surface of the countertop. Cut off the countertop with a jig saw, using a clamped straight-edge as a guide.

3 Attach the battens from the endcap kit to edge of countertop, using carpenter's glue and small brads. Sand out any unevenness with belt sander.

(continued next page)

4 Hold endcap laminate against end, slightly over-lapping edges. Activate adhesive by pressing an iron set at medium heat against endcap. Cool with wet cloth, then file endcap laminate flush with edges.

5 Position countertop on base cabinets. Make sure front edge of countertop is parallel to cabinet face. Check countertop for level. Make sure that drawers and doors open and close freely. If needed, adjust countertop with wood shims.

6 Because walls are usually un-even, use a compass to trace wall outline onto backsplash scrib-bing strip. Set compass arms to match widest gap, then move compass along length of the wall to transfer outline to scribing strip.

7 Remove the countertop. Use a belt sander to grind the back-splash to the scribe line.

8 Mark cutout for self-rimming sink. Position sink upside down on countertop and trace outline. Remove sink and draw cutting line ⅝" inside sink outline. To install sink, see page 117.

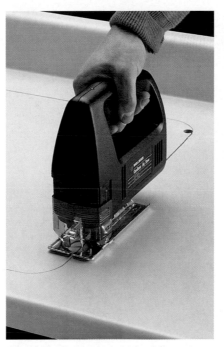

Variation for framed sink or cooktop: Position metal frame on countertop, and trace outline around edge of vertical flange. Remove frame. To install a framed sink or cooktop, see pages 117 or 135.

9 Drill pilot hole just inside cutting line. Make cutouts with jig saw. Support cutout area from below so that falling cutout does not damage cabinet.

10 Apply a bead of silicone caulk on edges of mitered countertop sections. Force countertop pieces tightly together.

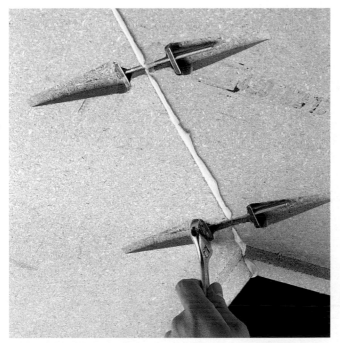

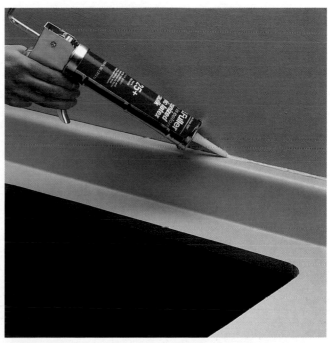

11 From underneath cabinet, install and tighten miter take-up bolts. Position countertop tightly against wall and fasten to cabinets by driving wallboard screws up through corner brackets into the countertop. Screws should be long enough to provide maximum holding power, but not long enough to puncture laminate surface.

12 Seal the seam between the backsplash and the wall with silicone caulk. Smooth the bead with a wet fingertip. Wipe away excess caulk.

Building a Custom Laminate Countertop

Building your own custom laminate countertop using sheets of plastic laminate and particleboard is a bit time-consuming. It does offer two advantages: It will be less expensive than a custom-ordered countertop, and it will allow you more options in terms of colors and edge treatments. A countertop made with laminates can be tailored to fit any space.

Laminates are sold in 6-, 8-, 10- or 12-foot lengths that are about 1/20" thick. Laminate sheets range in width from 30" to 48". Most new laminates have consistent color through the thickness of the sheet. Solid-color laminate countertops do not show dark lines at the trimmed edges as the older laminates did.

Choose nonflammable contact cement when building a countertop, and thoroughly ventilate your work area.

Tools and Materials

Tools: tape measure, framing square, straightedge, scoring tool, paint roller, 3-way clamps, caulk gun, J-roller, miter saw, scribing compass, circular saw, screwdriver, belt sander, file, router.

Materials: 3/4" particleboard, sheet laminate, contact cement and thinner, wood glue, drywall screws.

Laminate countertop: Countertop core is ¾" particleboard. Perimeter is built up with strips of particleboard screwed to the bottom of the core. For decorative edge treatments, hardwood strips can be attached to core.

Laminate pieces are bonded to the countertop with contact cement. Edges are trimmed and shaped with a router.

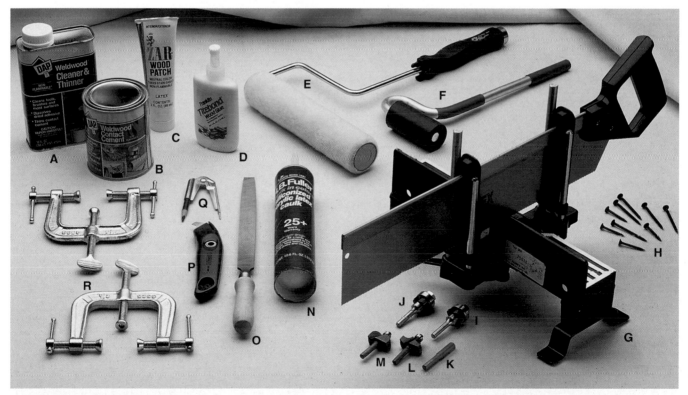

Specialty tools & supplies include: contact cement thinner (A), contact cement (B), latex wood patch (C), wood glue (D), paint roller (E), J-roller (F), miter box (G), drywall screws (H), flush-cutting router bit (I), 15° bevel-cutting router bit (J), straight router bit (K), corner rounding router bit (L), cove router bit (M), silicone caulk (N), file (O), scoring tool (P), scribing compass (Q), 3-way clamps (R).

How to Build a Custom Laminate Countertop

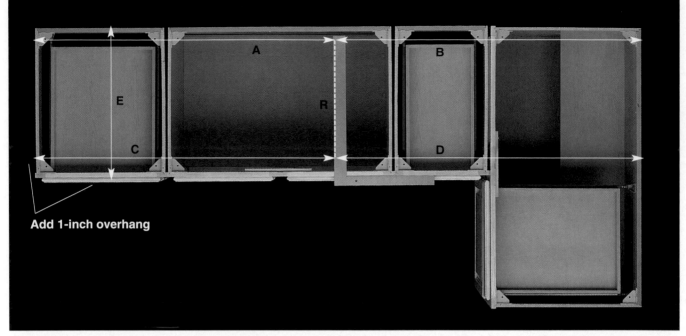

Add 1-inch overhang

1 Measure along tops of base cabinets to determine size of countertop. If wall corners are not square, use a framing square to establish a reference line (R) near middle of base cabinets, perpendicular to front of cabinets. Take four measurements (A, B, C, D) from reference line to cabinet ends. Allow for overhangs by adding 1" to the length for each exposed end, and 1" to the width (E). If an end butts against an appliance, subtract 1/16" from length to prevent scratching appliance.

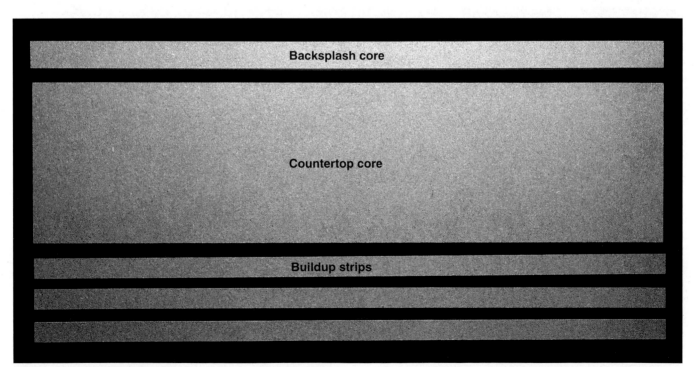

Backsplash core

Countertop core

Buildup strips

2 Transfer measurements from step 1, using a framing square to establish a reference line. Cut core to size using a circular saw with clamped straightedge as a guide. Cut 4" strips of particleboard for backsplash, and for joint support where sections of countertop core are butted together. Cut 3" strips for edge buildups.

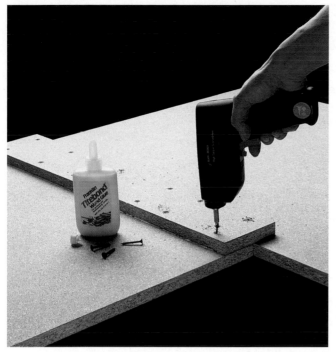

3 Join the countertop core pieces on the bottom side. Attach a 4" particleboard joint support across the seam, using carpenter's glue and 1¼" wallboard screws.

4 Attach 3" edge buildup strips to bottom of countertop, using 1¼" wallboard screws. Fill any gaps on outside edges with latex wood patch, then sand edges with belt sander.

5 To determine the size of the laminate top, measure countertop core. For strength, laminate seams should run opposite to core seam. Add ½" trimming margin to both the length and width of each piece. Measure laminate needed for face and edges of backsplash, and for exposed edges of countertop core. Add ½" to each measurement.

6 Cut laminate by scoring and breaking it. Draw a cutting line, then etch along the line with a scoring tool. Use a straightedge as a guide. Two passes of scoring tool will help laminate break cleanly.

(continued next page)

7 Bend laminate toward the scored line until the sheet breaks cleanly. For better control on narrow pieces, clamp a straightedge along scored line before bending laminate. Wear gloves to avoid being cut by sharp edges.

8 Create tight-fitting seams with plastic laminate by using a router and a straight bit to trim edges that will butt together. Measure from cutting edge of the bit to edge of the router baseplate (A). Place laminate on scrap wood and align edges. To guide the router, clamp a straightedge on the laminate at distance A plus 1/4", parallel to laminate edge. Trim laminate.

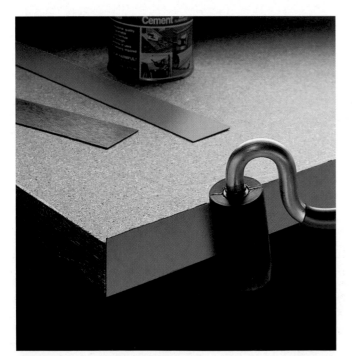

9 Apply laminate to sides of countertop first. Using a paint roller, apply two coats of contact cement to edge of countertop and one coat to back of laminate. Let cement dry according to manufacturer's directions. Position laminate carefully, then press against edge of countertop. Bond with J-roller.

10 Use a router and flush-cutting bit to trim edge strip flush with top and bottom surfaces of countertop core. At edges where router cannot reach, trim excess laminate with a file. Apply laminate to remaining edges, and trim with router.

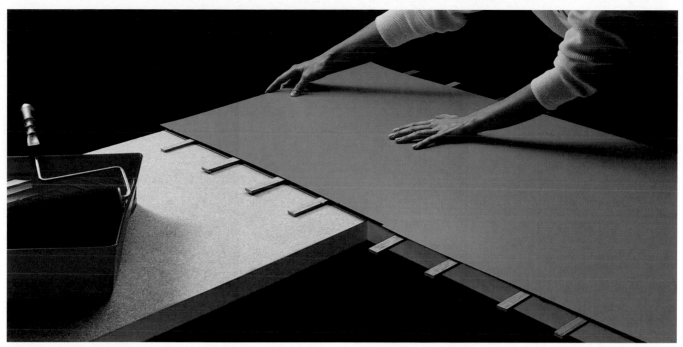

11 Test-fit laminate top on countertop core. Check that laminate overhangs all edges. At seam locations, draw a reference line on core where laminate edges will butt together. Remove laminate. Make sure all surfaces are free of dust, then apply one coat of contact cement to back of laminate and two coats to core. Place spacers made of ¼"-thick scrap wood at 6" intervals across countertop core. Because contact cement bonds instantly, spacers allow laminate to be positioned accurately over core without bonding. Align laminate with seam reference line. Beginning at one end, remove spacers and press laminate to countertop core.

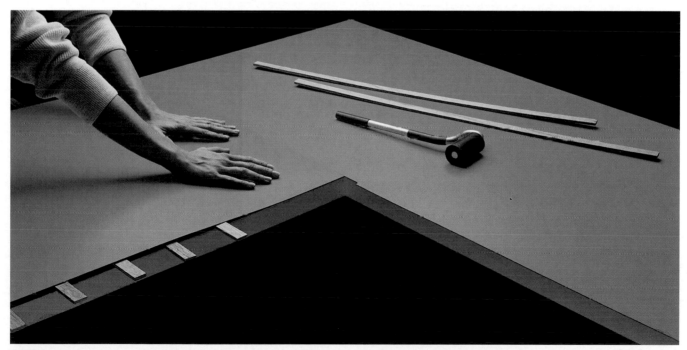

12 Apply contact cement to remaining core and next piece of laminate. Let cement dry, then position laminate on spacers, and carefully align butt seam. Beginning at seam edge, remove spacers and press laminate to countertop core.

(continued next page)

13 Roll entire surface with J-roller to bond laminate to core. Clean off any excess contact cement with a soft cloth and contact cement thinner.

14 Remove excess laminate with a router and flush-cutting bit. At edges where router cannot reach, trim excess laminate with a file. Countertop is now ready for final trimming with bevel-cutting bit.

15 Finish-trim the edges with router and 15° bevel-cutting bit. Set bit depth so that the bevel edge is cut only on top laminate layer. Bit should not cut into vertical edge surface.

16 File all edges smooth. Use downward file strokes to avoid chipping the laminate.

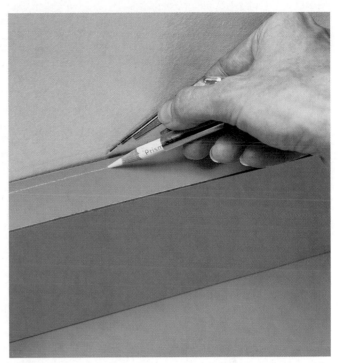

17 Cut 1¼"-wide strips of ¼" plywood to form an overhanging scribing strip for the backsplash. Attach to the top and sides of the backsplash core with glue and wallboard screws. Cut laminate pieces and apply to exposed sides, top and front of backsplash. Trim each piece as it is applied.

18 Test-fit countertop and backsplash. Because walls may be uneven, use compass to trace wall outline onto backsplash scribing strip. Use a belt sander to grind backsplash to scribe line (page 76).

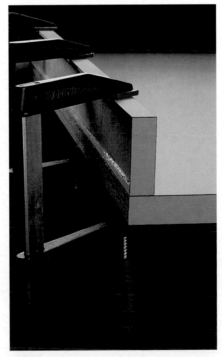

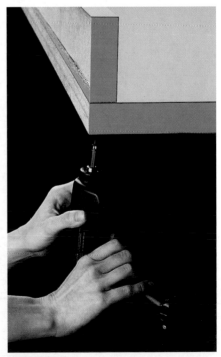

19 Apply bead of silicone caulk to the bottom edge of the backsplash.

20 Position the backsplash on the countertop, and clamp it into place with bar clamps. Wipe away excess caulk, and let dry completely.

21 Screw 2" wallboard screws through countertop into backsplash core. Make sure screw heads are countersunk completely for a tight fit against the base cabinet.

Creating Custom Wood Countertop Edges

For an elegant added touch on a laminate countertop, use hardwood edges and shape them with a router. Rout the edges before attaching the backsplash to the countertop.

Wood caps can also be added to the top edge of the backsplash. A simple edge is best for easy cleaning.

Tools and Materials

Tools: hammer, nail set, belt sander with 120-grit sanding belt, 3-way clamps, router.

Materials: 1 × 2 hardwood strips, carpenter's glue, finish nails.

How to Build Coved Hardwood Edges

1 Cut 1 × 2 hardwood strips to fit edges of countertop. Sand strips smooth. Miter-cut inside and outside corners.

2 Attach edge strips to countertop with carpenter's glue and 3-way clamps. Drill pilot holes, then attach strip with finish nails. Recess nail heads with a nail set.

3 Sand the edge strips flush with the top surface of the countertop, using a belt sander and 120-grit sandpaper.

4 Apply laminate to edge and top of countertop after hardwood edge has been sanded flush.

5 Cut cove edge with a router and cove bit with ball-bearing pilot. Smooth cove with 220-grit sandpaper. Stain and finish exposed wood as desired.

How to Build Solid Hardwood Edges

1 Laminate top of countertop before attaching edge strip. Attach the edge strip flush with the surface of laminate, using carpenter's glue and finish nails (opposite page).

2 Mold top and bottom edges of strip with router and edging bit, if desired. Stain and finish wood as desired.

Building a Stainless Steel Laminate Countertop

If you crave the look of stainless steel in your kitchen but find the price of custom-fabricated stainless steel countertops beyond your means, here's a possible solution. Metal laminates are available that incorporate metal foil attached to the same phenolic back as plastic laminates (see pages 78 to 85). These laminates are as easy to work with as plastic laminates, if you use high-quality carbide blades and tips while sawing and routing.

The stainless steel laminate must be rated for horizontal surface use. Many of the metal laminates available are for vertical, decorative use—which is suitable for a backsplash, but not a countertop. Just like their plastic counterparts, metal laminates are susceptible to heat and water damage.

Wear gloves when working with these metal laminates, as the edges of the metal foil are razor sharp. Be especially aware of this if you choose to create a self-edged countertop (as we have here) as opposed to a counter with a wood edge. File the edges carefully to eliminate all snags and sharp areas.

Stainless steel and other metal laminates are ideal for creating stove and sink backsplashes. A wide variety of colors, finishes and patterns are available. Laminates can be applied to wall surfaces using contact cement.

Tips for Cutting Metal Laminates

Use a jig saw with a carbide blade to cut laminate sheets to rough size. Masking tape prevents the saw base from scratching the laminate.

Use a router with a carbide flush-cutting bit to cut the metal laminate to exact size after it has been glued to the substrate.

Building a Tile Countertop

Ceramic tile is a popular choice for countertops and backsplashes for a number of reasons. It's available in a vast range of sizes, styles and colors; it's durable and can be repaired; and some tile—not all—is reasonably priced. With careful planning, tile is also easy to install, making a custom countertop a good do-it-yourself project.

The best tile for most countertops is glazed ceramic floor tile. Glazed tile is better than unglazed because of its stain resistance, and floor tile is better than wall tile because it's harder and more durable. Most residential floor tile has a hardness rating of Class 3 or better. Porcelain tile also is suitable for countertops; it's very hard and durable, but typically much more expensive than ceramic tile.

While glazing protects tile from stains, the grout between tiles is still vulnerable because it's so porous. To minimize staining, use a grout that contains a latex additive, or mix the grout using a liquid latex additive. After the grout cures fully, apply a quality grout sealer, and reapply the sealer once a year thereafter.

Photo courtesy of Crossville Porcelain Stone

The countertop in this project has a core of ¾" exterior-grade plywood that's cut to fit and fastened to the cabinets. (Treated plywood, particleboard and oriented-strand board are not acceptable tile backers.) The plywood is covered with a layer of plastic (for a moisture barrier) and a layer of ½"-thick cementboard. Cementboard is an effective backer for tile because it won't break down if water gets through the tile layer. The tile is adhered to the cementboard with thin-set adhesive. The overall thickness of the finished countertop is about 1½". If you want a thicker countertop, you can fasten an additional layer of plywood (of any thickness) to the core. Two layers of ¾" exterior-grade plywood without cementboard is also an acceptable substrate.

When laying out the tile for your countertop, account for the placement of the sink and any other fixtures. The tile should break evenly where it meets the sink and along the counter's perimeter. If you'll be installing a tile-in sink, make sure the tile thickness matches the rim of the sink to create a smooth transition.

Tools and Materials

Tools: tape measure, circular saw, drill, utility knife, straightedge, stapler, drywall knife, framing square, notched trowel, tile cutter, carpeted 2 × 4, mallet, rubber grout float, sponge, foam brush, caulk gun.

Materials: ceramic tile, tile spacers, ¾" exterior-grade (CDX) plywood, 4-mil polyethylene sheeting, packing tape, ½" cementboard, 1¼" galvanized deck screws, fiberglass mesh tape, thin-set mortar, grout with latex additive, silicone caulk, silicone grout sealer.

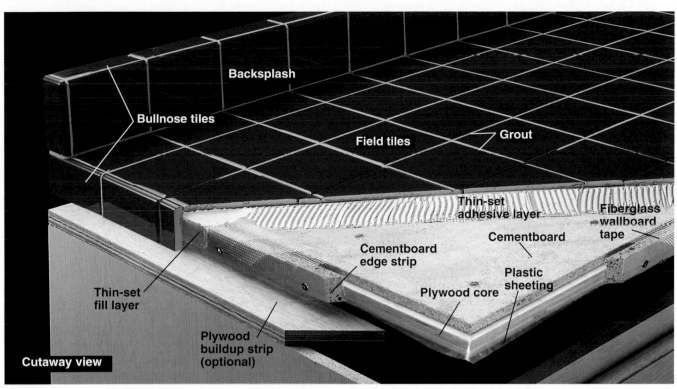

Labels on cutaway view:
- Backsplash
- Bullnose tiles
- Field tiles
- Grout
- Thin-set adhesive layer
- Fiberglass wallboard tape
- Cementboard edge strip
- Cementboard
- Plastic sheeting
- Plywood core
- Thin-set fill layer
- Plywood buildup strip (optional)
- Cutaway view

A ceramic tile countertop starts with a core of ¾" exterior-grade plywood that's covered with a moisture barrier of 4-mil polyethylene sheeting. Half-inch cementboard is screwed to the plywood, and the edges are capped with cementboard and finished with fiberglass mesh tape and thin-set mortar. Tiles for edging and back-splashes may be bullnose or another type of specialty tile (see below).

Options for Backsplashes & Countertop Edges

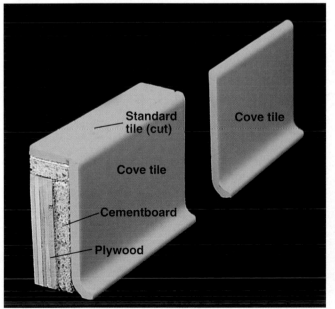

Labels:
- Standard tile (cut)
- Cove tile
- Cove tile
- Cementboard
- Plywood

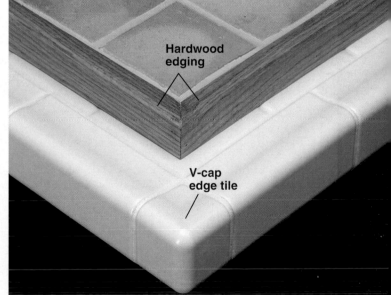

Labels:
- Hardwood edging
- V-cap edge tile

Backsplashes can be made from cove tile (right) attached to the wall at the back of the countertop. You can use the tile alone or build a shelf-type back-splash (left), using the same construction used for the countertop. Attach the plywood backsplash to the plywood core of the countertop. Wrap the front face and all edges of the plywood backsplash with cementboard before laying tile.

Edge options include V-cap edge tile and hardwood strip edging. V-cap tiles have raised and rounded corners that create a ridge around the countertop perimeter—good for containing spills and water. V-cap tiles must be cut with a tile saw. Hardwood strips should be prefinished with at least three coats of polyurethane finish. Attach the strips to the plywood core so the top of the wood will be flush with the faces of the tiles.

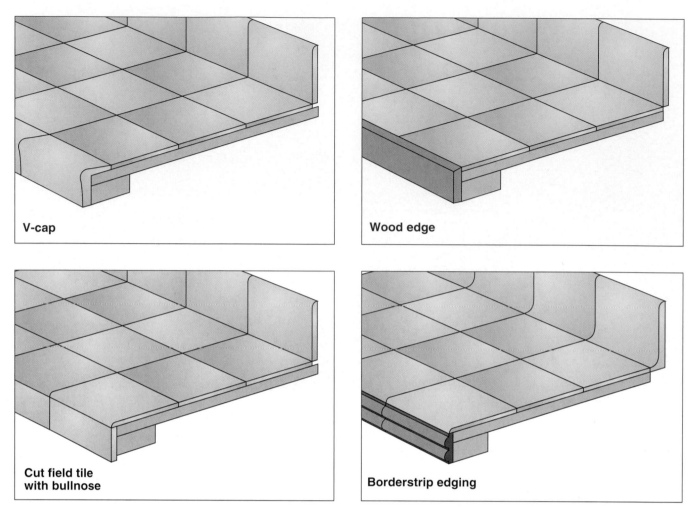

V-cap

Wood edge

Cut field tile with bullnose

Borderstrip edging

Before you select tile, consider how you want to handle the backsplash and edging, and find out what trim pieces are available in the tile you want to use. You'll probably want to use a combination of field tile and edge tile, trim or borders to create an attractive backsplash and edging.

Laying Out Tile Countertop Projects

You can lay tile over a laminate countertop that's square, level and structurally sound. Use a belt sander with 60- or 80-grit sandpaper to rough up the surface before setting the tiles. The laminate cannot have a no-drip edge. If you're using a new substrate and need to remove your existing countertop, see page 73. Make sure the base cabinets are level front to back, side to side and with adjoining cabinets. Unscrew a cabinet from the wall and use shims on the floor or against the wall to level it, if necessary.

Installing batten along the front edge of the countertop helps ensure the first row of tile is perfectly straight. For V-cap tiles, fasten a 1 × 2 batten along the reference line, using screws. The first row of field tile is placed against this batten. For bullnose tiles, fasten a batten that's

the same thickness as the edging tile, plus ⅛" for mortar thickness, to the face of the countertop so the top is flush with the top of the counter. The bullnose tiles are aligned with the outside edge of the batten. For wood edge trim, fasten a 1 × 2 batten to the face of the countertop so the top edge is above the top of the counter. The tiles are installed against the batten.

Before installing any tile, lay out the tiles in a dry run using spacers. If your counter is L-shaped, start at the corner and work outward. Otherwise, start the layout at a sink to ensure equal-sized cuts on both sides of the sink. If necessary, shift your starting point so you don't end up cutting very narrow tile segments.

How to Create Starting Lines for Countertops

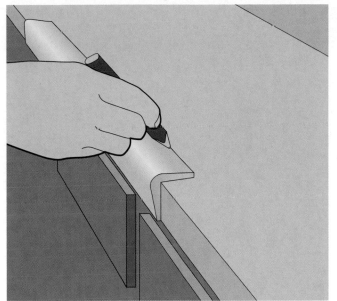

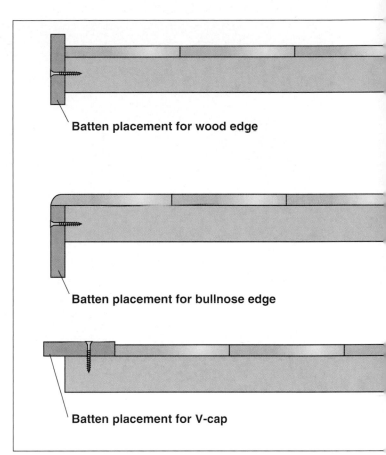

Batten placement for wood edge

Batten placement for bullnose edge

Batten placement for V-cap

1 If using V-cap tile, place it along the front edge of the substrate at one end of the countertop. Make a mark along the rear edge of the tile. Do the same at the opposite end of the countertop, then snap a chalk line between marks. Do this along the sides of the countertop as well.

2 Install battens along the edge of the countertop with screws to help line up the tile.

How to Lay Out Countertop Tile

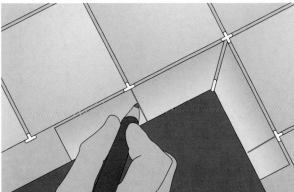
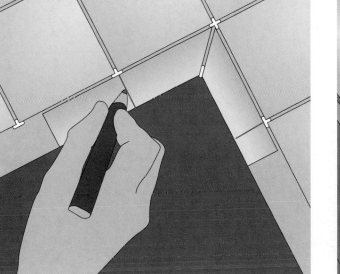

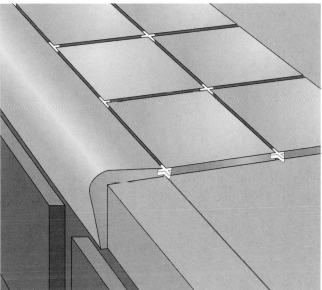

1 Lay out tiles and spacers in a dry run. Adjust starting lines, if necessary. If using battens, lay the field tile flush with the battens, then apply edge tile. Otherwise, install the edging first. If the countertop has an inside corner, start there by installing a ready-made inside corner or cutting a 45° miter in edge tile to make your own inside corner.

2 Place the first row of field tile against the edge tile, separating the tile with spacers. Lay out the remaining rows of tile. Adjust starting lines if necessary to create a layout using the least number of cut tiles.

How to Build a Tile Countertop

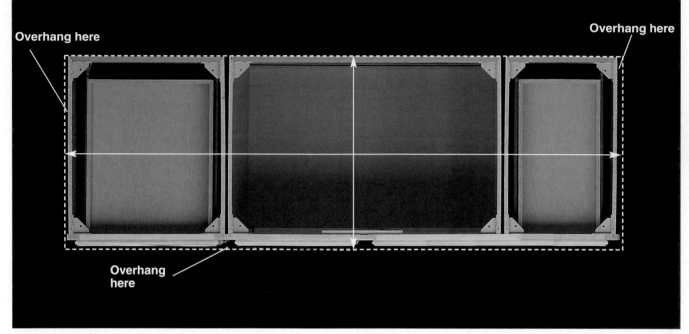

Overhang here

Overhang here

Overhang here

1 Determine the size of the plywood core by measuring across the top of the cabinets. The finished top should overhang the drawer fronts by at least ¼". Be sure to account for the thickness of the cementboard, adhesive and tile when deciding how large to make the overhang. Cut the core to size from ¾" plywood, using a circular saw. Also make any cutouts for sinks and other fixtures.

Corner bracket

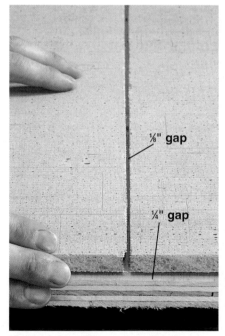

⅛" gap

¼" gap

2 Set the plywood core on top of the cabinets, and attach it with screws driven through the cabinet corner brackets. The screws should not be long enough to go through the top of the plywood core.

3 Cut pieces of cementboard to size, then mark and make the cutout for the sink. Dry-fit them on the plywood core with the rough sides of the panels facing up. Leave a ⅛" gap between the cementboard sheets and a ¼" gap along the perimeter.

Tip: Cut cementboard using a straightedge and utility knife or a cementboard cutter with a carbide tip. Hold the straightedge along the cutting line, and score the board several times with the knife. Bend the piece backward to break it along the scored line. Back-cut to finish.

4 Lay the plastic moisture barrier over the plywood core, draping it over the edges. Tack it in place with a few staples. Overlap seams in the plastic by 6", and seal them with packing tape.

5 Lay the cementboard pieces rough-side up on the plywood and attach them with cementboard screws driven every 6". Drill pilot holes using a masonry bit, and make sure all screw heads are flush with the surface. Wrap the countertop edges with 1¼"-wide cementboard strips, and attach them to the core with cementboard screws.

6 Tape all cementboard joints with fiberglass mesh tape. Apply three layers of tape along the front edge where the horizontal cementboard sheets meet the cementboard edging.

7 Fill all gaps and cover all of the tape with a layer of thin-set mortar. Feather out the mortar with a drywall knife to create a smooth, flat surface.

(continued next page)

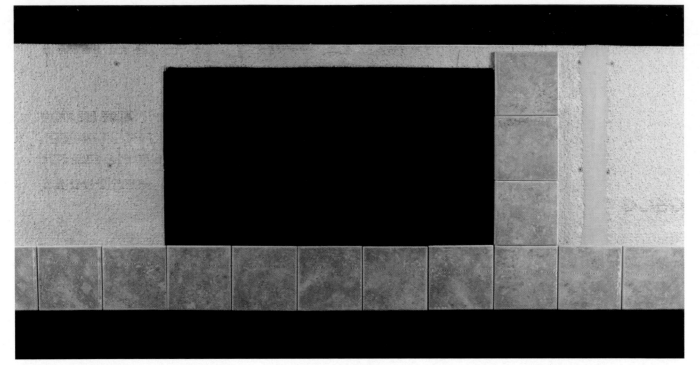

8 Dry-fit tiles on the countertop to find the layout that works best. If the tiles do not have spacing lugs on their edges, use plastic spacers to set the grout-joint gaps between tiles. Once the layout is established, make marks along the vertical and horizontal rows. Draw reference lines through the marks and use a framing square to make sure the lines are perpendicular.

9 Install the edge tiles by applying a layer of thin-set mortar to the back of the tile and the edges of the countertop, using a notched trowel. Use a dry tile set on top of the countertop to determine the height of the edge tiles. Place the tiles with a slight twisting motion. Add plastic spacers, if needed.

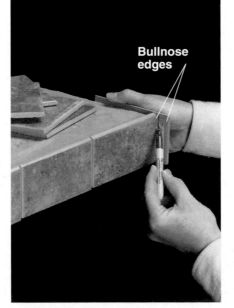

10 Use bullnose corner tile (with adjacent bullnose edges) to finish the corner edges of the countertop. Place dry tile glazed-side down on the edge face. Mark and cut the tile so the bullnose edge will sit directly on the corner. Install the piece with thin-set mortar.

Bullnose edges

11 Install the field tile after the edge tiles have set. Spread a layer of thin-set on the cement-board along the layout lines, and install perpendicular rows of tile. Make sure the spacing is correct, and use a framing square to check your work as you go.

12 To mark border tiles for cutting, allow space for backsplash tiles, grout and mortar by placing a tile against the back wall. Set another tile (A) on top of the last full tile in the field, then place a third tile (B) over tile A and hold it against the upright tile. Mark and cut tile A and install it with the cut edge toward the wall.

13 As you install small sections of tile, lay a carpeted 2 × 4 scrap over the tile and tap it lightly with a mallet. Run your hand over the tiles to make sure they are flush with one another. Remove any plastic spacers with a toothpick, and scrape any excess mortar from the grout joints. Let the mortar dry completely.

14 Mix a batch of grout with a latex additive and apply it with a rubber float, forcing the grout into the joints with a sweeping motion. Wipe away excess grout with a damp sponge. Wait one hour and wipe away the powdery haze. Let the grout cure fully.

15 Caulk along the backsplash and around penetrations with a fine bead of silicone caulk. Smooth the bead with a wet finger. After the grout cures completely, apply silicone sealer to the grout with a foam brush. Let the sealer dry, and apply a second coat.

Photo courtesy of Daltile

Tiling a Kitchen Backsplash

There are few spaces in your home with as much potential for creativity and visual impact as the space between your kitchen countertop and cupboards. A well-designed backsplash can transform the ordinary into the extraordinary.

Tiles for the backsplash can be attached directly to wallboard or plaster and do not require backerboard. When purchasing the tile, order 10 percent extra to cover breakage and cutting. Remove switch and receptacle coverplates and install box extenders to make up for the extra thickness of the tile. Protect the countertop from scratches by covering it with a drop cloth. See pages 180 to 181 for tile cutting tips.

Tools and Materials

Tools: level, tape measure, pencil, tile cutter, rod saw, notched trowel, rubber grout float, beating block, rubber mallet, sponge, bucket.

Materials: straight 1 × 2, wall tile, tile spacers (if needed), bullnose trim tile, mastic tile adhesive, masking tape, grout, caulk, drop cloth, grout sealer.

Tips for Planning Tile Layouts

Gather planning brochures and design catalogs to help you create decorative patterns and borders for the backsplash.

Photo courtesy of Hi-Ho Industries, Inc.

Break tiles into fragments and make a mosaic backsplash. Always use a sanded grout for joints wider than ⅛".

Photo courtesy of Fireclay Tile, Inc.

Add painted mural tiles to create a focal point. Mixing various tile styles adds an appealing contrast.

How to Tile a Kitchen Backsplash

1 Make a story stick by marking a board at least half as long as the backsplash area to match the tile spacing.

2 Starting at the midpoint of the installation area, use the story stick to make layout marks along the wall. If an end piece is too small (less than half a tile), adjust the midpoint to give you larger, more attractive end pieces. Use a level to mark this point with a vertical reference line.

3 While it may appear straight, your countertop may not be level and therefore is not a reliable reference line. Run a level along the counter to find the lowest point on the countertop. Mark a point two tiles up from the low point and extend a level line across the entire work area.

(continued next page)

How to Tile a Kitchen Backsplash (continued)

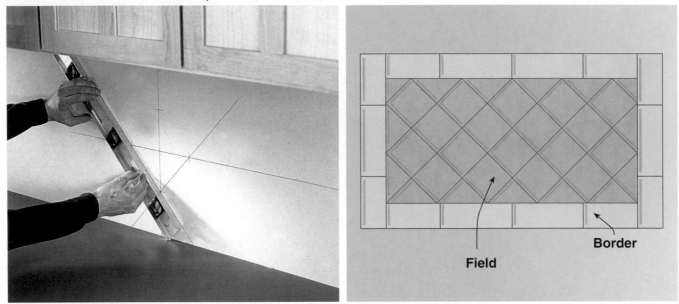

Variation: Diagonal Layout. Mark vertical and horizontal reference lines, making sure the angle is 90°. To establish diagonal layout lines, measure out equal distances from the crosspoint, then connect the points with a line. Additional layout lines can be extended from these as needed. To avoid the numerous, unattractive perimeter cuts common to diagonal layouts, try using a standard border pattern as shown. Diagonally set a field of full tiles only, then cut enough half tiles to fill out the perimeter. Finally, border the diagonal field with tiles set square to the field.

4 Apply mastic adhesive evenly to the area beneath the horizontal reference line, using a notched trowel. Comb the adhesive horizontally with the notched edge.

5 Starting at the vertical reference line, press tiles into the adhesive with a slight twisting motion. If the tiles are not self-spacing, use plastic spacers to maintain even grout lines. If the tiles do not hang in place, use masking tape to hold them in place until the adhesive sets.

6 Install a whole row along the reference line, checking occasionally to make sure the tiles are level. Continue installing tiles below the first row, trimming tiles that butt against the countertop as needed.

7 Apply adhesive to an area above the line and continue placing tiles, working from the center to the sides. Install trim tile, such as bullnose tile, to the edges of the rows.

8 When the tiles are in place, make sure they are flat and firmly embedded by laying a beating block against the tile and rapping it lightly with a mallet. Remove the spacers. Allow the mastic to dry for at least 24 hours, or as directed by the manufacturer.

9 Mix the grout and apply it with a rubber grout float. Spread it over the tiles, keeping the float at a low 30° angle, pressing the grout deep into the joints. Note: For grout joints ⅛" and smaller, be sure to use a non-sanded grout.

10 Wipe off excess grout, holding the float at a right angle to the tile, working diagonally so as not to remove grout from the joints. Clean any remaining grout from the tiles with a damp sponge, working in a circular motion. Rinse the sponge thoroughly and often.

11 Shape the grout joints by making slow, short passes with the sponge, shaving down any high spots; rinse the sponge frequently. Fill any voids with a fingerful of grout. When the grout has dried to a haze, buff the tile clean with a soft cloth. Apply a bead of caulk between the countertop and tiles. Reinstall any electrical fixtures you removed. After the grout has completely cured, apply a grout sealer.

FIXTURES & APPLIANCES

*S*electing the right appliances and fixtures for your kitchen update or remodeling project requires balancing cost, energy efficiency, performance, convenience and style. It's fun to look through magazines and at the trendy, cutting edge kitchens of model homes, but be prepared for sticker shock when you are ready to make your selections.

One way to ease this shock is to focus on the features you really need and want, and look for appliances and fixtures that offer those options. For instance, an all stainless kitchen may be appealing—but if your main goal is easy cleanup, you will be disappointed to discover that stainless steel prominently displays fingerprints and water marks.

This chapter gives basic information on appliance and fixture choices. As you read this section, consider what options you cannot live without as well as those you just don't need. Taking notes on these desires will help you narrow your choices when you begin looking at the costs of various options.

Photo courtesy of Kitchenaid

Appliance & Fixture Options

The cost of appliances and fixtures can quickly add up to be a major portion of your kitchen makeover budget. To take some of the sting out of the sticker shock, check your area for a "scratch and dent" appliance dealer. These dealers offer floor models, last year's models, returns and damaged items for significantly less. Many "damaged" items have cosmetic flaws that might actually be invisible depending on your particular arrangement.

Ranges, Cooktops & Ovens

A range, or stove, combines an oven and a cooktop in one unit. Ranges often cost less than two separate units, and take up less space. Choosing separate units, however, gives you flexibility in placement and may allow you access to features not available in a range. Cooktops can be placed in practically any enclosed cabinet with countertop. Ovens can be placed in islands, under counters and at varying heights on the wall.

The first decision to make for any of these items is what type of power. Gas is the favorite cooktop fuel of chefs and serious home cooks because it has immediate heat control. Electric cooktops are slower to heat and cool and are not as obviously "on" because there is no visible flame. Many bakers prefer an electric oven because the heat is more even. A solution is to either use separate components or to purchase a dual-fuel range that has an electric oven and a gas cooktop.

The gas cooktop has the reputation of being difficult to clean, though sealed burners make this less of an issue. All gas cooktops have some sort of grating to hold the pots above the flames; make sure you can move these easily for cleaning. With electronic ignition, gas cooktops and ovens do not have pilot lights, so the risks of extinguished pilot lights and the added heat are no longer an issue.

Gas ovens are often not as well insulated as self-cleaning electric ovens, so they may heat your kitchen space more. If you broil often, make sure the broiler is located in the main oven compartment, and not in a separate, lower compartment. This eliminates bending and allows for greater broiling capacity.

Electric cooktops come in a variety of burner

A double wall oven is a necessary convenience if you entertain often.

configurations. The traditional is the electric coil with drip plate. Solid disks are made of cast iron sealed to the cooktop. Halogen burners are underneath a glass cooktop and are heated by vacuum-sealed halogen lamps. Induction burners are also under a glass cooktop and have an electromagnetic coil that conducts electrical energy directly to the pot, requiring ferrous cookware (stainless steel, aluminum and ceramic cookware will not work). The flat ceramic tops are smooth, but may require special cleaners.

Electric ovens are conventional, convection or multi-mode. A conventional oven is the standard oven with a heating element at the bottom for

Professional-style gas ranges have the capabilities of restaurant stoves, but have important safety features necessary for home use.

baking and an element at the top for broiling. A true convection oven has no elements in the oven cavity. Instead, the baking element and a fan are located outside the cavity. The fan circulates the heated air to produce an absolutely balanced heat—you can bake as many trays of cookies as you have oven racks. The convection oven has its drawbacks, though. Many items will be dried out due to the constant airflow, the fan is noisy, and you will need to adjust all your recipes for different cooking times and temperatures. A multi-mode oven uses conventional, convection and microwave cooking. These units are expensive, and if you have the space it may be more economical in

---

GREEN DESIGN

Garbage disposers burden waste treatment systems, adding harmless food wastes to human wastes that need waste treatment. Waste treatment facilities in some areas were not engineered to handle the extra burden of food wastes. In homes with septic systems, the food waste adds to the solid waste load, requiring that you pump out the tank more often. The green solution? Compost your vegetable waste (meat waste shouldn't go in the disposer, anyway) and create a great, safe garden fertilizer while decreasing your contribution to the waste stream.

the long run to invest in two separate ovens.

If you entertain often, you may want to consider having two ovens, either as a double wall unit or as part of a dual range. Also popular now are the professional-style ranges and cooktops. These units produce high heat and generally have larger capacities than standard units. Be aware that they also require professional-style venting. Warming drawers are available as part of a range, or as separate units. These can be handy for dough raising, keeping courses warm or dealing with staggered meal times. If you do a great deal of wok cookery, you may want to invest in a specialized wok burner that generates the heat necessary in the proper configuration for this style.

Microwave Ovens

Microwaves have quickly become a standard kitchen appliance—both for their convenience and low price. Look for the features that you will use most often and an interior cavity that has the capacity you need. Though the space-saving microwave with integral exhaust fan installed over a range is popular, it is not necessarily a good idea. The ventilation provided is not optimal, the microwave impinges on the cooktop workspace and reaching over the cooktop to use the microwave can be hazardous—especially for children. If you are tight on counter space, a

cabinet-mounted microwave is a better idea.

Vent Fans

Vent fans protect your kitchen surfaces and your health by exhausting the heat, steam, grease and odors produced by cooking. Local codes may apply to venting systems, so check with a building inspector or HVAC contractor. To truly be effective, vent fans must vent to the outdoors, not filter and recirculate the air.

Vent fans are rated for airflow in cubic feet per minute (cfm) and by noise level measured in sones. Look for a high flow rating with a low noise rating. Large cooktops, specialty grills and wok burners require heavy-duty ventilation systems. Vent hoods over islands need to be more powerful because of the open, rather than enclosed, setting. Down-draft and pop-up vents pull the air down to exhaust, so they also need

Photo courtesy of Silestone by Cosentino

Separate components allow you to get exactly the features you want. Here, a gas cooktop is positioned over an electric drop-in oven.

Photo courtesy of Wilsonart International

Dual-fuel ranges combine a gas cooktop with an electric oven. A microwave with integrated exhaust hood completes this compact cooking station.

to be more powerful. Slide-out and low-profile vents are available, though they may not be as effective.

Each vent will have specific limitations concerning size and length of ductwork; make sure your planned vent outlet is within these limits.

Refrigerators

Buying a new refrigerator can be expensive, but running an older refrigerator will account for as much as 20% of your household electrical costs. New energy and pollution standards in the past 20 years have helped make refrigerators much more efficient.

Refrigerators come in a number of styles and configurations. Slide-in refrigerators are the traditional style, usually 28" to 34" deep, though some may be 24" deep. Built-in refrigerators are wider than slide-ins, but only 24" deep so they are flush with base cabinets. Built-ins need space above for venting. Refrigerator and freezer configurations include top freezer, bottom freezer and side-by-side. The top freezer is more efficient, and easier to access, but the bottom freezer puts more of the refrigerator at a usable height. Side-by-side configurations are popular because both are easily accessed, and in-door ice servers are only available on this style. The major drawback of the side-by-side is

the diminished width of the refrigerator side. A platter of hors d'oeuvres, a cookie sheet or a large roasting pan won't fit in this narrow compartment.

New freezer and refrigerator options include commercial-grade refrigerators, individual drawers that look like cabinet drawers and can be located anywhere, wine coolers and dedicated ice makers.

Dishwashers

Dishwashers, like refrigerators, have also become more efficient and quieter. A dishwasher that doesn't require hand rinsing before loading will also save water—enough so that using a dishwasher actually conserves water!

The key issues to consider in buying a dishwasher

Island cooktops require special island hoods to maintain adequate ventilation.

Glass-doored refrigerators allow you to easily view the contents without opening the door.

Placement and configuration of appliances can make them easier to use. Wall-mounted ovens and raised dishwashers make baking and cleanup easier by eliminating bending. In addition, moving the oven away from the cooktop makes it easier for two cooks to work at the same time. Side-swinging doors on a wall-mounted oven make them even easier and safer to use. Side-by-side refrigerators also cut down on bending, and the built-in water and ice dispensers conserve energy while allowing children to serve themselves. Avoid dangerous reaches across steaming stovetops by installing range hoods with wall- or counter-mounted controls and cooktops with front-mounted controls.

Photo courtesy of Wolf Appliance Company, LLC.

Photo courtesy of Sub-Zero Freezer Co., Inc.

(above) **Warming drawers** hold food at serving temperatures, freeing the oven for other tasks.

(left) **Refrigerated drawers** are convenient for snack foods or bar supplies. They can be located anywhere.

(right) **Dishwashers are available** in a wide variety of sizes—from standard units to extra-large sizes and also small drawer or countertop units.

(right, below) **A dishwasher knife drawer** holds your professional grade cutlery safely during cleaning.

Photo (right) courtesy of Maytag.

are the operating costs, noise reduction, cleaning power and features. Operating costs can be determined by looking at the yellow EnergyGuide tag. Noise reduction measures are often directly related to price. Look for sound-absorbent insulation around the tub, behind the door, over the top and behind the access panel and toe kick. Because you won't usually be able to hear a dishwasher run through its cycles in a showroom, refer to consumer ratings magazines for sound-level comparisons. A dishwasher's cleaning power depends on how it disperses and filters water. How the water jets are aimed can be as important as how many arrays of sprayers are present.

Food Disposers

The main consideration when looking at food disposers is horsepower. Models come with ⅓- to 1-horsepower motors, with the larger, more expensive models being quieter, carrying longer warranties and having more features. Most models are continuous feed, which means that a switch (usually on the wall, but occasionally sink or counter mounted) is flipped, the motor runs and items can be fed through the rubber gasket continuously. A batch-feed disposer does not have a switch. Instead, it is activated by twisting the lid in the mouth of the unit. No items can be added to the unit while it is running.

People with septic systems should be aware that a disposer adds to the overall load on the septic tank. Even though disposer units say they are safe for septic tanks and some even come with enzyme sprays to help promote the bacterial action, they will still add to the amount of sludge in the tank.

Sinks & Faucets

Stock sinks come in numerous bowl configurations, sizes and materials. The first choice to consider is the material. Stainless steel, cast

Photo courtesy of Asko

iron, enameled steel, solid surface, fireclay, acrylic and resin are all standard sink materials, each with its own advantages and disadvantages. Custom sinks are available in copper, brass, soapstone, concrete and granite.

Stainless steel sinks are easy to clean, attractive, long lasting and available in every possible bowl configuration (top mounts, undermounts and apron fronts) and in every price range. The only drawbacks are that stainless steel shows water spots and the sinks can be noisy if not properly undercoated with sound-deadening material.

Cast-iron sinks are actually cast iron with a fired-on porcelain finish. These sinks are durable, have a classy, rich appearance, and are available in a wide range of designs and colors including top mount, undermount and apron front. The only drawback of this type of sink is its hardness—you may break a few more glasses

than with a stainless, solid-surface or resin sink.

Enameled steel is the inexpensive cousin to cast iron. The metal is thinner, the enamel is less durable than porcelain, and the designs available may be limited. However, if you can find a steel sink with a porcelain finish and polyester-resin backing, you will have a sink that costs and weighs less than cast iron and absorbs shock better so you have fewer broken glasses.

Solid-surface sinks are available in a number of styles, but a limited range of colors. You will find more available undermount styles than drop-ins. This is because the majority are used as the sink component of a solid-surface counter, where they will be attached under the countertop in a seamless installation. Solid-surface sinks are shock absorbent, stain resistant and repairable. If you should happen to stain, gouge or scorch the material, a seamless, invisible repair through sanding or patching can be made.

(left) **This large utility sink** with integrated drain-board can handle the largest pots and pans with ease.

(left, below) **This one-piece stainless steel sink** with backsplash eliminates seams, making it easy to clean.

(right, below) **A fireclay or porcelain apron-front** sink is a beautiful addition to any kitchen.

Fireclay is a vitreous-china product that has a strong, smooth finish and a very hard, non-marking surface. These sinks are heavy and can be expensive, but they are available in a number of apron-front designs, which has increased their popularity.

Acrylic and fiberglass sinks are inexpensive, shock-absorbing sinks that are easy to clean but might not have good longevity.

Resin sinks are composites of resin, pigment and quartz or other minerals. This material does not chip, scratch, stain, crack or mar. The available colors are currently limited to slate, gray and two shades of white, but given the popularity of pigmented quartz-resin countertops, this is sure to change.

Sinks are mounted in a number of ways. They can be self-rimming (they rest on top of the countertop), rimmed (the sink and countertop

Above photo courtesy of Kohler

are flush and a separate steel rim joins the two) or undermounted (screwed into the underside of the countertop).

Self-rimming sinks are used in any type of countertop and are the most widely available. A variation of the self-rimming sink is the tile-in sink for tile countertops.

Top-mounted rimmed sinks have the disadvantage of having two seams, one between the rim and the counter and one between the rim and the sink, which means more areas for debris accumulation and possible leakage.

Undermount sinks are popular because of their clean lines—no part of the sink protrudes above the countertop—and because debris is less

likely to accumulate between the sink and countertop. A drawback is that undermount sinks cannot be used with laminate countertops.

Sinks are currently available in so many bowl configurations, that it would be impossible to list all of them here. Most sinks are single-, double- or triple-bowled, with the bowl depth and size ranging from a small bar sink to a large farm or utility sink. Using the undermount options allows you to create your own sink configuration using single bowls in the configuration most suited to your purposes.

When choosing a sink, remember that the primary sink should be roomy enough to easily fill or wash large pots and serving pieces. A sink (above) **Faucets with pull-out sprayers** are convenient and eliminate the need for another hole in the countertop for undermount sinks.

(left) **This dual-handled faucet** requires no cover plates, which gives it a clean, sleek look.

(right) **A pot-filler faucet** mounted over the stove is handy if you often cook pasta or fill stockpots.

that is more than 9" deep should be located in a raised countertop, because reaching into such a deep sink can cause back strain.

Faucets also come in a dizzying array of styles, materials and features. Though many kitchen faucets come with separate hot and cold taps, the single-handle lever faucets are much easier to use. Gooseneck and pull-out faucets make pot filling easier, but make sure that your sink is deep enough to accommodate the splashing from an extra-tall gooseneck. Most faucets require little or no maintenance and will retain their finish for many years, so it is mostly a matter of finding a style that suits you and your kitchen.

UNIVERSAL DESIGN

Sink depths of 8", 9" or 10" are becoming popular, but very tall or short users will find it difficult to reach the sink bottom comfortably. Raise or lower your sink countertop to enable the primary user to stand at the sink and easily reach the bottom without bending. Single-handle faucets are much easier to use, allowing for continuous temperature adjustment and easy on and off. Incorporating an anti-scald device makes the faucet safer for children.

Sinks & Faucets

Replacing a sink and faucet, or especially just the faucet, is a fast kitchen upgrade. The most difficult aspect of the project, aside from choosing which sink and which faucet, is the cramped working conditions under the sink.

Old fixtures often are corroded and stuck tight. It is easiest to remove the sink and faucet as one unit, rather than trying to remove the faucet mounting nuts while on your back inside the sink cabinet. Simply remove the tailpiece slip nut, the water connections and the sink mounting screws, and lift the whole unit free.

The same is true for installing a sink. Attach as many pieces, such as the strainer body, as you can before putting the sink into place. The exception would be a heavy, cast-iron sink. With these sinks, lift from the drain holes to avoid smashed fingers.

Sinks have pre-cut holes for faucets, sprayers and accessories. The most common options are single-, three- and four-hole. Decide on your faucet first, so you know which configuration sink to purchase. Don't forget to count a hole for a filtered water, hot water or soap dispenser. If you are placing a new single-hole faucet in an existing multiple-hole sink, coverplates are available to cover the extra holes.

SHOPPING TIPS

• *Stainless steel–wrapped, flexible supply hoses are slightly more expensive, but are burstproof.*
• *Before leaving the store, read the sink and faucet directions to make sure you have the tools and parts you need.*

Removing Sinks & Faucets

Removing an old sink or faucet can be a bit messy. Have rags and a bucket handy to catch water left in supply and drain pipes.

Turn off the water at the supply valves—if they stick, gently wiggle the handle back and forth to loosen scale deposits. A vise-style pliers around the handle will give you more leverage. If necessary, turn off the main water supply and replace the supply valves.

Tools and Materials

Tools: utility knife, channel-type pliers, basin wrench, spud wrench, hammer.

Materials: penetrating oil.

How to Remove an Old Sink

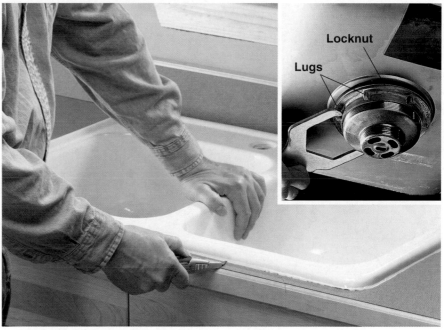

Use a utility knife to cut the caulk (if present) around the sink. Unscrew slip nuts from both ends of tailpiece, and remove tailpiece. Remove the locknut, using a spud wrench (inset). Tap stubborn locknut lugs with a hammer to loosen. Unscrew the locknut completely, and remove the strainer assembly. Release sink-mounting clips, remove the faucet, and lift out the sink. (See pages 123 to 124 to remove a food disposer.)

How to Remove an Old Sink Faucet

1 Spray penetrating oil on tailpiece mounting nuts and supply tube coupling nuts. Remove the coupling nuts with a basin wrench or channel-type pliers.

2 Remove the tailpiece mounting nuts with a basin wrench or channel-type pliers. Basin wrench has a long handle that makes it easy to work in tight areas.

3 Remove faucet. Use a putty knife to clean away old putty from surface of sink. If reusing the sink, clean the surface with mildly abrasive non-chlorine cleanser.

Installing a Kitchen Sink

Most top-mounted, self-rimming sinks are easily installed. Framed sinks are also fairly easy to install, but they are not as common. Under-mounted sinks are usually professionally installed as part of a countertop installation.

Kitchen sinks for do-it-yourself installation are made from cast iron coated with enamel, stainless steel, enameled steel, acrylic, fiberglass or resin composites.

Because cast-iron sinks are heavy, their weight holds them in place and they require no mounting hardware. Except for their weight, they are easy to install. Stainless steel and enameled-steel sinks weigh less than cast-iron and most require mounting brackets. Some acrylic and resin sinks rely on silicone caulk to hold them in place.

When choosing a sink, make sure the predrilled openings will fit your faucet. To make the countertop cutout for a kitchen sink installation, see page 76.

If you are replacing a sink, but not the counter-top, make sure the new sink is the same size or larger. All old silicone caulk residue must be removed with acetone or denatured alcohol, or else the new caulk will not stick.

SHOPPING TIPS

* *When purchasing a sink you also need to buy strainer bodies and baskets, sink clips and drain pipes.*
* *Look for basin dividers that are lower than the sink rim—this reduces splashing.*
* *Drain holes in the back or to the side make for more usable space under the sink.*

Tools and Materials

Tools: caulk gun, screwdriver.

Materials: sink, sink frame, plumber's putty or silicone caulk, mounting clips.

How to Install a Self-rimming Sink

1 After making countertop cutout, lay the sink up-side down. Apply a ¼" bead of silicone caulk or plumber's putty around the underside of sink flange.

2 Position front of sink in countertop cutout, by holding it through the drain openings. Carefully lower the sink into position. Press down to create a tight seal, then wipe away excess caulk. Install sink clips (if necessary) and tighten with a screwdriver.

How to Install a Framed Sink

1 Turn the sink frame upside down. Apply a ¼" bead of silicone caulk or plumber's putty around both sides of the vertical flange.

2 Set the sink upside down inside the frame. Bend frame tabs to hold the sink. Carefully set the sink into the cutout opening, and press down to create a tight seal.

3 Hook mounting clips every 6" to 8" around the frame from underneath countertop. Tighten mounting screws. Wipe away excess caulk from the frame.

Installing a Faucet & Drain

Most new kitchen faucets feature single-handle control levers and washerless designs that rarely require maintenance. Additional features include colorful enameled finishes, detachable spray nozzles or even digital temperature readouts.

Connect the faucet to hot and cold water lines with easy-to-install flexible supply tubes made from vinyl or braided steel. If your faucet has a separate sprayer, install the sprayer first. Pull the sprayer hose through the sink opening and attach to the faucet body before installing the faucet.

Where local codes allow, use plastic piping for drain hookups. A wide selection of extensions and angle fittings lets you easily plumb any sink configuration. Manufacturers offer kits that contain all the fittings needed for attaching a food disposer or dishwasher to the sink drain system.

Tools and Materials

Tools: adjustable wrench, basin wrench or channel-type pliers, hacksaw.

Materials: faucet, silicone caulk, plumber's putty, flexible vinyl or braided steel supply tubes, drain components.

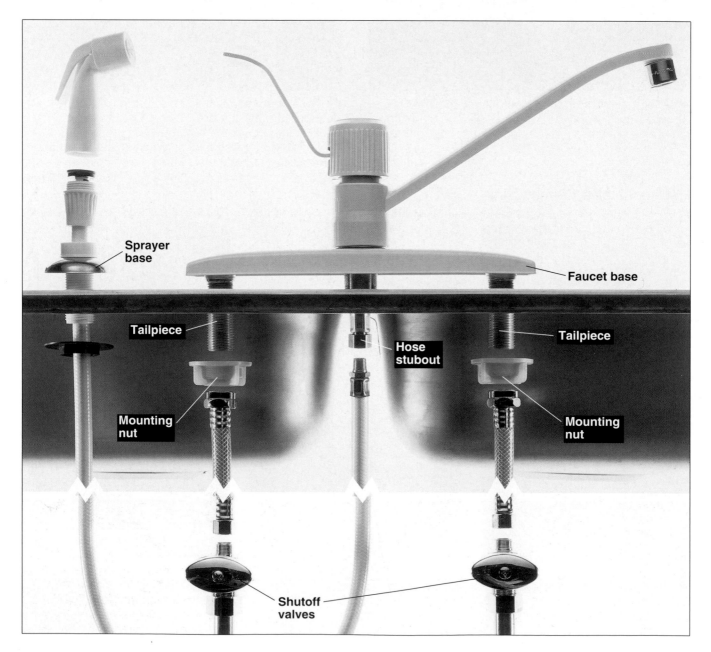

How to Install a New Sink Faucet

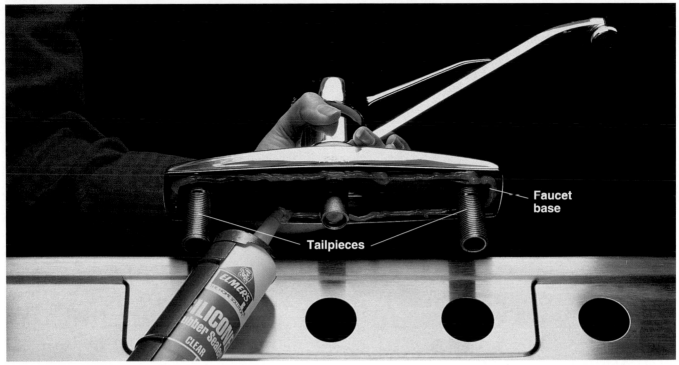

Faucet base

Tailpieces

1 Apply a ¼" bead of silicone caulk or plumber's putty around the base of the faucet. Insert the faucet tailpieces into the sink openings. Position the faucet so the base is parallel to the back of the sink, and press the faucet down to make sure caulk forms a good seal.

Mounting nut

Friction washer

2 Thread the metal friction washers and the mounting nuts onto the tailpieces, then tighten with a basin wrench or channel-type pliers. Wipe away excess caulk around base of faucet.

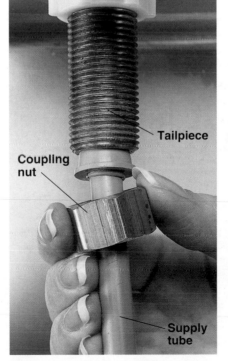

Tailpiece

Coupling nut

Supply tube

3 Connect flexible supply tubes to the faucet tailpieces. Tighten coupling nuts with a basin wrench or channel-type pliers.

Supply tube

Shutoff valve

4 Attach supply tubes to shutoff valves, using compression fittings. Hand-tighten nuts, then use an adjustable wrench to tighten nuts ¼ turn. If necessary, hold valve with another wrench while tightening.

How to Connect a Faucet with Preattached Supply Tubing

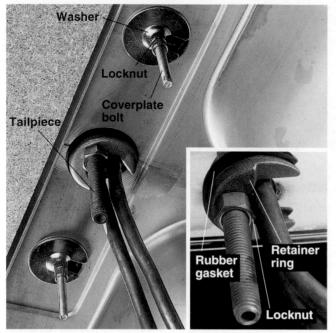

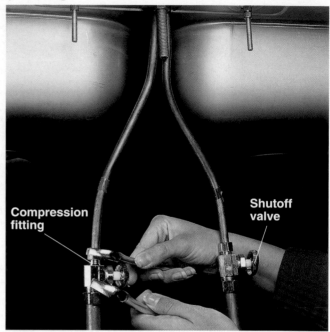

1 Attach faucet to sink by placing rubber gasket, retainer ring, and locknut onto threaded tailpiece. Tighten locknut with a basin wrench or channel-type pliers. Some center-mounted faucets have a decorative coverplate. Secure coverplate from underneath with washers and locknuts screwed onto coverplate bolts.

2 Connect preattached supply tubing to shutoff valves with compression fittings. If color-coded, the red tube should be attached to the hot water pipe, and the blue tube to the cold water pipe. Check the directions for non-color-coded tubes.

How to Attach a Sink Sprayer

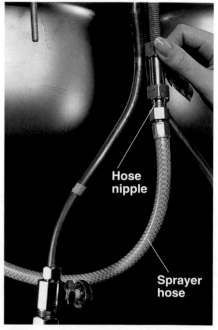

1 Apply a ¼" bead of plumber's putty or silicone caulk to bottom edge of sprayer base. Insert tailpiece of sprayer base into sink opening.

2 Place friction washer over tailpiece. Screw the mounting nut onto tailpiece and tighten with a basin wrench or channel-type pliers. Wipe away excess putty around base of sprayer.

3 Screw sprayer hose onto the hose nipple on the bottom of the faucet. Tighten ¼ turn, using a basin wrench or channel-type pliers.

How to Attach Drain Lines

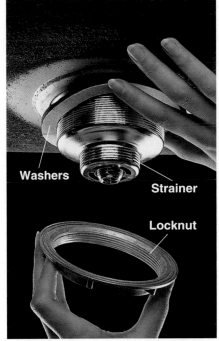

1 Install sink strainer in each sink drain opening. Apply ¼" bead of plumber's putty around bottom of flange. Insert strainer into drain opening. Place rubber and fiber washers over neck of strainer. Screw locknut onto neck and tighten with channel-type pliers.

2 Attach tailpiece to strainer. Place insert washer in flared end of tailpiece, then attach tailpiece by screwing a slip nut onto sink strainer. If necessary, tailpiece can be cut to fit with a hacksaw.

3 On sinks with two basins, use a continuous waste-T fitting to join the tailpieces. Attach the fitting with slip washers and nuts. Beveled side of washers face threaded portion of pipes.

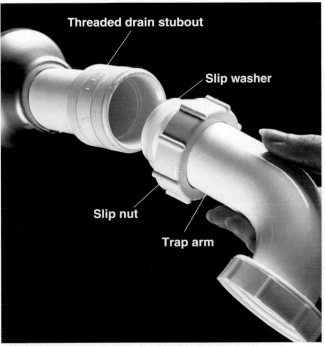

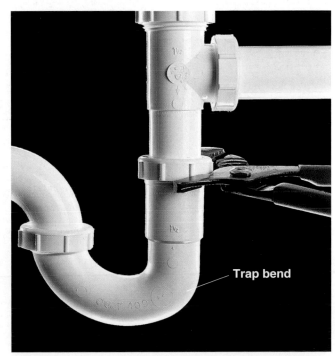

4 Attach the trap arm to the drain stubout, using a slip nut and washer. Beveled side of washer should face threaded drain stubout. If necessary, trap arm can be cut to fit with a hacksaw.

5 Attach trap bend to trap arm, using slip nuts and washers. Beveled side of washers should face trap bend. Tighten all nuts with channel-type pliers.

Appliances

A kitchen makeover or remodeling project usually includes adding or replacing appliances. In most cases this means removing a unit and sliding a new, similarly sized unit into place. However, retrofitting an older kitchen to handle a disposer or dishwasher requires plumbing changes and electrical updates, and adding a vent hood involves adding an electrical circuit, running ductwork and cutting through the exterior or roof of the house. Fortunately, these projects only require basic to moderate levels of do-it-yourself ability.

The most difficult aspect of many appliance projects is actually moving the appliance into the house and into the kitchen. As the following installation and removal projects show, it is important to protect the kitchen floor. Door frames and countertop edges can also be damaged during appliance moving—take it slowly and carefully and have plenty of help on hand.

SHOPPING TIPS

• *Scratch-and-dent appliance stores often have great deals on refrigerators, dishwashers, ranges, ovens and cooktops.*

• *Before you begin shopping, check consumer magazines for the latest ratings of appliance performance.*

• *Get the look of stainless steel without the expense or maintenance by purchasing coated steel appliances.*

•*Check energy ratings (the yellow label) especially on dishwashers and refrigerators.*

• *Most appliances come in standard dimensions, but always double-check the dimensions of the appliance and the space before purchasing.*

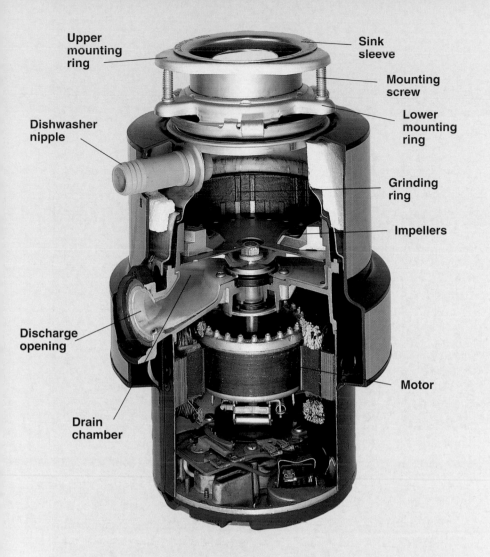

Upper mounting ring

Sink sleeve

Mounting screw

Dishwasher nipple

Lower mounting ring

Grinding ring

Impellers

Discharge opening

Motor

Drain chamber

Food disposers grind food scraps and kitchen waste so they can be flushed away through the sink drain system.

Removing & Installing a Food Disposer

Food disposers grind food waste so it can be flushed down the sink drain. They are convenient, but significantly increase the load handled by the sewage system—as much as adding another person to the household.

To prevent problems, choose a food disposer with at least a ½-horsepower motor, and a self-reversing feature to prevent jamming. Also look for foam sound insulation, a cast-iron grinding ring and overload protection that resets the motor if it overheats.

Removing the old food disposer is the first step if you're installing a new disposer or if you're replacing a sink. When replacing a disposer, bear in mind that both removal and installation will be easier if you replace the unit with another of the same make and model, since some parts can remain in place. However, if you end up buying a different model, you can still do the work yourself. The extra steps aren't difficult.

Tools and Materials

Tools: screwdriver, adjustable wrench, combination tool, hacksaw, putty knife.

Materials: food disposer, 12-gauge appliance cord with grounded plug, wire connectors, plumber's putty, dishwasher nipple, hose clamp, bucket.

If the disposer won't run and doesn't hum when you turn it on, push the reset button on the bottom of the unit.

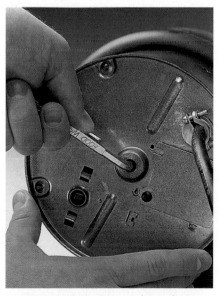

If the disposer hums but does not run when you turn it on, it's probably jammed. Free it by turning the impeller assembly.

How to Remove a Food Disposer

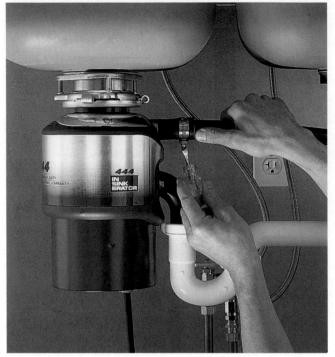

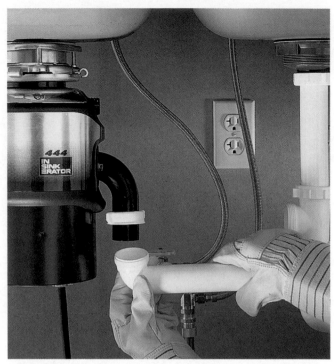

1 Using a screwdriver, loosen the screw on the hose clamp, then remove the dishwasher drain hose from the dishwasher nipple.

2 Place a bucket under the pipe. Use an adjustable wrench to loosen the slip nut connecting the continuous waste pipe and the discharge tube. Disconnect the pipe from the tube. If the slip nuts are stuck in place, use a hacksaw to cut the pipe loose, just past the elbow.

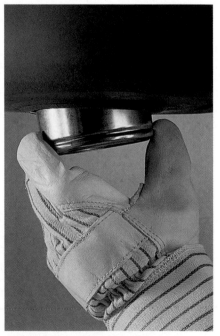

3 Insert a screwdriver or the disposer wrench into a mounting lug on the lower mounting ring. Turn counterclockwise until the mounting ears are unlocked.

4 If the mounting assembly in place is compatible with the new unit, you're done with the removal phase of the project. If it isn't, use a screwdriver to loosen the three mounting screws, then remove the mounting assembly.

5 Pry off the fiber gasket, the sink sleeve and flange. Scrape away the plumber's putty, using a putty knife and an abrasive pad. Thoroughly clean the sleeve, flange and sink opening.

124

How to Install a Food Disposer

1 Remove plate on bottom of disposer. Use combination tool to strip about ½" of insulation from each wire in appliance cord. Connect white wires, using a wire nut. Connect black wires. Attach green insulated wire to green ground screw. Gently push wires into opening. Replace bottom plate.

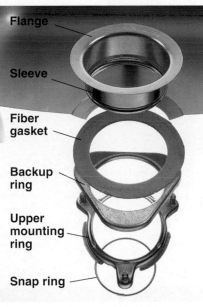

Flange
Sleeve
Fiber gasket
Backup ring
Upper mounting ring
Snap ring

2 Apply ¼-inch bead of plumber's putty under the flange of the disposer sink sleeve. Insert sleeve in drain opening, and slip the fiber gasket and the backup ring onto the sleeve. Place upper mounting ring on sleeve and slide snap ring into groove.

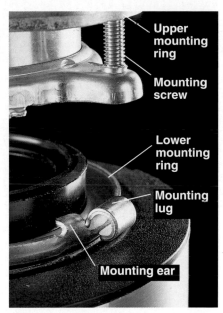

Upper mounting ring
Mounting screw
Lower mounting ring
Mounting lug
Mounting ear

3 Tighten the three mounting screws. Hold disposer against upper mounting ring so that the mounting lugs on the lower mounting ring are directly under the mounting screws. Turn the lower mounting ring clockwise until the disposer is supported by the mounting assembly.

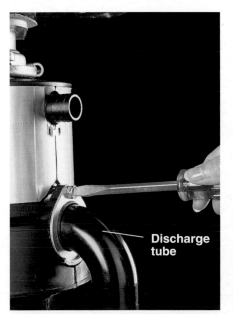

Discharge tube

4 Attach the discharge tube to the discharge opening on the side of the disposer, using the rubber washer and metal flange. If dishwasher will be attached, knock out the plug in the dishwasher nipple, using a screwdriver. Attach the dishwasher drain hose to nipple with hose clamp.

Continuous waste

5 Attach the discharge tube to continuous waste pipe with slip washer and nut. If discharge tube is too long, cut it with a hacksaw or tubing cutter.

Mounting lug
Lower mounting ring

6 Lock disposer into place. Insert a screwdriver or disposer wrench into a mounting lug on the lower mounting ring, and turn clockwise until the mounting ears are locked. Tighten all drain slip nuts with channel-type pliers.

Installing On-demand Hot Water

An on-demand hot water dispenser at your kitchen sink is especially useful if you regularly enjoy tea, or instant hot chocolate, cereals or soups. The dispensers can be set at a range of temperatures, but 190° is standard. Some dispensers are available with a dual faucet, so you can dispense heated water and filtered water from the same faucet. A note of caution: If you have young children, be aware that these faucets are easy to turn on and the water is instantly at 190° which will cause serious burns.

The dispenser head installs in the accessory hole in the sink, which means the sprayer hose will have to be removed if you have one. If you don't have a sprayer hose, you will have to install a sink with an accessory hole. The electric heating unit also requires an electrical outlet under the sink. If you already have a food disposer and dishwasher plugged in to your under sink outlet, you will need to add a fourplex outlet. Do not use extension cords, outlet extenders or power strips.

Tools and Materials
Tools: adjustable wrench, screwdriver.
Materials: ¼" soft copper tubing, saddle valve or dual-outlet valve.

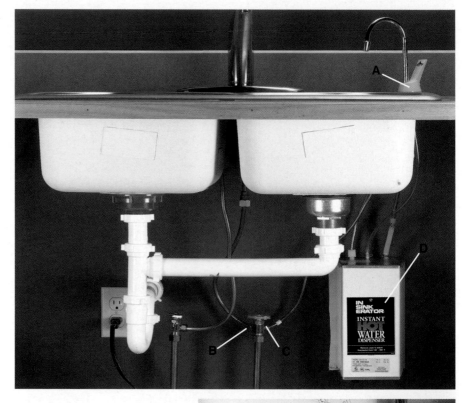

Place the dispenser head
(A) through the provided washers and into the sink accessory hole. From underneath, slip the washer and tightening nut over the threaded tube and tighten. (B) Turn off the water supply and attach a saddle valve (see page 133) or a ⅜" to ¼" dual-outlet valve to the cold water line.

(C) Place the nut and ferrule from the valve over the copper supply tubing line from the dispenser head. Push the tube into the valve opening as far as it will go. Finger-tighten the nut, making sure the supply tube is aligned in the hole. Tighten the nut firmly with a wrench, but do not over-tighten.

(D) Hold the heating unit against the back or side of the cabinet and mark its position, making sure the hoses from the dispenser head can reach it. Install the hanging bracket. Hang the heating unit. (E) Connect the inlet tube to the inlet fitting on the heating unit, carefully finger-tightening the nut before tightening it with a wrench. (F) Connect the vent line, if present, using the supplied hose clamp. (G) Connect the outlet tube to the outlet fitting with a hose clamp. Turn on the water supply and follow the manufacturer's directions for filling the unit and starting the heating element.

Installing Water Filtration Systems

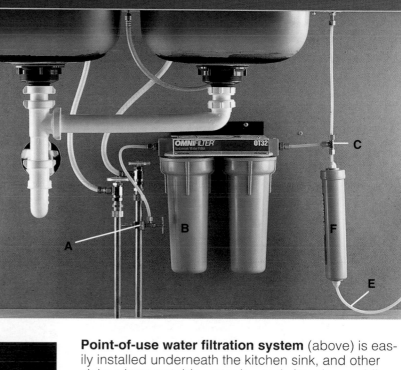

Water filtration systems are available for the whole house and for point-of-use locations. Whole-house systems are effective for reducing amounts of sediment and chlorine. Point-of-use systems are very effective at reducing lead and bacteria. Installing both provides the best-tasting and safest water.

Tools and Materials

Tools: adjustable wrench, channel-type pliers.
Materials: ¼" soft copper tubing, saddle valve, brass compression fittings.

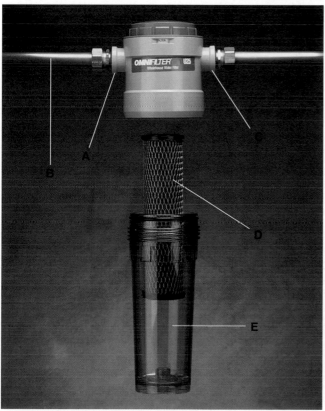

Point-of-use water filtration system (above) is easily installed underneath the kitchen sink, and other sinks where potable water is used. Attach a saddle valve (A) to the cold water supply pipe. Tubing connects the intake side of the filtration unit (B) to the saddle valve. Tubing connects the outtake side of the filtration unit to a T-valve (C). Additional tubing connects this valve to the faucet (D) and to the refrigerator/ice-maker line (E). Another filter (F) can be installed in the tubing for the refrigerator/ice maker for additional protection.

Whole-house filtration system (shown in exploded view, left) is installed in the pipe carrying water to the house from the water meter. The intake side of the filtration unit (A) is connected to the pipe to the water meter (B). Pipe supplying filtered water to the house is connected to the outtake side of the unit (C). Filters (D) must be replaced every few months, depending on type and manufacturer. The filtration unit cover (E) unscrews for filter access.

Removing & Installing a Dishwasher

A dishwasher requires a hot water supply connection, a drain connection and an electrical hookup. These connections are easiest to make when the dishwasher is located next to the sink.

Hot water reaches the dishwasher through a supply tube. With a multiple-outlet shutoff valve or brass T-fitting on the hot water pipe, you can control water to the sink and dishwasher with the same valve.

To prevent drain water from backing up into the dishwasher, the drain hose needs to be attached to the underside of the countertop. Some local codes require the installation of an air gap.

A dishwasher requires its own 20-amp electrical circuit. For convenience, have this circuit wired into one-half of a split duplex receptacle. The other half of the receptacle powers the food disposer.

Tools and Materials

Tools: screwdriver, utility knife, drill with 2" hole saw, adjustable wrench, channel-type pliers, combination tool.

Materials: drain hose, waste-T tailpiece, braided steel supply tube, rubber connector for food disposer, hose clamps, brass L-fitting, 12-gauge appliance power cord, wire connectors.

How to Remove a Dishwasher

Remove the toe kick and access panel (if present) by unscrewing the attachment screws. Unplug the dishwasher or, if it is wired directly, turn off the power at the service panel. Remove the junction box cover and remove the wire connectors and the cable clamp. Turn off the water supply. Disconnect the water supply line from the 90° elbow. Disconnect the drain line from the waste-T or disposer. Remove the mounting screws inside the door (inset). Lower leg levelers and slide out dishwasher.

How to Install a Dishwasher

1 Cut openings in side of sink base cabinet for electrical and plumbing lines, using a drill and hole saw. Dishwasher instructions specify size and locations of openings. Slide dishwasher into place, feeding rubber drain hose through hole in cabinet. Level the dishwasher.

2 Attach the dishwasher drain hose to the nipple on the food disposer with hose clamps. On sinks without food disposer, attach a special waste-T sink tailpiece to sink strainer (shown above). Attach the drain hose to the waste-T nipple with a hose clamp.

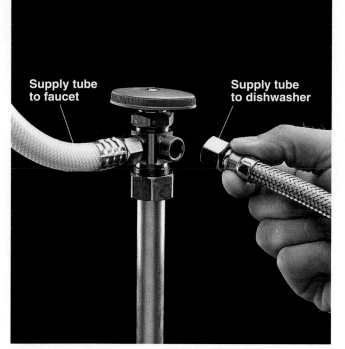

Supply tube to faucet

Supply tube to dishwasher

3 Connect the dishwasher supply tube to the hot water shutoff, using channel-type pliers. This connection is easiest with a multiple-outlet shutoff valve or a brass T-fitting.

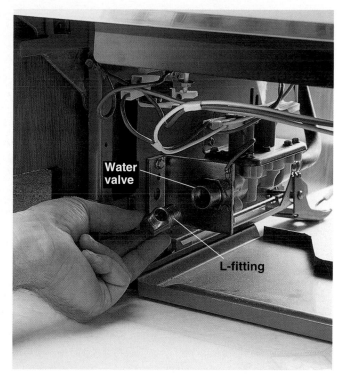

Water valve

L-fitting

4 Remove the access panel on the front of the dishwasher. Connect a brass L-fitting to the threaded opening on the dishwasher water valve, and tighten with channel-type pliers.

5 Run the braided steel supply tube from the hot water pipe to the dishwasher water valve. Attach supply tube to L-fitting, using channel-type pliers.

6 Remove the cover on the electrical box. Run power cord from outlet through to electrical box. Strip about ½" insulation from each cord wire, using a combination tool. Connect black wires, using a wire connector. Connect white wires. Connect green insulated wire to ground screw. Replace box cover and dishwasher access panel.

Installing a Raised Dishwasher

Raising the dishwasher 6" to 9" makes it much easier to load and unload. You'll eliminate a lot of stooping, which is especially important for those of us with sore backs. A raised dishwasher is also much easier for wheelchair users to operate.

These directions are for raising an existing dishwasher 8¼"—the height of a 2 × 8 and a sheet of ½" plywood. These directions cover the new extra space above the toe kick with a piece of matching cabinetry. Because the platform will cover the previous access holes, you will need to cut new access holes in the side cabinets.

A raised dishwasher ideally should have 12" of countertop available on one side as a "landing" area for dish unloading. If your dishwasher currently abuts the sink, you will need to move it, since the sink needs to have clearance of 12" on one side and 21" on the other.

Because dishwashers are meant to be built in, the directions include the creation of side panels to house the portion of the dishwasher that extends above the countertop.

See pages 128 to 129 for installing a dishwasher. The easiest way to move the dishwasher into the new space is to make another, temporary box of 2 × 8 lumber and plywood the same size as the dishwasher footprint. Push this box against the dishwasher opening, pick up the dishwasher and place it on the box, then slide the dishwasher into the new opening.

Tools and Materials

Tools: circular saw, drill, framing square, jig saw, jamb saw.

Materials: 2 × 8 lumber, 1 × 3 lumber, ½" plywood, 2", 1¼" & ¾" screws, ½" × 2" angle irons, ½" × 4" mending plates, masking tape, edge banding, drawer panel.

Cutting List				
Part	Name	Measurements	Material	No.
A	Platform sides	24"*	2 × 8	2
B	Platform cross braces	21"*	2 × 8	2
C	Platform top	24" × 24"	½" plywood	1
D	Side panels	24" × 8¼"*	½" plywood	
E	Cleats	21"	1 × 3	1

*approximate measurement, cut to fit.

How to Install a Raised Dishwasher

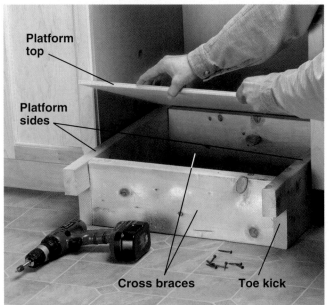

Platform top

Platform sides

Cross braces   Toe kick

1 Remove the dishwasher completely. Cut a 4" × 4" notch in each platform side piece. (Make sure this matches your existing toe kick space. Most toe kick cutouts are 4" × 4" and covered with molding.) Place the cross brace to align with the back of the toe kick cutout. Place the other cross brace at the back. Drill pilot holes and attach with 2" screws. Cut the ½" plywood to fit the platform and attach with 1¼" screws. Place the platform into the dishwasher opening.

2 Put masking tape on top of the counter and use a framing square to mark cutting lines flush with the cabinet edges on each side of the opening. Use a jig saw to cut the countertop. To cut the backsplash, use a jamb saw or a reciprocating saw. The masking tape prevents the laminate from chipping.

3 Cut the plywood side panels to size. **For frameless cabinets,** cut length to match front edge of cabinet sides. Use a compass to scribe the backsplash cutouts for the side panels and cut, using a jig saw. Apply edge banding to exposed edge and install with mending plates.

For framed cabinets, cut length to match the cabinet front edge minus the face frame. Use a compass to scribe the backsplash cutouts for the side panels and cut, using a jig saw. Install a matching face frame filler strip. Use scrap lumber and mending plates to set the panels back from the edge.

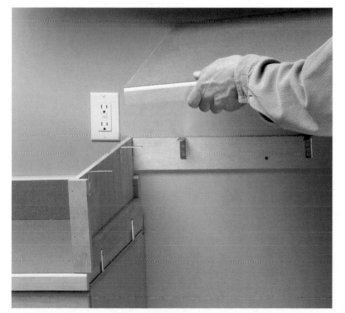

4 Cut the new countertop to size and apply edge trim to match. Attach a 1 × 3 cleat to the wall, using 2" screws. Install the countertop, using two angle irons per side and ¾" screws.

5 Make the necessary connections and slide the dishwasher into the new space. Make the final connections (see page 129). Reattach the access panel cover (if present), but leave off the toe kick plate. Purchase a door or drawer panel to match your cabinets and install across the front of the platform and the dishwasher toe kick space. Install toe kick molding to match.

Photo courtesy of Maytag

Removing & Installing a Refrigerator

Refrigerators are heavy and bulky, and their compressors and cooling coils make them sensitive to jarring. Before moving, refer to the manufacturer's information for specific directions for your model.

If moving a refrigerator a short distance for cleaning or painting, you do not need to empty it. Otherwise, empty the refrigerator. Even if you are simply sliding the fridge out a short distance, protect the floor surface from being scratched, using heavy-duty cardboard, wood paneling or thin plywood. Tilt the refrigerator backward and slide the floor protection under the front wheels or leveling legs. Carefully continue sliding or rolling the refrigerator out. Lift the back wheels or levelers onto the floor protection. Once the refrigerator is out from the wall, unplug it. If a water supply is present, locate the shutoff valve (which may be in the basement) and turn it off. Disconnect the water supply.

Use an appliance dolly to lift the fridge from the side only—not the front or the back. If it will not fit through doorways, remove the door handles. Refer to the manufacturer's instructions before removing doors, as in-door dispensers have water lines that must be disconnected.

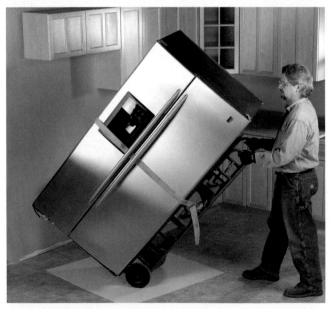

Protect flooring by placing heavy cardboard, wood paneling or thin plywood on the floor in front of the refrigerator location.

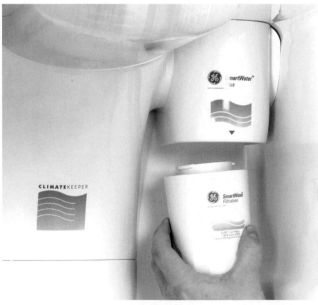

Refrigerators with water dispensers often have their own water filter. This filters the dispenser water and the ice-maker water, eliminating the need for an in-line water filter.

Installing a Refrigerator Ice Maker

Many refrigerators come with ice makers, which need to be attached to a water supply. The most difficult aspect is locating a water supply close to the refrigerator. Most installations involve drilling a hole through the floor and attaching the tubing to a nearby supply line in the basement.

Parts for ice-maker installation are available separately, or as kits containing saddle valve, tubing and compression fittings. Appliance stores, service centers and home centers have kits available with copper or plastic tubing. The plastic tubing can become brittle over time and possibly break, so most appliance centers recommend using copper tubing.

Tools and Materials

Tools: adjustable wrench.

Materials: ¼" soft copper tubing, saddle valve, brass compression fittings.

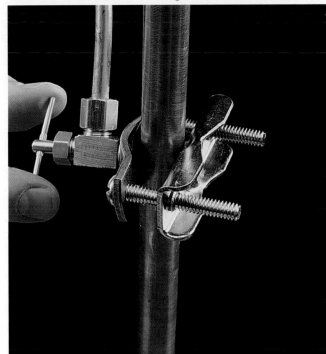

1 Shut off water at main shutoff valve. Attach a ¼" saddle valve to cold water pipe. Connect ¼" soft copper tubing to saddle valve with compression ring and coupling nut. Closing spigot fully causes spike inside valve to puncture water pipe. Allow 2 to 3 ft. of extra copper tubing to create a coil (see step 3).

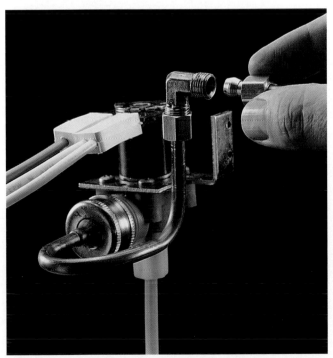

2 Run copper tubing to refrigerator. Connect water supply tube to the water valve tube, using a ¼" compression elbow. Slide coupling nuts and compression rings over tubes, and insert tubes into elbow. Tighten coupling nuts.

3 Arrange the copper coil so it won't be pinched when the refrigerator is moved back into place. Carefully roll the refrigerator into place and lock the wheels.

Removing & Installing a Range

When moving a range for painting or cleaning, removing it for replacement, or installing a new range, make sure you protect the flooring as shown below. Use an appliance dolly to lift the range from the side only—not the front or the back. If the range will not fit through doors, remove the oven door handle.

An electric range or cooktop must have its own dedicated 240-volt circuit. A gas range or cooktop must have the gas connections made by an authorized installer. Contact your gas provider or plumbing contractor for service in your area. Gas ranges and cooktops also need a grounded 3-hole electrical outlet to power the electronic ignition, clock and timers.

SHOPPING TIPS

• *Smooth-surface cooktops require special care and cleaning supplies.*

• *Self-cleaning ovens (electric ranges only) are better insulated.*

Photo courtesy of General Electric

How to Move a Range

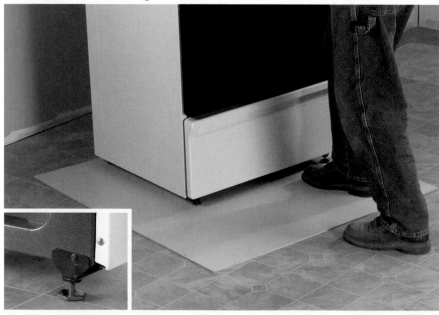

1 To prevent the leveling legs (inset) from scratching or tearing the floor covering, use heavy-duty cardboard or wood paneling as protection. Tilt the range back and slide the floor protection under the front leveling legs. Slide the range out and lift the back legs onto the floor protection.

2 Once the range is away from the wall, unplug it or turn off and disconnect the gas line. NOTE: Some codes require gas connectors to be handled only by licensed contractors.

Installing a Cooktop

How to Install an Electric or Gas Cooktop

Each individual cooktop will have specific minimum clearances. Carefully read the manufacturer's instructions before beginning any cooktop installation. Installation in solid-surface (Corian) material and stone counters requires different cutout clearances (listed in the cooktop instructions) and the use of reflective aluminum tape. Check with your countertop manufacturer to make sure your cooktop installation will not damage the countertop.

Tools and Materials

Tools: framing square, drill, jig saw, screwdriver, combination tool.

Materials: cooktop with installation kit, masking tape, marker, junction box, NM cable, wire connectors.

1 Using the dimensions from the installation instructions, draw the cutting lines on masking tape on the countertop. Use a framing square to ensure all corners are square and aligned properly. Drill pilot holes, then use a jig saw to make the cuts.

2 Place the cooktop upside down on a protected surface and attach the foam tape as directed. Attach the mounting brackets in the specified holes.

3 Insert the cooktop into the countertop and attach the brackets to the cabinet sides, countertop or wood blocks, depending on stove type.

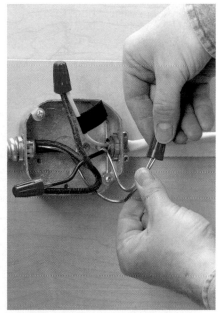

4 Install a junction box under the counter within the distances specified in the directions. Insert the wires from the stove conduit through a cable clamp and into the junction box. Connect the black wires; connect the red wire from the stove conduit to the white supply wire and tag the white wire with black electrical tape; connect the bare or green grounds. Close the junction box.

135

Installing a Vent Hood

A vent hood eliminates heat, moisture and cooking vapors from your kitchen. It has an electric fan unit with one or more filters and a system of metal ducts to vent air to the outdoors. A ducted vent hood is more efficient than a ductless model, which filters and recirculates air without removing it.

Metal ducts for a vent hood can be round or rectangular. Elbows and transition fittings are available for both types of ducts. These fittings let you vent around corners, or join duct components that differ in shape or size.

Tools and Materials

Tools: tape measure, screwdrivers, hammer, drill, reciprocating saw, combination tool, metal snips, masonry drill and masonry chisel (for brick or stucco exterior).

Materials: duct sections, duct elbow, duct cap, vent hood, ¾", 1½", 2½" sheetmetal screws, 1¼" drywall screws, silicone caulk, metallic duct tape, wire connectors, eye protection, pencil, 2" masonry nails (for brick or stucco exterior).

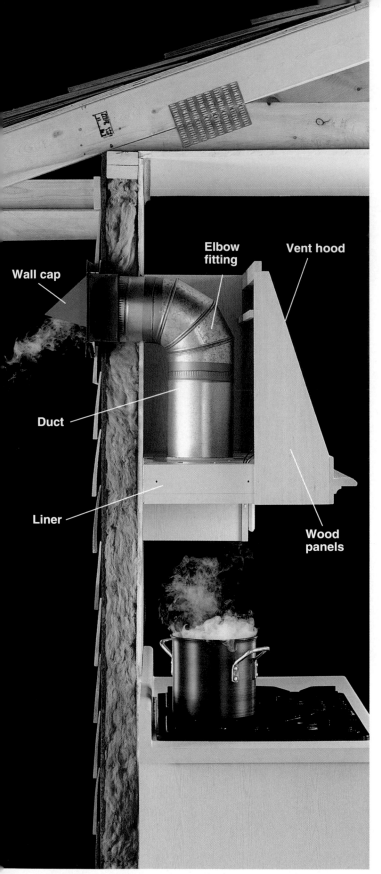

A wall-mounted vent hood (shown in cutaway) is installed between wall cabinets. The fan unit is fastened to a metal liner that is anchored to cabinets. Duct and elbow fitting exhaust cooking vapors to the outdoors through a wall cap. The vent fan and duct are covered by wood or laminate panels that match the cabinet finish.

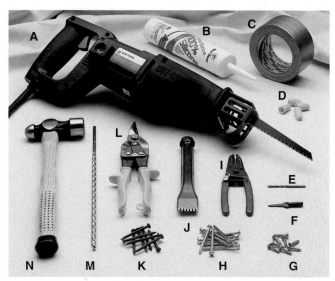

Tools & materials include: reciprocating saw with coarse wood-cutting blade (A), silicone caulk (B), duct tape (C), wire connectors (D), ⅛" twist bit (E), No. 9 counterbore drill bit (F), ¾" sheetmetal screws (G), 2½" sheetmetal screws (H), combination tool (I), masonry chisel (J), 2" masonry nails (K), metal snips (L), masonry drill bit (M), ball peen hammer (N).

How to Install a Wall-mounted Vent Hood

1 Attach ¾" × 4" × 12" wooden cleats to sides of the cabinets with 1¼" wallboard screws. Follow manufacturer's directions for proper distance from cooking surface.

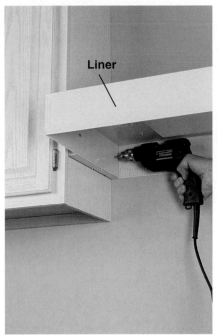

Liner

2 Position the hood liner between the cleats and attach with ¾" sheetmetal screws.

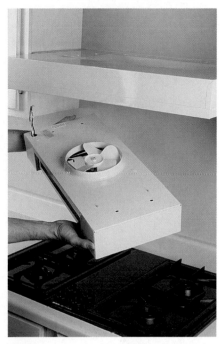

3 Remove cover panels for light, fan and electrical compartments on fan unit, as directed by manufacturer. Position fan unit inside liner and fasten by attaching nuts to mounting bolts inside light compartments.

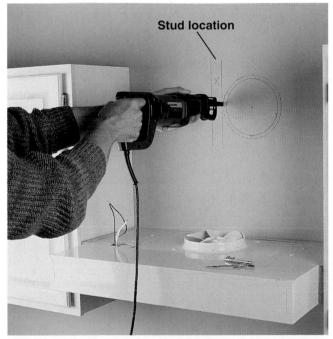

Stud location

4 Locate studs in wall where duct will pass, using a stud finder. Mark hole location. Hole should be ½" larger than diameter of duct. Complete cutout with a reciprocating saw or jig saw. Remove any wall insulation. Drill a pilot hole through outside wall.

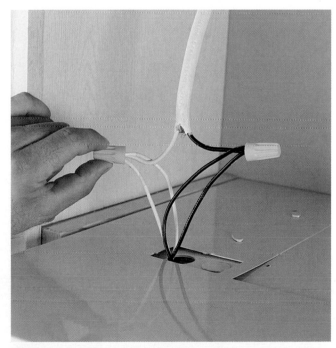

5 Strip about ½" of plastic insulation from each wire in the circuit cable, using combination tool. Connect the black wires, using a wire connector. Connect the white wires. Gently push the wires into the electrical box. Replace the cover panels on the light and fan compartments.

(continued next page)

Outlet flange

6 Make duct cutout on exterior wall. On masonry, drill a series of holes around outline of cutout. Remove waste with a masonry chisel and ball peen hammer. On wood siding, make cutout with a reciprocating saw.

7 Attach first duct section by sliding the smooth end over the outlet flange on the vent hood. Cut duct sections to length with metal snips.

8 Drill three or four pilot holes around joint through both layers of metal, using a ⅛" twist bit. Attach duct with ¾" sheetmetal screws. Seal joint with duct tape.

9 Join additional duct sections by sliding smooth end over corrugated end of preceding section. Use an adjustable elbow to change directions in duct run. Secure all joints with sheetmetal screws and duct tape.

10 Install duct cap on exterior wall. Apply a thick bead of silicone caulk to cap flange. Slide cap over end of duct.

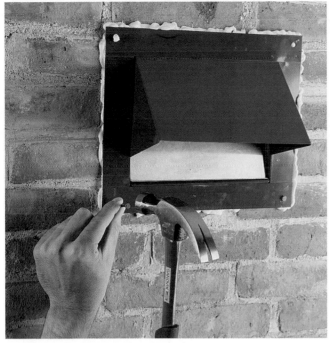

11 Attach cap to wall with 2" masonry nails, or 1½" sheetmetal screws (on wood siding). Wipe away excess caulk.

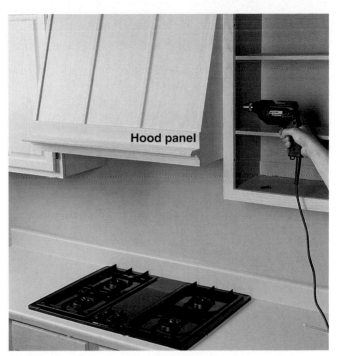

Hood panel

12 Slide the decorative hood panel into place between the wall cabinets. Drill pilot holes through the cabinet face frame with a counterbore bit. Attach the hood panel to the cabinets with 2½" sheetmetal screws.

Vent Hood Variations

Blower unit

Downdraft cooktop has a built-in blower unit that vents through the back of the bottom of a base cabinet. A downdraft cooktop is a good choice for a kitchen island or peninsula.

Cabinet-mounted vent hood is attached to the bottom of a short, 12"- to 18"-tall wall cabinet. Metal ducts run inside this wall cabinet.

Installing an Island Vent Hood

Photo courtesy of General Electric

An island vent hood installation is a bit more complicated because the unit must be supported from above, and because of the extra ductwork. Before installation, read the manufacturer's instructions carefully for recommended heights for cooktop and hood installation.

Most island vents weigh over 100 pounds, so you will need assistance during parts of the installation. Install the vent hood prior to installing the cooktop, if possible, to prevent damage to the cooktop. If not possible, protect the cooktop and countertop with a heavy moving pad.

This installation is vented directly through the roof through attic space above the kitchen. You can also install the ductwork between ceiling joists and out to a side wall, or you can build a soffit around the ductwork (see page 235).

All vent hoods have a maximum permissible length for duct runs. The installation instructions will contain a chart giving equivalent lengths for each type of duct fitting. For example, a 90° elbow is the equivalent of 15 feet of round straight duct. A round roof cap is the equivalent of 26 feet of round straight duct.

SHOPPING TIPS

• *Professional-style cooktops require heavy-duty vent hoods. Check your cooktop manual for venting requirements.*

Tools and Materials

Tools: measuring tape, plumb bob, ladder, wallboard saw, drill, reciprocating saw, screwdriver, wire stripper.

Materials: 6" round duct, roof vent, 2 × 4 lumber, 3" #10 wood screws, sheetmetal screws, NM cable, wire connectors, tape, metallic duct tape, duct straps.

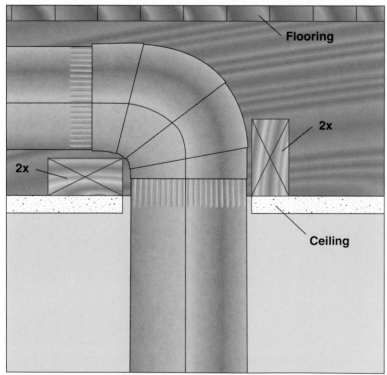

Flooring

2x

2x

Ceiling

Variation: If you must install ductwork in the ceiling joists, turn one 2 × 4 brace flat to allow the duct to fit between the 2 × 4 and the flooring above.

How to Install an Island Vent Hood

1 The manufacturer's directions will tell you the distance from the front of the vent to the duct centerline and the necessary vent hood alignment over the cooktop. Use a plumb bob to find the position of the duct centerline over the cooktop. Mark the location of the duct centerline on the ceiling by poking a 12" length of hanger wire through the ceiling. In the attic, pull back the insulation surrounding the wire and the adjoining joists. Center a section of 6" duct over the wire hole and trace around it to mark the cutout for the duct. Using a wallboard saw or a rotary saw, cut out the hole.

2 Cut two lengths of 2 × 4 to fit between the joists. Check the manufacturer's instructions for the correct distance between the braces. Place the braces flush against the ceiling top. Drill pilot holes and install with a minimum of two 3" #10 wood screws driven through the joist and into the brace. The cross bracing and the ceiling surface must be level for proper installation of the vent hood. Insert the 6" round duct through the ceiling so it extends down 3 or 4 inches. This must be a female or external connection. Attach lengths of duct until you reach the roof deck.

3 Draw an outline of the duct on the roof deck. Drill a pilot hole, then saw through the sheathing and roofing material with a reciprocating saw to make the cutout for the vent tailpiece.

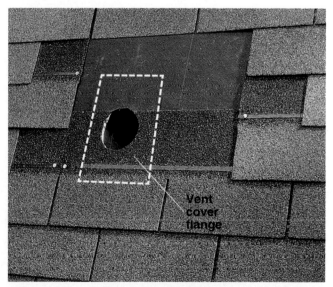

Vent cover flange

4 Remove a section of shingles from around the cutout, leaving the roofing paper intact. Remove enough shingles to create an exposed area that is at least the size of the vent cover flange.

(continued next page)

5 If the hole for the vent does not abut a rafter, attach a 2 × 4 brace between the roof rafters. Attach a hose clamp to the brace or rafter about 1" below the roof sheathing (top). Insert the vent tailpiece into the cutout and through the hose clamp, then tighten the clamp screw (bottom).

6 Apply roofing cement to the bottom of the vent cover flange, then slide the vent cover over the tailpiece. Nail the vent cover flange into place with self-sealing roofing nails, then patch in shingles around the cover.

7 Complete installation of the ductwork by securing each joint with self-tapping sheetmetal screws. Wrap each joint with metallic duct tape. Support the duct as it passes through the ceiling with duct straps.

8 Secure the upper support frame to the ceiling joists or the cross bracing with the screws provided. The screws must be driven into the center of the joists or cross braces. Check to make sure the frame is level in all directions. Insert the lower support frame and secure loosely. Adjust the lower support frame to the desired height above the countertop and tighten the screws. Check again that the support frame is level and plumb.

9 In the attic, run a branch circuit from a nearby junction box. (This may be a job for an electrician.) Route the cable through the ceiling hole. Pull the cable to reach the junction box, approximately 6" below the frame support. Tape the cable to the frame support.

10 Measure from the bottom of the duct flange in the ceiling to the bottom of the support frame. Add 1" for insertion into the ceiling duct and subtract 1¾" for the hood insertion. (This will vary; check the manufacturer's dimensions.) Cut 6" round duct to this length. Install the duct and attach with sheetmetal screws and metallic duct tape.

11 Slide the top decorative duct cover over the support frame to the ceiling and attach it to the support frame using the supplied decorative screws. Slide the bottom decorative duct cover over the support frame and the top duct cover. Secure with the provided stop screw to hold it in place while the hood is installed.

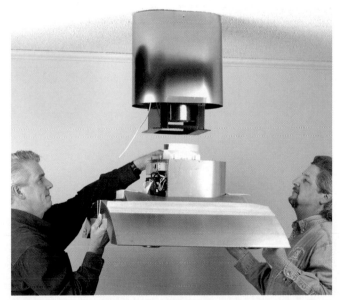

12 With a helper, lift the hood up to the support frame. Align the hood mounting studs with the support frame holes and guide the hood duct connector into the house duct. Install the nuts and lock washers to the mounting studs and tighten. Check that the hood is level in all directions. Make sure the duct is positioned over the hood connector. Seal the joint with metallic duct tape, not screws.

13 Strip 8" of cable. Thread the cable through a cable clamp and through a knockout into the junction box. Connect the white supply wire to the white vent wire with a wire connector. Connect the black supply wire to the black vent wire. Connect the green or bare supply wire to the green or yellow vent wire. Push the wires into the junction box and replace the cover without pinching the wires. Remove the stop screw and slide down the decorative cover.

FLOORING

The floor is often the largest single surface in a kitchen, and therefore has great potential for setting the kitchen's tone. Options for kitchen flooring have expanded immensely in the past few years. Many of these options are perfect for do-it-yourselfers looking to give their kitchen a stylish face-lift.

Perhaps your kitchen has a resilient sheet floor that is in good shape but is of a dated pattern. A new floating floor can be installed over existing resilient flooring in a weekend. This chapter contains information on what floating floor options are available and how to install them.

Or maybe you are more adventurous and want to install the ceramic tile floor you have always dreamed of. Information on ceramic tile options and directions on how to prepare for, cut, place and finish a ceramic tile floor are included here as well.

You'll also find information on resilient tile and sheet installation, how to remove old flooring, tips on measuring and trimming your finished floor, and many other pointers.

Photo courtesy of Wilsonart Flooring

Because they are often damp, kitchen floors tend to be hazardous. To avoid slips and falls, make sure any flooring you use has a coefficient of friction of at least 0.6. Natural wood flooring and solid vinyl flooring with a matte finish may offer the best traction. Adding ceramic tile to your kitchen floor may make the transition from kitchen to other rooms abrupt. Use transition strips to ease the transition. All area rugs should have non-skid backing. Reduce glare by using matte finishes or textured tile, rather than highly polished surfaces.

(above) **Prefinished wood flooring** is available in a variety of woods and finishes. This floor is teak.

(right) **The rich tones** of stained wood flooring are perfect for setting off painted cabinets in the kitchen.

(left) **Resilient sheet and tile flooring** is available in styles that resemble ceramic tile.

Flooring Options

Your kitchen floor is more than just a walking surface—it also helps to create the room's style by adding color, texture and personality. You can use flooring to complement your countertops and cabinets, or create a point of contrast. Flooring can define task and traffic areas, giving a large kitchen floor a bit more style. Flooring choices can help the kitchen flow into other rooms or create more visible boundaries.

Almost any material can and has been used as kitchen flooring, and with new processes of factory lamination, many inexpensive and easy-to-install options are available. The only floor covering that is truly not suited to kitchen use is carpeting. Non-slip area rugs, however, are a good option in many kitchens. Different flooring options have different merits, especially in the kitchen. It pays to think carefully about what you want, because the cost and labor involved in flooring projects mean you won't soon want to change it.

Vinyl Flooring

Vinyl flooring, also known as "resilient flooring," is a versatile, flexible surface. Vinyl flooring is available in both sheets and tiles, in thicknesses ranging from ⅟₁₆" to ⅛". Sheets come in 6-ft.-wide or 12-ft.-wide rolls, with either a felt or a polyvinyl chloride (PVC) backing, depending on the type of installation. Tiles typically come in 12" squares and are available with or without self-adhesive backing.

Installation is easy. Sheet vinyl with felt backing is glued to the floor using the full-spread method, meaning the entire project area is covered with

adhesive. PVC-backed sheet vinyl is glued only along the edges (perimeter-bond method). Tiles are the easiest to install, but because tile floors have a lot of seams, they're less suitable for high-moisture areas. All vinyl flooring must be installed over a smooth underlayment.

Sheet vinyl is priced per square yard, while tile is priced per square foot. Cost for either style is comparable to carpet and less expensive than ceramic tile or hardwood. Prices vary based on the percentage of vinyl in the material, the thickness of the product and the complexity of the pattern.

(left) **Resilient sheet vinyl** has long been a kitchen standard. It is available in hundreds of colors and patterns.

(right) **Slate floor tiles** in irregular shapes and sizes create a unique and rustic look for kitchens.

(below) **Earth-toned ceramic tile** adds to the warmth of this kitchen.

Photo courtesy of Koechel Peterson and Associates for Plato Woodwork, Inc.

Ceramic Tile

Ceramic tile is a hard, durable, versatile material that's available in a wide variety of sizes, patterns, shapes and colors. This all-purpose flooring is an excellent choice for high traffic and high-moisture areas.

Common ceramic tiles include unglazed quarry tile, glazed ceramic tile and porcelain mosaic tile. As an alternative to traditional ceramic tiles, natural stone tiles are available in several materials, including marble, slate and granite. Thicknesses for most floor tiles range from ³⁄₁₆" to ¾".

In general, ceramic tile is more expensive than other types of floor coverings, with natural stone tile ranking as the most expensive. While tile is more time-consuming to install than other materials, it offers the most flexibility of design.

Floor preparation is critical to the success of a tile installation. All floors that support tile must be stiff and flat to prevent cracking in the tile surface. Tile is installed following a grid-pattern layout and adhered to the floor with thin-set mortar. The gaps between individual tiles are filled with grout, which should be sealed periodically to prevent staining.

(above) **A herringbone pattern** gives this wood floor a distinctive look.

(left) **Cork flooring** is easy on the feet because it is resilient. It is available in many shades of natural brown.

Other Flooring Options

Other flooring options available for kitchens are concrete, stone tile, cork, bamboo and linoleum.

Concrete is a low-maintenance flooring that can look quite sophisticated. It can be dyed and scored to resemble stone or tile. Most installations include in-floor heating.

Stone tile is similar to ceramic tile. It is available as cut square shapes or irregular pieces. Techniques for setting are the same as for ceramic tile, but stone tiles must always be sealed.

Cork is available in a variety of colors and patterns, many of which use cork's natural brown shadings. Cork provides comfort because it "gives" slightly and has noise-reducing properties. Cork flooring is available in sheets, tiles or planks for floating installations.

Though bamboo is actually a grass, it is harder than oak. It does not accept stain, so it is available only in a light yellow-brown and a caramel brown. Thin bamboo strips are laminated and are milled into planks for floating installation.

Linoleum is made from linseed oil, fabric backing, and cork or wood dust. It is an excellent option for people with chemical sensitivities. Available in many colors and styles, it resembles vinyl resilient flooring and is available in sheets or tiles.

Wood Flooring

Wood floors are resilient and durable, yet they still look warm and elegant. They hold up well in high-traffic areas.

Traditional solid wood planks are the most common type of wood flooring, but there's a growing selection of plywood-backed and synthetic-laminate products (also called laminated wood) that are well suited for do-it-yourself installation. Oak and maple are the most common wood species available, and size options include narrow strips, wide planks and parquet squares. Most wood flooring has tongue-and-groove construction, which helps to provide a strong, flat surface.

In general, hardwood flooring is slightly less expensive than ceramic tile, and laminated products are typically less expensive than solid hardwood. Most types of wood flooring can be installed directly over a subfloor and sometimes over vinyl flooring. Installation of laminated wood flooring is simple. It can be glued or nailed down, or "floated" on a foam cushion. Parquet squares typically are glued down. Solid hardwood planks must be nailed to the subfloor.

GREEN DESIGN

A number of choices are available in flooring if you desire an environmentally friendly option. The old standby, linoleum, is an excellent choice. Made from linseed oil, fabric backing, and cork or wood dust, this old favorite is currently produced in an eye-popping array of colors and patterns.

Cork is harvested from cork oak trees every 9 to 15 years. The trees can grow for up to 250 years. Because of this, cork plantations are home to diverse wildlife populations.

Bamboo is a renewable resource. It is harvested every 3 to 5 years, with the rootstock left to produce another crop.

In terms of outgassing, linoleum and ceramic tile are the safest, though some ceramic tile sealers may be problematic. Cork and bamboo are generally laminated to a substrate, or, in the case of bamboo, many layers of bamboo are glued together. These glues should be safe for everyone except the most chemically sensitive.

Project Preparation

Before your new floor goes in, your old flooring will probably need to be taken out and the subfloor carefully prepared for a finished surface. Project preparation is just as important as installing your floor covering and requires the same attention to detail.

If your new floor is part of a larger kitchen remodeling project, removing the existing floor is one of the first steps in the overall project, while installing the new floor is one of the last steps in the process. All other demolition and construction should be finished in the room before the floor is installed to avoid damaging the surface.

Underlayment is an important part of the preparation step. It is a layer of sheeting that's screwed or nailed to the subfloor to provide a smooth, stable surface for the floor covering. The type of underlayment you choose depends in part on the type of floor covering you plan to install.

Ceramic and natural stone tile floors usually require an underlayment that stands up to moisture, such as cementboard. Fiber/cementboard is a thin, high-density underlayment used under ceramic tile and vinyl flooring in situations where floor height is a concern. Isolation membrane is used to protect ceramic tile installations from movement that may occur on cracked concrete floors. For vinyl flooring, use a quality-grade plywood since most manufacturers' warranties are void if the flooring is installed over substandard underlayments. If you're using your old sheet vinyl flooring as underlayment, apply an embossing leveler to prepare it for the new installation (see opposite page, bottom). Most wood flooring does not require underlayment and is often placed directly on a plywood subfloor.

This section shows how to remove sheet vinyl, vinyl tile, ceramic tile, and underlayment, and how to install new plywood or cementboard underlayment. Cutting door casings, establishing reference lines and measuring for materials needed are also covered.

Plywood

Fiber/cement-board

Cementboard

Isolation membrane

Latex patching compound fills gaps, holes and low spots in underlayment. It's also used to cover screw heads, nail heads and seams in underlayment. Some compounds include dry and wet ingredients that need to be mixed, while others are premixed. The compound is applied with a trowel or wallboard knife.

Preparation Tools & Materials

Tools for flooring removal and surface preparation include: power sander (A), jamb saw (B), putty knife (C), floor roller (D), circular saw (E), hammer (F), hand maul (G), reciprocating saw (H), cordless drill (I), flat edged trowel (J), notched trowel (K), stapler (L), cat's paw (M), flat pry bar (N), heat gun (O), masonry chisel (P), crowbar (Q), nippers (R), wallboard knife (S), wood chisel (T), long-handled floor scraper (U), phillips screwdriver (V), standard screwdriver (W), utility knife (X), carpenter's level (Y).

Turn old flooring into a smooth underlayment layer for new flooring by applying an embossing leveler. Embossing leveler is a mortar-like substance that can prepare resilient flooring or ceramic tile, provided it's well adhered to the subfloor, for use as an underlayment for a new floor covering. Mix the leveler following manufacturer's directions, then spread it thinly over the floor, using a flat-edged trowel. Wipe away excess leveler with the trowel, making sure all dips and indentations are filled. Embossing leveler begins setting in 10 minutes, so work quickly. Once it dries, scrape away ridges and high spots with the trowel edge.

How to Remove Sheet Vinyl

1 Use a utility knife to cut the old flooring into strips about a foot wide to make removal easier.

2 Pull up as much flooring as possible by hand. Grip the strips close to the floor to minimize tearing.

3 Cut stubborn sheet vinyl into strips about 6" wide. Starting at a wall, peel up as much of the floor covering as possible. If the felt backing remains, spray a solution of water and liquid dishwashing detergent under the surface layer to help separate the backing. Use a wallboard knife to scrape up particularly stubborn patches.

4 Scrape up the remaining sheet vinyl and backing with a floor scraper. If necessary, spray the backing with the soap solution to loosen it. Sweep up the debris, then finish the cleanup using a wet/dry vacuum. **Tip:** Fill the vacuum with about an inch of water to help contain dust.

How to Remove Vinyl Tiles

1 Starting at a loose seam, use a long-handled floor scraper to remove tiles. To remove stubborn tiles, soften the adhesive with a heat gun, then use a wallboard knife to pry up the tile and scrape off the underlying adhesive.

2 Remove stubborn adhesive or backing by wetting the floor with a mixture of water and liquid dishwashing detergent, then scrape it with a floor scraper.

How to Remove Ceramic Tile

1 Knock out tile using a hand maul and masonry chisel. If possible, start in a space between tiles where the grout has loosened. Be careful when working around fragile fixtures, such as drain flanges, so you don't damage them.

2 If you plan to reuse the underlayment, use a floor scraper to remove any remaining adhesive. You may have to use a belt sander with a coarse sanding belt to grind off stubborn adhesive.

Remove the underlayment and floor covering as though they're a single layer. This is an effective removal strategy with any floor covering that's bonded to the underlayment.

Removing & Installing Underlayment

Flooring contractors routinely remove the underlayment along with the floor covering before installing new flooring. This saves time and makes it possible to install new underlayment that's ideally suited to the new flooring. Do-it-yourselfers using this technique should make sure to cut the flooring into pieces that can be easily handled.

Warning: This floor removal method releases flooring particles into the air. Be sure the flooring you are removing does not contain asbestos.

Tools and Materials

Tools: circular saw, flat pry bar, reciprocating saw, wood chisel, hammer.

Materials: goggles, gloves, ear and eye protection, dust mask.

Removal Tip

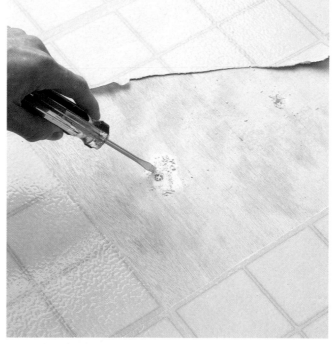

Examine fasteners to see how the underlayment is attached. Use a screwdriver to expose the heads of the fasteners. If the underlayment has been screwed down, you'll need to remove the floor covering and then unscrew the underlayment.

How to Remove Underlayment

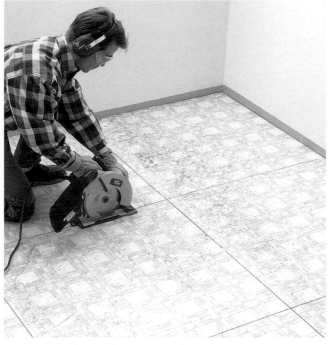

1 Adjust the cutting depth of a circular saw to equal the combined thickness of your floor covering and underlayment. Using a carbide-tipped blade, cut the floor covering and underlayment into squares measuring about 3 feet square. Be sure to wear safety goggles and gloves.

2 Use a reciprocating saw to extend the cuts to the edges of the walls. Hold the blade at a slight angle to the floor and be careful not to damage walls or cabinets. Don't cut deeper than the underlayment. Use a wood chisel to complete cuts near cabinets.

3 Separate the underlayment from the subfloor using a flat pry bar and hammer. Remove and discard the sections of underlayment and floor covering immediately, watching for exposed nails.

Variation: If your existing floor is ceramic tile over plywood underlayment, use a hand maul and masonry chisel to chip away the tile along the cutting lines before making cuts.

How to Install Plywood Underlayment

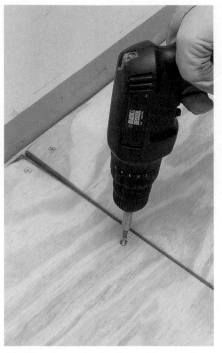

1 Install a full sheet of plywood along the longest wall, making sure the underlayment seams are not aligned with the subfloor seams. Fasten the plywood to the subfloor using 1" deck screws driven every 6" along the edges and at 8" intervals in the field of the sheet.

2 Continue fastening sheets of plywood to the subfloor, driving the screw heads slightly below the underlayment surface. Leave ¼" expansion gaps at the walls and between sheets. Offset seams in subsequent rows.

3 Using a circular saw or jig saw, notch the plywood to meet the existing flooring in doorways. Fasten the notched sheets to the subfloor.

4 Mix floor-patching compound and latex or acrylic additive following the manufacturer's directions. Spread it over seams and screw heads, using a wallboard knife.

5 Let the patching compound dry, then sand the patched areas, using a power sander.

How to Install Cementboard

1 Mix thin-set mortar according to the manufacturer's directions. Starting at the longest wall, spread the mortar on the subfloor in a figure-eight pattern using a ¼" notched trowel. Spread only enough mortar for one sheet at a time. Set the cementboard on the mortar with the rough side up, making sure the edges are offset from the subfloor seams.

2 Fasten the cementboard to the subfloor using 1¼" cementboard screws driven every 6" along the edges and 8" throughout the sheet. Drive the screw heads flush with the surface. Continue spreading mortar and installing sheets along the wall. **Option:** If installing fiber/cementboard underlayment, use a ³⁄₁₆" notched trowel to spread the mortar, and drill pilot holes for all screws.

3 Cut cementboard pieces as necessary, leaving an ⅛" gap at all joints and a ¼" gap along the room perimeter. For straight cuts, use a utility knife to score a line through the fiber-mesh layer just beneath the surface, then snap the board along the scored line.

4 To cut holes, notches or irregular shapes, use a jig saw with a carbide blade. Continue installing cementboard sheets to cover the entire floor.

5 Place fiberglass-mesh wallboard tape over the seams. Use a wallboard knife to apply thin-set mortar to the seams, filling the gaps between sheets and spreading a thin layer of mortar over the tape. Allow the mortar to set for two days before starting the tile installation.

Cutting Door Casing & Jambs

For best results, your new flooring should fit beneath the door case molding and frame jambs, not against them. It also creates a more finished look and eliminates the intricate fitting and cutting necessary to fit flooring around molding.

It only takes a few minutes to cut the casing and jambs. If you're installing ceramic tile or parquet, keep in mind you'll be placing the flooring over adhesive, so cut about ⅛" above the top of the tile to allow for the height of the adhesive.

These directions show the casing and jambs being cut to accommodate ceramic tile. Because the tile will be placed on top of cementboard, a piece of cementboard is placed under the tile when the casing is marked.

Cut the bottom of door casings and jambs the thickness of your flooring and underlayment so your floor covering will fit under it.

Tools and Materials

Tools: jamb saw, floor covering.

How to Cut Door Casing

1 Place a piece of flooring and underlayment against the door casing. Mark the casing about ⅛" above the top of the flooring.

2 Cut the casing at the mark using a jamb saw. Mark the jambs and door stops, and cut them as well.

3 Slide a piece of flooring under the door jamb to make sure it fits easily.

Measuring Your Kitchen

You'll need to determine the total square footage of your kitchen before ordering your floor covering. To do this, divide the room into a series of squares and rectangles that you can easily measure. Be sure to include all areas that will be covered, such as pantries and space under your refrigerator and other movable appliances.

Measure the length and width of each area in inches, then multiply the length times the width. Divide that number by 144 to determine your square footage. Add all of the areas together to figure the square footage for the entire room, then subtract the areas that will not be covered, such as cabinets and other permanent fixtures.

When ordering your floor covering, be sure to purchase 10 to 15% extra to allow for waste and cutting. For patterned flooring, you may need as much as 20% extra.

Measure the area of the project room to calculate how much flooring you will need.

How to Measure Your Kitchen

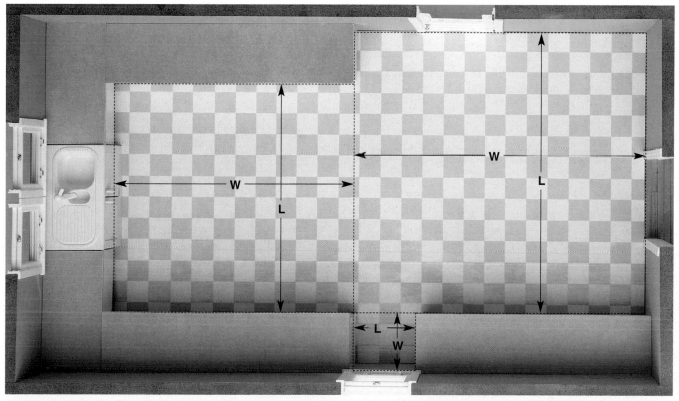

Divide the room into rectangles or squares. Include pantries and areas where movable appliances are installed. Measure the length and width of each area in inches, then multiply the length times the width. Divide that number by 144 to determine your square footage.

To check your reference lines for squareness, use the 3-4-5 triangle method. Measuring from the centerpoint, make a mark along a reference line at 3 ft. and along a perpendicular reference line at 4 ft. The distance between the two points should be exactly 5 ft. If it's not, adjust your lines accordingly.

Establishing Reference Lines

Your first row of flooring, your first few tiles or your first piece of sheeting sets the direction for the rest of your floor. It's critical, therefore, to get off to a perfect start. You can do this by carefully planning your layout and establishing accurate reference lines.

In general, tile flooring begins at the center of the room and is installed in quadrants along layout lines, also called working lines. After establishing reference lines that mark the center of the room, lay the tile in a dry run along those lines to ensure you won't have to cut off more than half of a tile in the last row. If necessary, adjust your reference lines by half the width of the tile to form the layout lines.

For most floating floors and tongue-and-groove floors, you only need a single reference line along the starting wall. If your wall is straight, you don't even need a working line. You can place spacers along the wall and butt the first row of flooring against the spacers. However, this only works if your wall is straight. If it's bowed or out of square, it will affect the layout.

The photos on the next page show options for establishing reference lines.

Tools and Materials

Tools: tape measure, chalk line, framing square, hammer.
Materials: 8d finish nails, spacers.

Two Methods for Establishing Reference

Mark the centerpoint of two opposite walls, then snap a chalk line between the marks. Mark the centerpoint of the chalk line. Place a framing square at the centerpoint so one side is flush with the chalk line. Snap a perpendicular reference along the adjacent side of the framing square.

Snap chalk lines between the centerpoints of opposite walls to establish perpendicular reference lines. Check the lines for squareness using the 3-4-5 triangle method.

How to Establish Reference Lines for Wood & Floating Floors

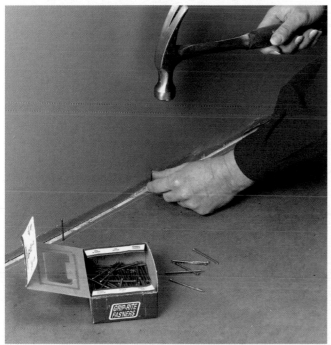

If your wall is out of square or bowed, make a mark on the floor ½" from the wall at both ends and snap a chalk line between these points. Drive 8d finish nails every 2" to 3" along the line. Use this as the reference line and butt the first row of flooring against the nails.

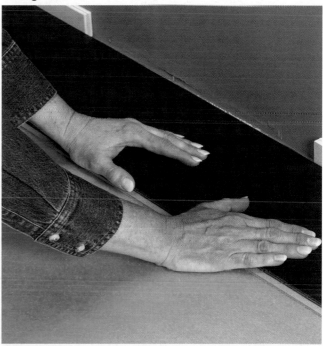

If your wall is straight, place ½" spacers along the wall, then butt your flooring up against the spacers.

Installing Floating Floors

Floor installation doesn't get any easier than this. Floating floors have revolutionized the way floor coverings are installed, since they require no nails, staples, tackless strips or adhesive. The advent of floating floors with their special tongue-and-groove fastening system has helped flooring become a popular do-it-yourself project rather than a job for professionals.

Floating floors are most often associated with laminates, although other products can be used. Hardwood, cork and bamboo are other choices for floating floors that are just as easy to install.

Part of the appeal of floating floors is that they don't require a special subfloor. The actual floor covering is not fastened or adhered to the subfloor in any way. Instead, it "floats" above the subfloor and is held in place solely by its own weight.

This technology allows you to install a floating floor over most existing floors. Floating floors simply click together at the tongue-and-groove joints. This allows for quick installation, and you can walk on the floor immediately.

Although laminates are resistant to scratching, denting, fading, scuffing, staining and burning, they are not resistant to water. After the floor is installed, apply caulk along the bottom edge of panels that could come into contact with water, such as in front of a dishwasher, sink or exterior door.

Tools and Materials

Tools: tape measure, utility knife, circular saw, straightedge, hammer, floor pull bar, jig saw.

Materials: underlayment, floor panels, chalk.

The grain pattern in this laminate floor features the look of real wood and harmonizes with the wood accessories in the room.

How to Install a Floating Floor

1 Choose the manufacturer's recommended underlayment and roll it out to fit the entire floor. Do not overlap seams.

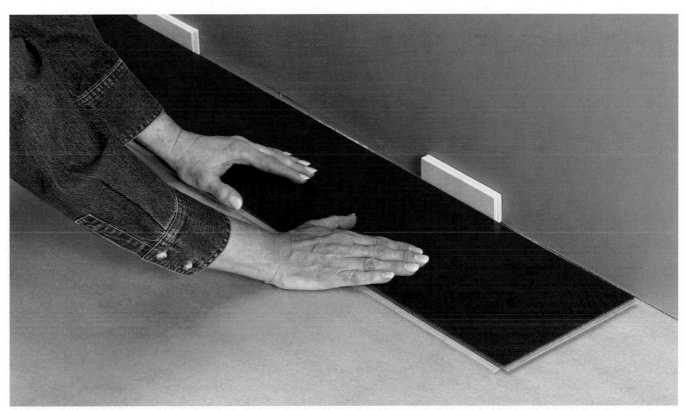

2 Place ½" spacers along the starting wall to provide a gap for expansion of the flooring. Set the first row of flooring against the spacers with the groove side facing the wall. If wall is uneven, create a reference line using 8d finish nails every 2" to 3" (see page 163).

(continued next page)

3 Install successive rows of flooring by lifting the panels at a 45° angle and sliding them into the tongue of the preceding panels until they lock into place. Stagger joints by at least 8".

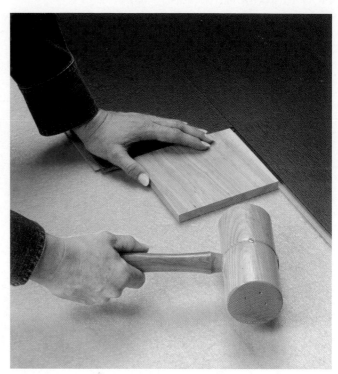

4 After locking the long edge of the panel in place, slide the panel back to fit the short edge into the tongue of the last panel in the row. Use a mallet and scrap piece of wood to gently tap it into place.

5 At the end of the rows, use a floor pull bar and hammer to fit the last board into place. Leave a ½" gap along walls.

Cut panels by turning the panel facedown. Mark the appropriate length, then cut along the mark using a circular saw. Cut-off pieces can be used to begin the next row, provided they are at least 10" long.

6 For the last row of flooring, place panels directly over the last installed row. Place a third panel on top of the second and butt the side against the ½" spacers along the wall. Trace along the edge of the panel onto the second panel, then cut the second panel to size.

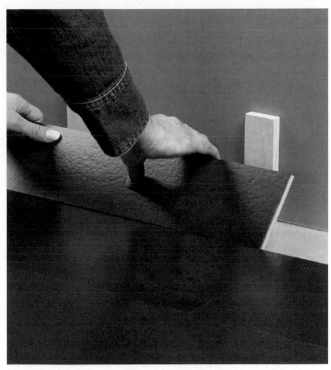

7 Set the last row of panels in place. If needed, use the floor pull bar to pull the panels in place.

8 Apply a bead of caulk along the edge of the flooring to prevent water intrusion.

To fit panels around obstacles place the board next to the obstacle, mark it, and cut it with a jig saw. Set the board in place by locking the tongue-and-groove joints with the preceding board.

Most resilient flooring is made from vinyl. The higher the percentage of vinyl in the product, the higher the quality of the floor. In solid vinyl flooring (left), the design pattern is built up from solid layers of vinyl. Vinyl composition flooring (center) combines vinyl with filler materials. Printed vinyl flooring (right) relies on a screen print for its color and pattern. The print is protected by a vinyl-and-urethane wear layer.

Installing Resilient Sheet Vinyl

Preparing a perfect underlayment is the most important phase of resilient sheet vinyl installation. Cutting the material to fit the contours of the room is a close second. The best way to ensure accurate cuts is to make a cutting template. Some manufacturers offer template kits, or you can make one by following the instructions on the opposite page. Be sure to use the recommended adhesive for the sheet vinyl you are installing. Many manufacturers require that you use their glue for installation. Use extreme care when handling the sheet vinyl, especially felt-backed products, to avoid creasing and tearing.

Tools and Materials

Tools: linoleum knife, framing square, compass, scissors, non-permanent felt-tipped pen, utility knife, straightedge, ¼" V-notched trowel, J-roller, stapler, flooring roller, chalk line, heat gun, ¹⁄₁₆" V-notched trowel.

Materials: vinyl flooring, masking tape, heavy butcher or kraft paper, duct tape, flooring adhesive, ⅜" staples, metal threshold bars, nails.

How to Cut Vinyl

Use a linoleum knife or utility knife and a straightedge to cut resilient flooring. Make sure to use a sharp knife blade, and change blades often. Always make cuts on a smooth surface, such as a scrap of hardboard placed under the flooring.

How to Make a Cutting Template

1 Place sheets of heavy butcher paper or brown wrapping paper along the walls, leaving a ⅛" gap. Cut triangular holes in the paper with a utility knife. Fasten the template to the floor by placing masking tape over the holes.

2 Follow the outline of the room, working with one sheet of paper at a time. Overlap the edges of adjoining sheets by about 2" and tape the sheets together.

3 To fit the template around pipes, tape sheets of paper on either side. Measure the distance from the wall to the center of the pipe, then subtract ⅛".

4 Transfer the measurement to a separate piece of paper. Use a compass to draw the pipe diameter on the paper, then cut out the hole with scissors or a utility knife. Cut a slit from the edge of the paper to the hole.

5 Fit the hole cutout around the pipe. Tape the hole template to the adjoining sheets.

6 When completed, roll or loosely fold the paper template for carrying.

How to Install Perimeter-bond Sheet Vinyl

1 Unroll the flooring on any large, flat, clean surface. To prevent wrinkles, sheet vinyl comes from the manufacturer rolled with the pattern side out. Unroll the sheet and turn it pattern-side up for marking.

2 For two-piece installations, overlap the edges of the sheets by at least 2". Plan to have the seams fall along the pattern lines or simulated grout joints. Align the sheets so the pattern matches, then tape the sheets together with duct tape.

3 Position the paper template over the sheet vinyl and tape it in place. Trace the outline of the template onto the flooring using a non-permanent felt-tipped pen.

4 Remove the template. Cut the sheet vinyl with a sharp linoleum knife or a utility knife with a new blade. Use a straightedge as a guide for making longer cuts.

5 Cut holes for pipes and other permanent obstructions. Cut a slit from each hole to the nearest edge of the flooring. Whenever possible, make slits along pattern lines.

6 Roll up the flooring loosely and transfer it to the installation area. Do not fold the flooring. Unroll and position the sheet vinyl carefully. Slide the edges beneath undercut door casings.

7 Cut the seams for two-piece installations using a straightedge as a guide. Hold the straightedge tightly against the flooring, and cut along the pattern lines through both pieces of vinyl flooring.

8 Remove both pieces of scrap flooring. The pattern should now run continuously across the adjoining sheets of flooring.

(continued next page)

9 Fold back the edges of both sheets. Apply a 3" band of multipurpose flooring adhesive to the underlayment or old flooring, using a ¼" V-notched trowel or wallboard knife.

10 Lay the seam edges one at a time onto the adhesive. Make sure the seam is tight, pressing the gaps together with your fingers, if needed. Roll the seam edges with a J-roller or wallpaper seam roller.

11 Apply flooring adhesive underneath flooring cuts at pipes or posts and around the entire perimeter of the room. Roll the flooring with the roller to ensure good contact with the adhesive.

12 If you're applying flooring over a wood underlayment, fasten the outer edges of the sheet with ⅜" staples driven every 3". Make sure the staples will be covered by the base molding.

How to Install Full-spread Sheet Vinyl

1 Cut the sheet vinyl using the techniques described on pages 170 and 171 (steps 1 to 8).

2 Pull back half of the flooring, then apply a layer of flooring adhesive over the underlayment or old flooring using a ¼" V-notched trowel. Lay the flooring back onto the adhesive.

3 Roll the floor with a heavy flooring roller, moving toward the edges of the sheet. The roller creates a stronger bond and eliminates air bubbles. Fold over the unbonded section of flooring, apply adhesive, then lay the flooring down and roll it. Wipe up any adhesive that oozes up around the edges of the vinyl, using a damp rag.

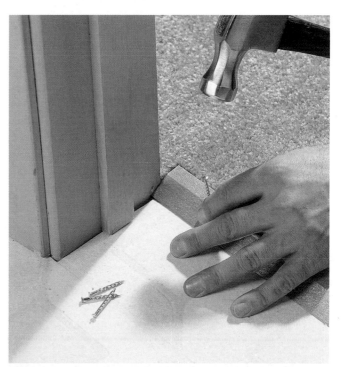

4 Measure and cut metal threshold bars to fit across doorways. Position each bar over the edge of the vinyl flooring and nail it in place.

Installing Resilient Tile

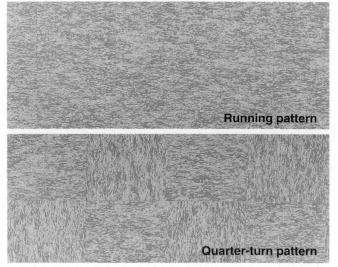

Running pattern

Quarter-turn pattern

As with any tile installation, resilient tile requires carefully positioned layout lines. Before committing to any layout and applying tile, conduct a dry run to identify potential problems.

Keep in mind there's a difference between reference lines (see page 162) and layout lines (see below). Reference lines mark the center of the room and divide it into quadrants. If the tiles don't lay out symmetrically along these lines, you'll need to adjust them slightly, creating layout lines.

Once layout lines are established, installing the tile goes fairly quickly, especially if you're using self-adhesive tile. Be sure to keep joints between the tiles tight and lay the tiles square.

Tiles with an obvious grain pattern can be laid so the grain of each tile is oriented identically throughout the installation. You can also use the quarter-turn method, in which each tile has its pattern grain running perpendicular to that of adjacent tiles. Whichever method you choose, be sure to be consistent throughout the project.

Check for noticeable directional features, like the grain of the vinyl particles. You can set the tiles in a running pattern so the directional feature runs in the same direction (top), or in a checkerboard pattern using the quarter-turn method (bottom).

Tools and Materials

Tools: tape measure, chalk line, framing square, utility knife, 1/16" notched trowel (for dry-back tile).

Materials: resilient tile, flooring adhesive (for dry-back tile).

How to Establish Tile Layout Lines

1 Snap perpendicular reference lines with a chalk line. Dry-fit tiles along layout line Y so a joint falls along reference line X. If necessary, shift the layout to make the layout symmetrical or to reduce the number of tiles that need to be cut.

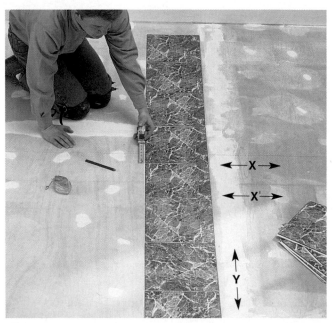

2 If you shift the tile layout, create a new line that's parallel to reference line X and runs through a tile joint near line X. The new line, X', is the line you'll use when installing the tile. To avoid confusion, use a different colored chalk to distinguish between lines.

3 Dry-fit tiles along the new line, X'. If necessary, adjust the layout line as in steps 1 and 2.

4 If you adjusted the layout along X', measure and make a new layout line, Y', that's parallel to reference line Y and runs through a tile joint. Y' will form the second layout line you'll use during installation.

How to Install Self-adhesive Resilient Tiles

1 Once your reference lines are established, peel off the paper backing and install the first tile in one of the corners formed by the intersecting layout lines. Lay three or more tiles along each layout line in the quadrant. Rub the entire surface of each tile to bond the adhesive to the floor underlayment.

2 Begin installing tiles in the interior area of the quadrant, keeping the joints tight between tiles.

(continued next page)

Note: Tile to be cut shown inverted for clarity; tiles should be faceup for marking.

3 Finish setting full tiles in the first quadrant, then set the full tiles in an adjacent quadrant. Set the tiles along the layout lines first, then fill in the interior tiles.

4 To cut tiles to fit along the walls, place the tile to be cut (A) faceup on top of the last full tile you installed. Position a ⅛"-thick spacer against the wall, then set a marker tile (B) on top of the tile to be cut. Trace along the edge of the marker tile to draw a cutting line.

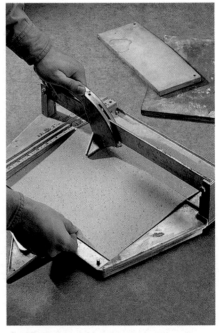

Tip: To mark tiles for cutting around outside corners, make a cardboard template to match the space, keeping a ⅛" gap along the walls. After cutting the template, check to make sure it fits. Place the template on a tile and trace its outline.

5 Cut tile to fit using a utility knife and straightedge. Hold the straightedge securely against the cutting line to ensure a straight cut.

Option: You can use a ceramic-tile cutter to make straight cuts in thick vinyl tiles.

6 Install cut tiles next to the walls. If you're pre-cutting all tiles before installing them, measure the distance between the wall and installed tiles at various points in case the distance changes.

7 Continue installing tile in the remaining quadrants until the room is completely covered. Check the entire floor. If you find loose areas, press down on the tiles to bond them to the underlayment. Install metal threshold bars at room borders where the new floor joins another floor covering.

How to Install Dry-back Tile

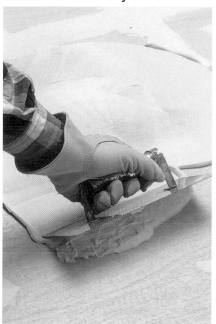

1 Create perpendicular reference lines and dry-fit tiles to establish the final layout. Apply adhesive around the intersection of the layout lines using a trowel with 1/16" V-shaped notches. Hold the trowel at a 45° angle and spread adhesive evenly over the surface.

2 Spread adhesive over most of the installation area, covering three quadrants. Allow the adhesive to set according to the manufacturer's instructions, then begin to install the tile at the intersection of the layout lines. You can kneel on installed tiles to lay additional tiles. When the first three quadrants are completely tiled, spread adhesive over the remaining quadrant, then finish setting the tile.

Thin-set mortar is a fine-grained cement product used to bond floor tile to underlayment. It is prepared by adding liquid, a little at a time, to the dry powder and stirring the mixture to achieve a creamy consistency. Some mortars include a latex additive in the dry mix. With others, you'll need to add liquid latex additive when you prepare the mortar.

Ceramic Tile Tools & Materials

The tools required to cut tiles and to apply mortar and grout are generally small and fairly inexpensive.

The materials needed for tile installation include adhesive thin-set mortar, used to fasten the tiles to the underlayment; grout, used to fill the joints between tiles; and sealers, used to protect the tile surface and grout lines. Make sure to use the materials recommended by the tile manufacturer.

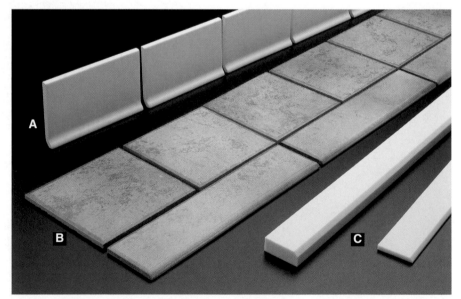

Trim and finishing materials for tile installation include: base-trim tiles (A), which fit around the room perimeter, and bullnose tiles (B), used at doorways and other transition areas. Doorway thresholds (C) are made from either synthetic materials or natural materials, such as marble, and come in thicknesses ranging from ¼" to ¾" to match different floor levels. The longest-lasting thresholds are made from solid-surface mineral products. If the threshold is too long for the doorway, cut it to fit with a jig saw or circular saw and a tungsten-carbide blade.

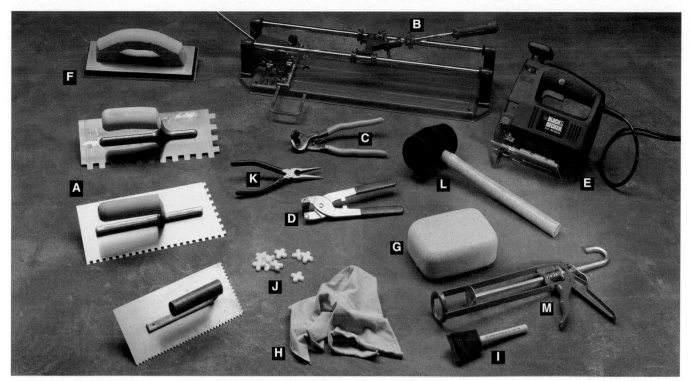

Tile tools include adhesive-spreading tools, cutting tools and grouting tools. Notched trowels (A) for spreading mortar come with notches of varying sizes and shapes. The size of the notch should be chosen based on the recommendations of the manufacturer. Cutting tools include a tile cutter (B), tile nippers (C), hand-held tile cutter (D) and jig saw with carbide blade (E). Grouting tools include a grout float (F), grout sponge (G), buff rag (H) and foam brush (I), for applying grout sealer. Other tile tools include spacers (J), available in different sizes to create grout joints of varying widths; needlenose pliers (K), for removing spacers; rubber mallet (L), for setting tiles into mortar; and caulk gun (M).

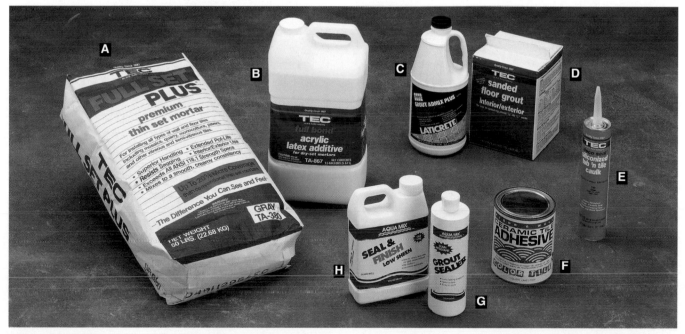

Tile materials include adhesives, grouts and sealers. Thin-set mortar (A), the most common floor-tile adhesive, is often strengthened with latex mortar additive (B). Grout additive (C) can be added to floor grout (D) to make it more resilient and durable. Grout fills the spaces between tiles and is available in pre-tinted colors to match your tile. Silicone caulk (E) should be used in place of grout where tile meets another surface, like a bathtub. Use wall-tile adhesive (F) for installing base-trim tile. Grout sealer (G) and porous-tile sealer (H) ward off stains and make maintenance easier.

How to Cut Tile Using a Tile Cutter

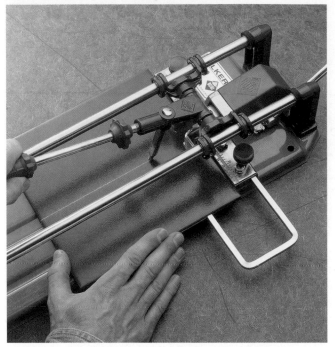

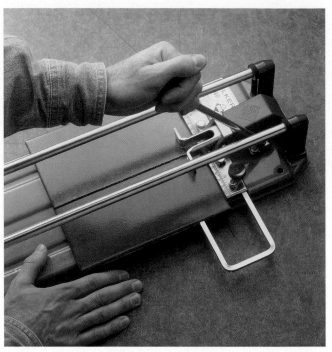

1 Mark a cutting line on the tile with a pencil, then place the tile in the cutter so the cutting wheel is directly over the line. While pressing down firmly on the wheel handle, run the wheel across the tile to score the surface. For a clean cut, score the tile only once.

2 Snap the tile along the scored line as directed by the tool manufacturer. Snapping the tile is usually accomplished by depressing a lever on the tile cutter.

How to Cut Tile Using Power Tools

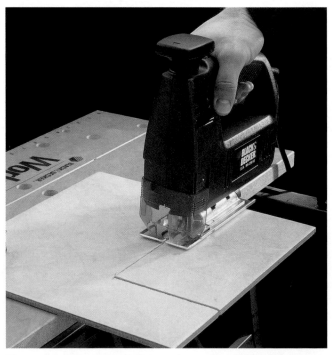

Tile saws, also called "wet saws" because they use water to cool blades and tiles, are used primarily for cutting natural-stone tiles. They're also useful for quickly cutting notches in all kinds of hard tile. Wet saws are available for rent at tile dealers and rental shops.

To make square notches, clamp the tile down on a worktable, then use a jig saw with a tungsten-carbide blade to make the cuts. If you need to cut several notches, a wet saw is more efficient.

How to Cut Tile Using Tile Nippers

1 Mark a cutting line on the tile face, then use the scoring wheel of a hand-held tile cutter to score the cut line. Make several parallel scores, no more than ¼" apart, in the waste portion of the tile.

2 Use tile nippers to nibble away the scored portion of the tile. To cut circular holes in the middle of a tile, score and cut the tile so it divides the hole in half, then remove waste material from each half of the circle.

Tips for Cutting Tile

To cut mosaic tiles, use a tile cutter to score tiles in the row where the cut will occur. Cut away excess strips of mosaics from the sheet, using a utility knife, then use a hand-held tile cutter to snap tiles one at a time. Use tile nippers to cut narrow portions of tiles after scoring.

Cut holes for plumbing stub-outs and other obstructions by marking the outline on the tile, then drilling around the edges using a ceramic tile bit (inset). Gently knock out the waste material with a hammer. The rough edges of the hole will be covered by protective plates on fixtures, called "escutcheons."

Installing Ceramic Tile

Ceramic tile installation starts with the same steps as installing resilient tile. You snap perpendicular reference lines and dry-fit tiles to ensure the best placement.

Work in small sections so the mortar doesn't dry before the tiles are set. Use spacers between tiles to ensure consistent spacing. Plan an installation sequence to avoid kneeling on set tiles. Be careful not to kneel or walk on tiles until the designated drying period is over.

Tools and Materials

Tools: ¼" square-notched trowel, rubber mallet, tile cutter, tile nippers, hand-held tile cutter, needle-nose pliers, grout float.

Materials: grout sponge, soft cloth, small paintbrush, thin-set mortar, tile, tile spacers, grout, latex grout additive, wall adhesive, 2 × 4 lumber, grout sealer, tile caulk.

How to Install Ceramic Floor Tile

1 Make sure the subfloor is smooth, level and stable. Spread thin-set mortar on the subfloor for one sheet of cementboard. Place the cementboard on the mortar, keeping a ¼" gap along the walls. Fasten it in place with 1¼" cementboard screws. Place fiberglass-mesh wallboard tape over the seams. Cover the remainder of the floor (see page 159).

2 Draw reference lines and establish the tile layout (see pages 162 to 163). Mix a batch of thin-set mortar, then spread the mortar evenly against both reference lines of one quadrant, using a ¼" square-notched trowel. Use the notched edge of the trowel to create furrows in the mortar bed.

3 Set the first tile in the corner of the quadrant where the reference lines intersect. When setting tiles that are 8" square or larger, twist each tile slightly as you set it into position.

4 Using a soft rubber mallet, gently tap the central area of each tile a few times to set it evenly into the mortar.

Variation: For large tiles or uneven stone, use a larger trowel with notches that are at least ½" deep.

Variation: For mosaic sheets, use a ³⁄₁₆" V-notched trowel to spread the mortar and a grout float to press the sheets into the mortar. Apply pressure gently to avoid creating an uneven surface.

(continued next page)

How to Install Ceramic Floor Tile (continued)

5 To ensure consistent spacing between tiles, place plastic tile spacers at the corners of the set tile. With mosaic sheets, use spacers equal to the gaps between tiles.

6 Position and set adjacent tiles into the mortar along the reference lines. Make sure the tiles fit neatly against the spacers.

7 To make sure the tiles are level with one another, place a straight piece of 2 × 4 across several tiles, then tap the board with a mallet.

8 Lay tile in the remaining area covered with mortar. Repeat steps 2 to 7, continuing to work in small sections, until you reach walls or fixtures.

9 Measure and mark tiles to fit against walls and into corners (see page 176). Cut the tiles to fit. Apply thin-set mortar directly to the back of the cut tiles, instead of the floor, using the notched edge of the trowel to furrow the mortar.

10 Set the cut pieces of tile into position. Press down on the tile until each piece is level with adjacent tiles.

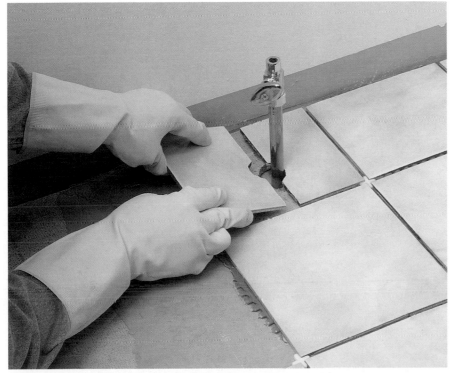

11 Measure, cut and install tiles that require notches or curves to fit around obstacles, such as exposed pipes or toilet drains.

12 Carefully remove the spacers with needlenose pliers before the mortar hardens.

(continued next page)

13 Apply mortar and set tiles in the remaining quadrants, completing one quadrant before starting the next. Inspect all of the tile joints and use a utility knife or grout knife to remove any high spots of mortar that could show through the grout.

14 Install threshold material in doorways. If the threshold is too long for the doorway, cut it to fit with a jig saw or circular saw and a tungsten-carbide blade. Set the threshold in thin-set mortar so the top is even with the tile. Keep the same space between the threshold as between tiles. Let the mortar set for at least 24 hours.

15 Prepare a small batch of floor grout to fill the tile joints. When mixing grout for porous tile, such as quarry or natural stone, use an additive with a release agent to prevent grout from bonding to the tile surfaces.

16 Starting in a corner, pour the grout over the tile. Use a rubber grout float to spread the grout outward from the corner, pressing firmly on the float to completely fill the joints. For best results, tilt the float at a 60° angle to the floor and use a figure-eight motion.

17 Use the grout float to remove excess grout from the surface of the tile. Wipe diagonally across the joints, holding the float in a near-vertical position. Continue applying grout and wiping off excess until about 25 square feet of the floor has been grouted.

18 Wipe a damp grout sponge diagonally over about 2 square feet of the floor at a time. Rinse the sponge in cool water between wipes. Wipe each area only once since repeated wiping can pull grout back out of joints. Repeat steps 15 to 18 to apply grout to the rest of the floor.

19 Allow the grout to dry for about 4 hours, then use a soft cloth to buff the tile surface and remove any remaining grout film.

20 Apply grout sealer to the grout lines, using a small sponge brush or sash brush. Avoid brushing sealer on to the tile surfaces. Wipe up any excess sealer immediately.

Variation: Use a tile sealer to seal porous tile, such as quarry tile or unglazed tile. Following the manufacturer's instructions, roll a thin coat of sealer over the tile and grout joints, using a paint roller and extension handle.

Filling in the Gaps

With most flooring projects you will have gaps between walls and floor that need to be covered, as well as at thresholds, between rooms and around small obstacles, such as pipes. For every situation, there is a molding to fit your needs.

A floor isn't truly finished until all of the pieces are in place. These moldings help give your floors a professional look. The names for moldings may differ slightly between manufacturers. Marble thresholds and vinyl cove molding (not pictured) are available for tile and resilient flooring applications.

Wood molding is used for a smooth transition between the hardwood in the dining area and the tile in the adjoining room.

T-moldings span transitions between hardwood floors and other floors of equal height. These products are usually glued in place.

Reducer strips provide a transition between a wood floor and an adjacent floor of a lower height. One edge is grooved to fit the tongue in the hardwood.

Carpet reducers (A) are used to finish off and create a smooth transition between flooring and carpeting.

Stair nosing (B) is used to cover the exposed edges of stairs where the risers meet the steps. It is also used between step-downs and landings.

Baby threshold (C) is used in place of baseboards and quarter round in front of sliding glass doors or door thresholds, to fill the gap between the floor and door.

Reducer strips (D), also called transition strips, are used between rooms when the floors are at different heights and composed of different materials.

Overlap reducers (E) are also used between rooms when one floor is at a different height than an adjoining room.

T-moldings (F) are used to connect two floors of equal height. They are also used in doorways and thresholds to provide a smooth transition. T-moldings do not butt up against the flooring, allowing the wood to expand and contract under it.

Baseboards (G) are used for almost all types of floors and are available in a wide variety of designs and thicknesses. They are applied at the bottom of walls to cover the gap between the floor and walls.

Quarter round (H), similar to shoemolding, is installed along the bottom edge of baseboard and sits on top of the floor. It covers any remaining gaps between the floor and walls.

A

B

C

D

E

F

G

H

LIGHTING

*L*ighting does many jobs in the kitchen. It can set the mood, illuminate the task at hand, highlight a detail, or simply be beautiful to look at. Important as lighting is, a great many kitchens are poorly lit.

One common kitchen lighting problem is the centrally placed ceiling fixture with no other lighting sources. Unfortunately, this central fixture creates strong shadows at every workstation because the cook's body is always between the light source and the work area. Fortunately, this can be remedied in a number of creative and beautiful ways highlighted in this chapter.

Another kitchen lighting scheme, considered a step up from the single fixture, was the suspended ceiling with banks of fluorescent lights. The problem with fluorescent lighting is that it can make everything look green. In this chapter you will learn that light sources have different effects on color.

We'll cover lighting for tasks, accent and ambient lighting, and decorative lighting, using photo examples of each. Also included are how-to directions for installing track and cable lighting, under-, in-, and above-cabinet lighting, recessed lights and a ceiling fan with light fixture.

Add as much natural light as you can to your kitchen to lower your energy usage. Consider adding a tube-style skylight, standard skylights, clerestories, larger windows or greenhouse windows.

Fluorescent bulbs are more energy efficient and have much longer life than incandescent bulbs. Remember that they need to be disposed of properly— they contain traces of hazardous substances that can be recovered for future use.

Xenon bulbs have a longer life expectancy than halogen bulbs and provide the same type light.

Using dimmer switches saves energy by allowing you to select the appropriate level of light for the occasion.

Of course, turning the lights off when not in use will save energy and prolong the life of the bulbs.

(above) **Skylights** provide additional natural light to a kitchen.

(left) **Decorative lighting** for the kitchen might include a whimsical piece such as this.

(right) **Lighting is ample in this kitchen:** rope lights in the toe kicks, under-cabinet lights, recessed task lights and a hanging fixture.

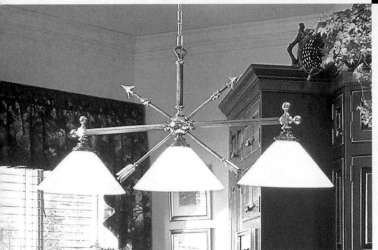

Lighting Options

Designers divide light sources into four basic layers: task, accent, ambient and decorative. Each layer has an important function when it comes to lighting your kitchen.

Task lighting is lighting directed at a specific area to aid in illuminating the job at hand. Basically, it helps you see what you are doing. But task lighting also helps define and emphasize working spaces. In a kitchen, you have numerous areas where specific task lighting is necessary—the sink, cooktop, countertop and other food prep areas, the dining area, and desk or study area.

Begin by putting a recessed light or track lights over the sink. Most range hoods have a lighting option—if you don't have a range hood, consider adding one for proper ventilation and lighting. Add pendants or spotlights over an island to brighten this valuable work and eating space. Don't use just one fixture, however, because this can create distracting shadows. To eliminate shadows, use cross lighting. Cross lighting is the use of two or more light sources directed at a space from different angles. Using a dimmer switch on these fixtures allows you to switch from bright lighting for prep work to subdued lighting for dining. Add strip lights under cabinets to shorten the distance light has to travel and reduce the number of shadows. Use pen-

dants with chrome-bottomed bulbs over the breakfast table for a softly lit eating space. A small clip-on or desktop halogen light illuminates a desk or study area.

Accent lighting is basically lighting for emphasis rather than lighting for a task. Careful accent lighting draws attention to an object or a space. For kitchens, this might be lighting a display of antique plates or focusing a spotlight on an alcove that holds a flowering plant.

Shadows are as important as the lighted spaces when using accent lights. Tight beams of light from small spotlights are ideal for accent lighting. Direct light from below gives bold, dramatic shadows. Lighting small objects from the side creates large shadows. You may want to light architectural features—accent lights can bring out the details of a rough brick chimney or a textured plaster wall.

Accent light fixtures are not the center of attention, so they can be small and inconspicuous. Tiny, inexpensive, low-voltage recessed fixtures are perfect for ceilings and cabinets. For glass-front cabinets, in-cabinet lighting rather than external spotlighting is necessary to prevent glare off the glass fronts.

Ambient lighting is the diffuse light that illuminates a room from several sources and sets the minimum level of lighting. This layer is considered last in designing because the task and accent layers of lighting will provide some ambient light. The ambient layer provides a background by gently lighting areas not illuminated by specific task and accent lights, reducing the eye-straining contrast between brightly lit task areas and dim, unlit surroundings. If your kitchen needs more ambient light, above-cabinet or cove lighting are excellent options.

Decorative lighting is lighting simply to show off the beauty of light. Decorative lighting in a kitchen may be candles or a string of paper lanterns. This type of light is not meant to be the only source of light in the room—creating too great a contrast between light and dark diminishes the decorative impact.

In addition to the layers of lighting design, it is important to consider light sources. Until recently, fluorescent bulbs cast what is called cool light and produced poor color rendering. If you always thought fluorescent light made everything look a little greenish, you were correct. The older tubes produced an excess of green and yellow light, which meant everything illuminated looked slightly green. New, color-corrected fluorescent tubes do not have this problem.

The other common lightbulb is the incandescent—the standard globe with metal filament that looks very much like what Thomas Edison invented. The light produced by incandescent bulbs is a much warmer light, with more reds and yellows. This warmer light is perceived as being cozier and more inviting. Lighting your dining nook with standard incandescent lighting will make it a more inviting space.

The latest in lighting is the use of halogen or xenon bulbs. These bulbs are actually incandescent bulbs, with halogen or xenon gas filling the globe. They produce a very bright, very cool light. This light is excellent for task lighting, but isn't always suitable for accent or decorative lighting. For example, halogen bulbs would be perfectly suited for your stainless and glass upscale loft kitchen, but might not yield the desired homey feel of a country-style kitchen.

Daylight is also an important light source in the kitchen. If you are contemplating a complete kitchen remodel, make sure you consider adding sources of daylight in the form of skylights, clerestories, larger windows or greenhouse windows. Daylight can be diffuse and provide excellent ambient light, but it can also be harsh and create glaring bright spots on highly polished surfaces. Cooking supper in your west-facing stainless steel kitchen might necessitate pulling the shades.

UNIVERSAL DESIGN

Lighting your kitchen properly makes it a safer and more welcoming space for all users. If you have provided ample task lighting and sufficient ambient light, you have already made it a more accessible place. Other factors to consider are reducing glare by using anti-glare film on windows and having matte or brushed surfaces for floors, countertops and appliance facings. Glare reduction is important for people with vision problems and for many elderly people, who find it takes longer for their eyes to recover after looking at a bright light. Choosing long-life bulbs for your fixtures decreases the number of times the bulbs need to be changed, which is important for someone with limited mobility. Automated window shade openers also are a great help for people with limited mobility. Rocker switches are easier for everyone to operate (you'll appreciate the ease of using your elbow to turn on the lights when your arms are full of groceries). Lighted rocker switches are easier to locate in a dim or dark room, and voice- or motion-activated switches are the best of all. Low wattage under- or above-cabinet lighting makes an ideal night-light to make late-night kitchen trips safer.

LIGHTBULB SHOPPING TIPS

• *Choose longer-life bulbs—they usually are more energy efficient and don't need to be changed as often.*

• *Look for fluorescent bulbs labeled "rare-earth" or "triphosphor."*

• *Full-spectrum bulbs give the best color rendering.*

• *Halogen bulbs burn very hot—they can be a burn or fire hazard if not properly installed.*

• *Xenon bulbs produce the same bright, white light as halogens, but last longer and burn cooler.*

(right) **Pendant lighting** defines the peninsula in this kitchen. Recessed lights provide task lighting without interrupting the look of the paneled ceiling.

(below) **Lots of natural light floods this kitchen.** When the sun goes down, low-voltage cable lights and recessed lights supply task and accent lighting.

Rocker switch

Dimmer switch

Motion sensor

Controls & Fixtures

A huge variety of controls and fixtures for lighting is available to suit all needs and tastes. The following represents what is generally available.

Controls

Rocker switches are the direct descendants of the original toggle switch. Perfect for turning lights on and off with elbows when fingers are greasy or arms are burdened with groceries. They're easier to use for those with limited hand strength. Lighted versions are easy to locate in the dark.

Dimmer switches are the lighting designer's most important control. No lighting design can work if it can't be controlled to a finer degree than simply on and off. If you have easy control over the level of light, you'll be more likely to take time to set the lighting levels to suit the occasion. Dimmers also lengthen bulb life. Replacing a switch with a dimmer is a ten dollar—ten minute home improvement worth its weight in gold.

Motion sensing switches turn on lights as soon as you enter the room. They're perfect for midnight snacking trips where fumbling for a light switch in the dark could be hazardous.

Integrated control panels are the home version of theatrical lighting control boards. By controlling several fixtures at once, you can create lighting schemes for specific times of day or situations using several fixtures dimmed to specific levels. Once you've created a scheme, all you have to do is press a button. Instead of switching on a light, these devices let you switch on the room.

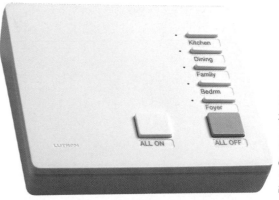

Integrated control panel

Photo Courtesy of Hubbardton Forge®

Photo Courtesy of Hubbardton Forge®

Photo Courtesy of MIRAGE Prefinished Hardwood Floors

Fixtures

Chandeliers and pendants (A) hang from the ceiling. Focused pendants provide light for tasks; fixtures mounted flush to the ceiling reflect light off the ceiling surface for ambient light; chandeliers provide decorative light.

Wall sconces (B) are any fixtures that can be mounted on the wall. They provide ambient illumination by directing light up to the ceiling or down the wall.

Track lighting systems (C) are flexible tracks installed on the ceiling that supply power to fixtures anywhere along the track. Fixtures include spotlights, pendants and decorative fixtures.

Recessed lights (D) are fixtures mounted inside a ceiling. They vary in size from 1½" to 8". Depending on the trim (the part that directs the light), they can provide any light from very focused to diffused.

Strip lights (E) are strips of small lightbulbs that can be installed under cabinets or shelves to create large task-lit spaces.

Torchieres (F) are floor lamps that direct light up toward the ceiling to provide ambient illumination. They are generally placed near walls and in corners.

Cove lights (G) are fluorescent tubes, flexible rope lights or other small fixtures installed in coves, above cabinets or behind trim to turn architectural features into light sources.

Removing Electrical Fixtures

1 Shut off the electrical power to the kitchen circuits at the main service panel.

Many of the following lighting projects begin with removing an electrical fixture—either a receptacle or a lighting fixture. Whenever you remove an electrical fixture, carefully follow the instructions on this page. The neon circuit tester is an inexpensive yet vital tool for preventing potentially fatal electrical shocks. Remember that simply turning a wall switch off does not guarantee that all wires in a fixture will be without power.

Tools and Materials

Tools: circuit tester, screwdriver.

2 Loosen the mounting screws, then remove the bases and coverplates from lights and other electrical fixtures. Be careful not to touch the wires until they have been tested for power.

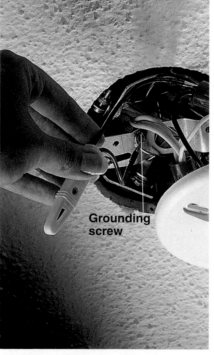

Grounding screw

3 Test the circuit wires for power, using a neon circuit tester. Touch one probe to a grounding screw, and the other to each circuit wire connection. If the circuit tester light glows, turn off the main circuit breaker, and retest.

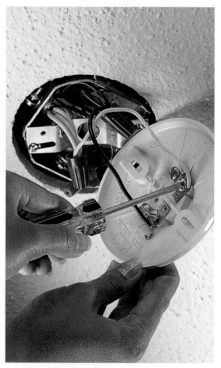

4 When you are sure the power is off, disconnect the fixture or receptacle from the circuit wires.

Installing Track Lighting

Track lights give you the ability to precisely aim light fixtures. They are ideal for illuminating work areas and dining spaces.

It's easy to replace your central ceiling fixture with a surface-mounted lighting track. Additional tracks can be added, using L- or T-connectors.

Shopping Tips

• *A variety of fixtures are available, including pendants ideal for lighting islands.*

• *Fixtures come in black, white and brushed steel.*

Tools and Materials

Tools: circuit tester, screwdriver.

Materials: track lighting kit.

Photo courtesy of Mill's Pride

Track lighting makes it easy to create custom lighting effects. The individual fixtures can be arranged to provide focused task lighting or supply indirect lighting to brighten a dark corner.

How to Install Track Lighting

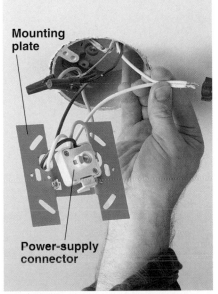

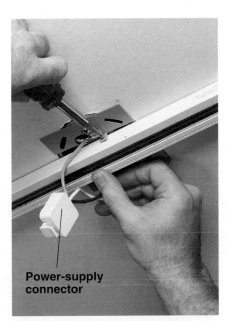

1 Connect the power-supply connector to the circuit wires, using wire connectors. Then, attach the mounting plate to the electrical box.

2 Mount the first track to the ceiling, screwing it into framing members or using toggle bolts. Secure the track to the mounting plate with screws. Snap the power-supply connector into the track.

3 Install additional tracks, connecting them to the first track with L- or T-connectors. Install the power-supply cover. Cap bare track ends with dead-end pieces. Position the light fixtures as desired.

Installing Low-voltage Cable Lighting

This unique fixture system is a mainstay of retail and commercial lighting and is now becoming common in homes. Low-voltage cable systems consist of a transformer and two parallel, current-carrying cables to suspend and provide electricity to fixtures mounted anywhere on the cables. The system's ease of installation, flexibility and the wide variety of whimsical and striking individual lights available make it perfect for all kinds of spaces. Low-voltage cable light systems are ideal for situations where surface-mounted track is undesirable or impossible to install. Most fixtures use the MR16 halogen bulb, which provides very white, focused light—excellent for accent lighting.

SHOPPING TIPS

• *Individual fixtures can be purchased at lighting stores, and you can generally mix and match manufacturers.*

• *Plug-in transformers are available if you don't want to install a hard-wired kit.*

Tools and Materials

Tools: neon circuit tester, screwdriver.

Materials: low-voltage cable lighting system, wire connectors.

How to Install Low-voltage Cable Lighting

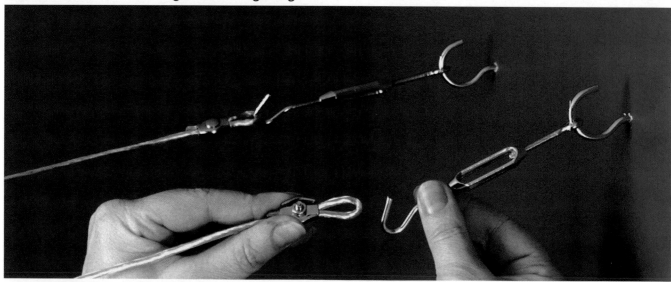

1 Screw the cable hooks into the walls, 6 to 10" apart. (Make sure the hooks hit wall framing, or use wall anchors.) Cut the cable to the length of the span plus 6" extra for loops. Make loops with the provided fasteners, and attach the cables. Adjust the turnbuckles until cables are taut. Turn off the power at the service panel, and test the circuit with a neon tester. Remove the old fixture if you are replacing an existing fixture.

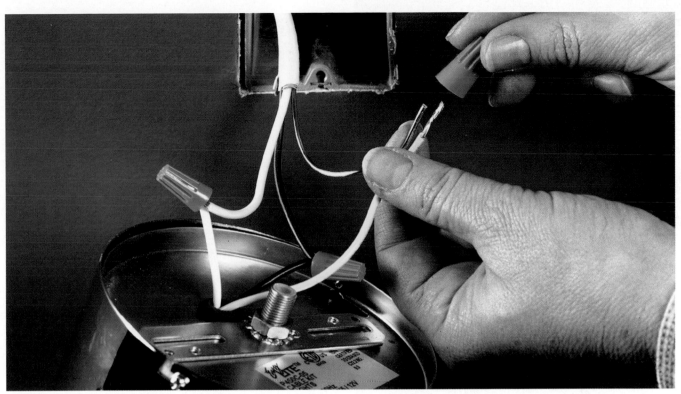

2 If you are not replacing an old fixture, install a new electrical box for the power supply and route cable to it from nearby receptacle (see pages 202 to 203). Leave 11" of extra cable for making connections, and secure it in the box with a cable clamp. Remove 10½" of sheathing from the end, and strip ¾" of insulation from the ends of the wires.

Install the mounting strap for the transformer onto the fixture box with the provided screws. Remove the cover from the transformer, and connect the black transformer wire to the black circuit wire. Connect the white transformer wire to the white circuit wire, and connect the ground transformer wire to the grounding wire. Attach the transformer to the wall, and replace the cover.

3 Connect the two low-voltage leads from the transformer to the parallel cables. The low-voltage leads can be connected at any point on the cable and can be cut to any length. Connect the leads to the cables using the screw-down connectors provided. (It doesn't matter which lead is connected to which cable.) Make sure the screw is tight enough to pierce the insulation. Once the leads are attached, it's safe to restore the power. The 12-volt current is safe, and it's easier to adjust the lights when they're on.

4 Attach the fixtures with the connectors supplied by the manufacturers (fixtures connect in a variety of ways), and adjust the beams as necessary. Make sure you don't add more fixtures than the transformer can support.

Installing Under-cabinet Lighting

Under-cabinet lights come in numerous styles, including mini-track lights, strip lights, halogen puck lights, flexible rope lights and fluorescent task lights (covered here).

This installation shows hard-wiring a series of fluorescent under-cabinet lights and installing a new wall switch control.

Consult your electrical inspector about code requirements regarding the type of cable required (some may require armored cable) and the power source from which you draw. Some codes may not allow you to draw power for light fixtures from small appliance circuits. Also make sure the wattage of the new lights does not exceed the safe capacity of the circuit.

SHOPPING TIPS

• *Look for low-profile fixtures—some slim fixtures are only ¾" × 1⅜".*

• *Choose rapid-start lamps with rapid-start ballasts—these are the best quality.*

• *Avoid inexpensive "utility" ballasts that buzz or hum.*

Tools and Materials

Tools: neon circuit tester, utility knife, wallboard saw, hammer, screwdriver, drill and hole saw, jig saw, wire stripper.

Materials: under-cabinet lighting kit, 12-2 NM cable, pigtail wiring, twist-on wire connectors, plastic switch box, switch.

How to Install Hard-wired Under-cabinet Lighting

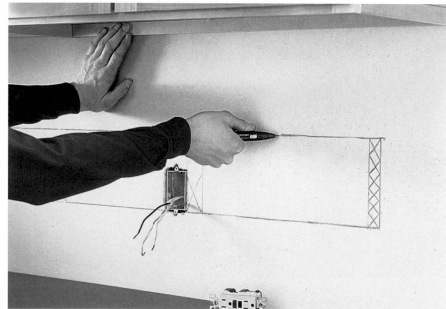

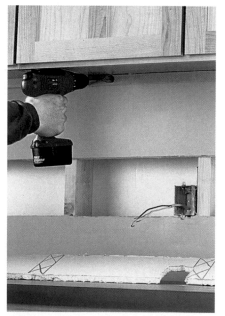

1 Shut off the power to the receptacle you plan to draw power from, then use a neon circuit tester to confirm the power is off. Disconnect the receptacle from its wiring. Locate and mark the studs in the installation area. Mark and cut a channel to route the cable, using a utility knife. In order to ease repair of the wallboard when finished, we cut a 6"-wide channel in the center of the installation area.

2 Drill holes through the cabinet edging and/or wall surface directly beneath the cabinets where the cable will enter each light fixture. Drill ⅝" holes through the studs to run the cable.

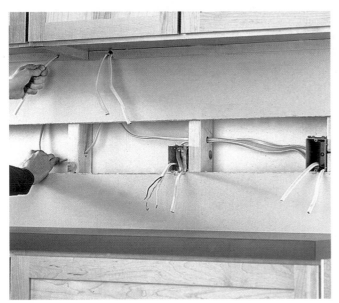

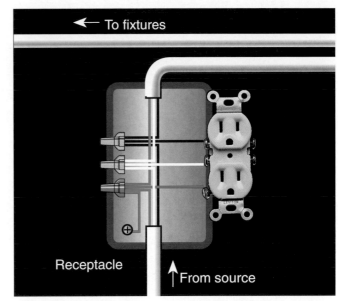

3 Install a plastic switch box by nailing it to the stud. Route a piece of 12-2 cable from the switch location to the power source. Route another cable from the switch to the first fixture hole. If you are installing more than one set of lights, route cables from the first fixture location to the second, and so on.

4 Strip 8" of sheathing from the ends of the switch-to-power cable. Clamp the cable into the receptacle box. Using plastic wire connectors, pigtail the white wires to the silver terminal on the receptacle and the black wires to the brass terminal. Pigtail the grounding wires to the grounding screw in the electrical box. Tuck wiring into the electrical box and re-attach the receptacle.

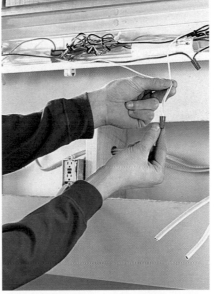

5 Remove the access cover, lens and bulb from the light fixture. Open the knockouts for running cables into the fixture. Insert the cables into the knockouts and secure the clamps. Strip 8" of sheathing from the cables. Attach the light fixture to the bottom of the cabinet with screws.

6 Use wire connectors to join the black, white and ground leads from the light fixture to each of the corresponding cable wires from the wall, including any cable leading to additional fixtures. Re-attach the bulb, lens and access cover to the fixture. Repeat this process for any additional fixtures.

7 Strip 8" of sheathing from each cable at the switch and clamp the cables into the switch box. Join the white wires together with wire connectors. Connect each black wire to a screw terminal on the switch. Pigtail the ground wires to the grounding screw on the switch. Install the switch and coverplate; restore power. Patch removed wallboard.

Installing In-cabinet & Above-cabinet Lighting

Cabinets are great places for a variety of lighting. While under-cabinet lights make great task and accent lighting, cabinet tops and insides are great for concealing ambient sources.

SHOPPING TIPS

• *Halogen fixtures require a mounting hole that extends completely through the stock for ventilation.*

• *Xenon bulbs are cooler than halogen bulbs and burn longer. They do not require a through-cut mounting hole.*

Tools and Materials

Tools: neon circuit tester, drill, hole saw, fish tape, cable stripper, combination tool.

Materials: mini low-voltage recessed light, 120 volt-12 volt transformer, fluorescent light fixture, wire connectors, non-metallic cable.

How to Install In-cabinet Lights

1 Use a hole saw to make a hole in the top of the cabinet or in a shelf. Depress the spring clips on the side of the light and fit it into the hole. The two wires should be on top.

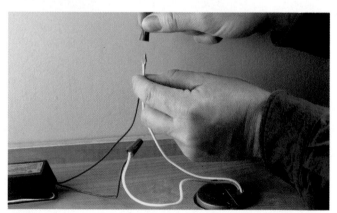

2 Connect the light to transformer wires or to the next light in the series with wire connectors. The simplest way to install a transformer for these lights is to use a plug-in transformer. You can install a switch for the receptacle or you can use a plug-in transformer with a built-in switch. For larger, built-in cabinets, hardwire the transformer and use a standard or dimmer switch as with under- or above-cabinet lights.

How to Install Above-cabinet Lights

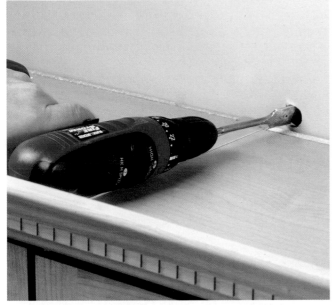

1 Turn off power to the circuit and confirm that the power is off, using a neon circuit tester. Drill a ⅝" hole through the wall surface directly above the cabinets where the cable will enter each light fixture.

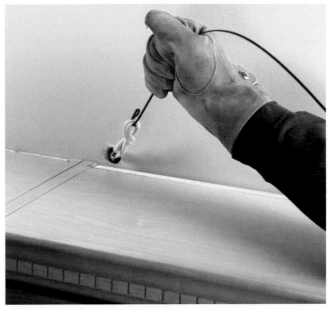

2 Route an NM cable from a nearby receptacle to a switch, as you would for under-cabinet lighting (see pages 202 to 203). Route cable from the switch to the hole above the cabinet. Use a fish tape to pull the cable up through the wall behind the cabinet. Pull about 16" of cable through the hole.

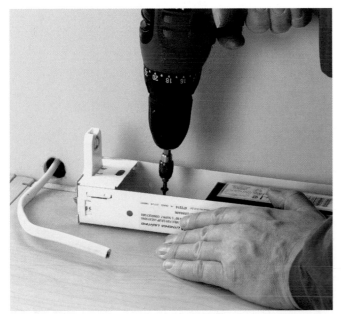

3 Use a fluorescent fixture that will be entirely concealed by the trim on the front edge of the cabinet top. (Lighting stores sell low-profile fluorescent fixtures.) Remove the lens and the cover from the fluorescent fixture. Attach the light fixture to the back of the cabinet top with screws.

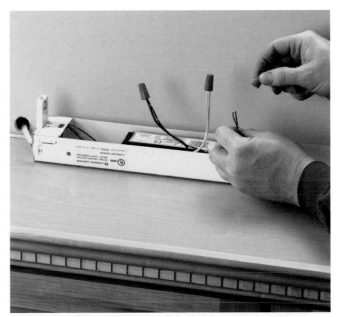

4 Remove a knockout from the fixture, and route the cable into the fixture, leaving 11" extra for making connections. Secure it with a cable clamp. Remove 10½" of sheathing from the cable and strip ¾" of insulation from each of the wires. Using wire connectors, connect the black circuit wire to the black fixture wire, the white circuit wire to the white fixture wire, and the grounding circuit wire to the fixture grounding wire. Tuck the wires into the fixture, replace the cover and lens, and install a bulb. Install the switch, and restore the power.

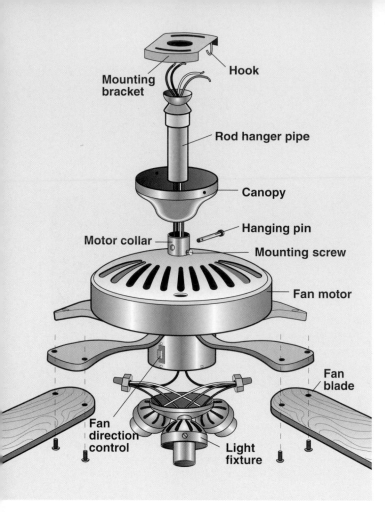

Mounting bracket
Hook
Rod hanger pipe
Canopy
Hanging pin
Motor collar
Mounting screw
Fan motor
Fan blade
Fan direction control
Light fixture

Installing a Ceiling Fan & Light

A combination fan and light is a great choice for a kitchen ceiling fixture. Using the wiring from an existing light fixture, you can easily install it yourself. The best fans have forward and reverse speeds—counterclockwise for summer and clockwise for winter.

Most standard ceiling fans work with a wall switch functioning as master power for the unit. Pull chains attached to the unit control the fan and lights. If you would like to eliminate the pull chains, consider a remote-control device.

SHOPPING TIPS

• *A longer warranty indicates a higher quality, quieter motor.*

Tools and Materials

Tools: stepladder, screwdrivers, wire stripper, pliers or adjustable wrench, neon circuit tester, hammer.

Materials: ceiling fan-light kit, 2 × 4 lumber or adjustable ceiling fan cross brace, 1½" and 3" wallboard screws.

How to Install a Ceiling Fan & Light

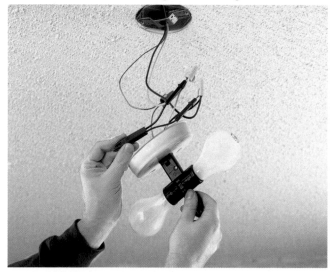

1 Shut off the power to the circuit at the service panel. Unscrew the existing fixture and carefully pull it away from the ceiling. Do not touch bare wires. Test for power by inserting the probes of a neon circuit tester into the wire connectors on the black and white wires. If the tester lights, return to the service panel and turn off the correct circuit. Disconnect the wire connectors and remove the old fixture.

2 Due to the added weight and vibration of a ceiling fan, you must determine whether the existing electrical box will provide adequate support. If you can access the box from the attic, check to see that it is a metal, not plastic, box and that it has a heavy-duty cross brace rated for ceiling fans. If the box is not adequately braced, cut a 2 × 4 to fit between the joists and attach it with 3" screws. Attach a metal electrical box to the brace from below with at least three 1½" wallboard screws. Attach the fan mounting bracket to the box.

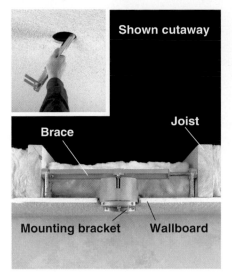

Variation: If the joists are inaccessible from above, remove the old box and install an adjustable ceiling fan brace through the rough opening in the ceiling. Insert the fan brace through the hole, adjust until it fits tightly between the joists, then attach the box with the included hardware. Make sure the lip of the box is flush with the ceiling wallboard before attaching the mounting bracket.

3 Run the wires from the top of the fan motor through the canopy and then through the rod hanger pipe. Slide the rod hanger pipe through the canopy and attach the pipe to the motor collar using the included hanging pin. Tighten the mounting screws firmly.

4 Hang the motor assembly by the hook on the mounting bracket. Connect the wires according to manufacturer's directions, using wire connectors to join the fixture wires to the circuit wires in the box. Gather the wires together and tuck them inside the fan canopy. Lift the canopy and attach it to the mounting bracket.

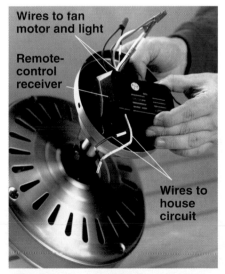

Remote Control Variation: To install a remote control, fit the receiver inside the fan canopy. Follow the manufacturer's wiring diagram to wire the unit. The receiver has a set of three wires that connects to the corresponding wires from the fan motor and lights, and another set that connects to the two circuit wires from the electrical box.

5 Attach the fan blades one at a time with the included hardware. Follow the manufacturer's directions.

6 Connect the wiring for the fan's light fixture according to the manufacturer's directions. Tuck all wires into the switch housing and attach the fixture. Install light bulbs and globes. Restore power and test the fan. If the fan vibrates excessively, check the manufacturer's documentation to adjust the balance. If the fan doesn't run at all, turn off the power and check the wiring connections.

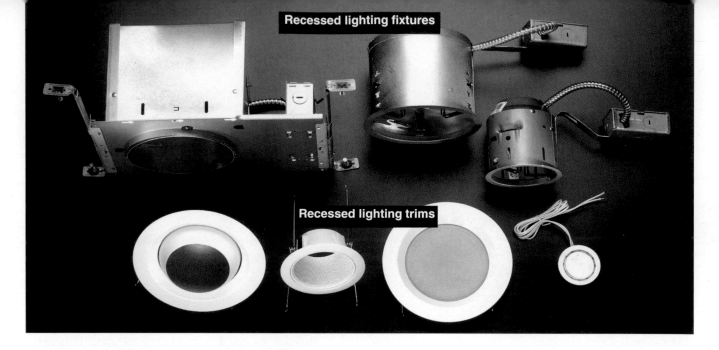

Recessed lighting fixtures

Recessed lighting trims

Installing Recessed Lighting

Recessed lights are versatile fixtures, suited for providing focused task and accent lighting or ambient lighting. Installing a single recessed fixture with a spot trim can provide task lighting for a work area or subtle accent lighting for artwork or an architectural feature.

There are recessed lighting cans in all shapes and sizes for almost every type of ceiling or cabinet. Cans are rated as either insulation-compatible or for uninsulated ceilings. Be sure to use the correct one for your ceiling to prevent creating a fire hazard. Low-voltage models are also available.

Tools and Materials

Tools: hammer, screwdriver, drywall saw, fish tape, cable stripper, combination tool.

Materials: recessed light can and trim, nonmetallic cable, wire connectors.

How to Mount a Recessed Light Fixture in Soffit Framing

1 Extend the mounting bars on the recessed fixture to reach the framing members. Adjust the position of the light unit on the mounting bars to locate it properly. Align the bottom edges of the mounting bars with the bottom face of the framing members.

2 Nail or screw the mounting bars to the framing members. Remove the wire connection box cover, open knockouts and install cable clamps. Run cable and make connections, using wire connectors.

How to Install a Recessed Light Fixture in a Finished Ceiling

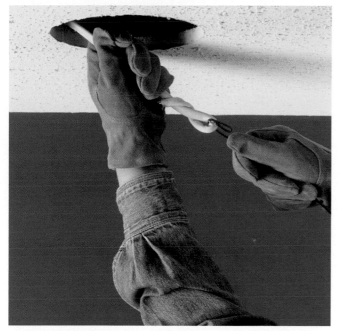

1 Turn off the power at the service panel. Make the hole for the can with a drywall saw or hole saw. Most fixtures will include a template for sizing the hole. Use a fish tape to run the cable from the switch box to the hole (see page 273 for instructions on running cable). Pull about 16" of cable out of the hole for making the connection.

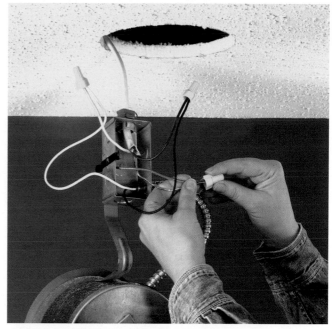

2 Remove a knockout from the electrical box attached to the can, and thread about 14" of the cable into the box and secure it with a cable clamp. Remove 12" of the sheathing from the cable, and strip ¾" of insulation from the wires. Using wire connectors, connect the black fixture wire to the black circuit wire, the white fixture wire to the white circuit wire, and then connect the ground wire to the grounding screw or grounding wire (shown) attached to the box

3 Install the can in the ceiling, depressing the mounting clips so the can will fit into the hole. Insert the can so that its edge is tight to the ceiling. Push the mounting clips back out so they grip the drywall and hold the fixture in place.

4 Install the trim by pressing the trim into the can until its spring clips snap into place. Restore the power and adjust the trim.

PAINTING & WALLCOVERING

*W*hat could be a quicker and easier kitchen makeover than a fresh coat of paint? Many people underestimate what a color change or a fresh coat of paint can do for a kitchen.

Choosing a color for your kitchen can be a tricky decision. Some colors can make a warm kitchen seem cooler, and others can make a large space seem more intimate. Our color overview gives you valuable information on color theory to help you make your color choices.

Painting kitchen walls and ceilings is perhaps the easiest of kitchen remodeling projects, but there are still important preparation steps, which you'll learn about in this section. Complete information on brush and roller painting is also given.

Wallcovering border trim and stencils are very popular for kitchen décor. They can tie together a decorative motif, add whimsy or formality or define spacial boundaries. If you have always wanted to add a border or stencil, this chapter shows just how easy it is to include these highlights in your kitchen.

Using Color

Decorating kitchen walls with paint and wallcoverings can change the appearance of the room, and affect its tone or "feel." Even with the limited amount of available wall space in most kitchens, you still need to consider what overall effect you desire. Here are some pointers about choosing colors and patterns.

Colors have an emotional effect, especially when vivid colors are used. Red is associated with passion and actually speeds up the metabolism. It is a warm color, and using it in the kitchen may add to the "heat" of the room. According to the principles of feng shui, using red, pink or purple in the kitchen is not positive. Because these colors are associated with fire, they are believed to increase the emotional level in negative directions. If these are colors you like and wish to use in the kitchen, use lighter or darker shades, or use vivid red as an accent. A crimson pot or a folk-art plate is an excellent accent that will immediately draw the eye.

Yellow is a cheery color, and often used for kitchens. Beware of covering large areas with vivid, glossy yellow. Its cheerfulness can quickly become tiring. Instead, use a lighter shade to create a mellow positive feeling rather than an intense one.

Green and blue are soothing, cool colors. Used in conjunction with white, they "offset" the heat of cooking. As with red and yellow, intense or vivid shades of blue and green on large surfaces can become tiring. Green is often associated with jealousy (bile) and poison—not necessarily a positive choice for a kitchen. Used as an accent, however, it can convey the calmness of green outdoor spaces. The ivy border is a common use of green in a white kitchen. White and blue are perceived as cleaner colors, and a white kitchen certainly sparkles. An intensely white kitchen, however, can seem sterile and forbidding in addition to revealing each speck of dust.

Purple was the color of royalty because it is rare in nature. Because of this rarity, purple is often seen as artificial. Again, it is an excellent accent color and can be used to excellent effect in its darker shades. Brown, on the other hand, is found extensively in nature, but is still considered a rich color. Dark stains and aging copper combined with tan or beige can give a kitchen a rich but comfortable feel. Black is elegant, and trendy, but can be as harsh as white. You wouldn't want to paint a kitchen wall black, but many countertops, appliances and fixtures are available in glossy black finishes.

Lighting affects our perception of color. Make sure you view your selections in daylight as well as under artificial lighting.

Because our eyes are sensitive to gradations in shade, the shade you choose may have more effect on the feel of the kitchen than the actual color. In general, lighter shades create a greater feeling of spaciousness, while darker shades increase the feeling of intimacy. A ceiling painted with a light shade seems higher than one painted a dark shade. Just as with lighting, consider the task areas of your kitchen. If you have a seating nook where you often eat, you may want to set it off with a cozier, dark shade. Work areas should be light shades to reflect more task lighting, and to make the area seem larger.

Because cabinet, floor and appliance colors are more difficult to change, it is important to factor these colors into your choices unless you are doing a complete remodeling project. Be aware that vivid colors can impart their hue to neutral surfaces. A hot pink wall will give a rosy glow to neighboring white cabinets. Whichever color you choose, begin by buying a small quantity and painting a 2 × 2-foot sample square on the wall. Some paint companies actually sell small paint packets for this purpose.

Basic Color Theory

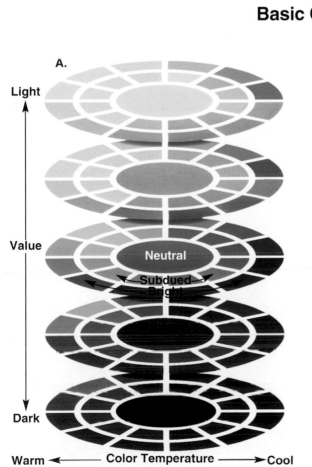

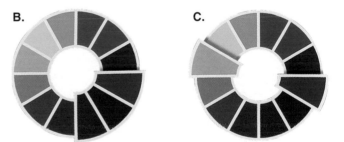

A: Red, yellow and blue are the primary colors and all colors are made from combinations of these three along with black and white. Colors come in many values, or shades; light shades contain more white and dark shades contain more black. A color's vividness or brightness is dulled by adding gray. Colors are also classified by their temperature—warm colors are reds and yellows, cool colors are greens and blues.

Relationships between colors are illustrated by the color wheel. **B:** Similar, or related, colors are together on the color wheel. **C:** Complementary colors are directly opposite each other, and contrasting colors have three colors between them.

213

Wash kitchen walls thoroughly before painting. Grease and dirt will prevent paint from adhering fully.

Surface Preparation Tips

Apply lightweight spackle to holes with a putty knife or your fingertip. This keeps repair areas small. Let the spackle dry. Sand until smooth.

Water or rust stains may indicate water damage. Check for leaking pipes and soft plaster, make needed repairs, then seal the area with stain-covering sealer.

Painting Preparation & Projects

Kitchen walls need to be washed before painting. A dirty, greasy wall will absorb paint unevenly and is more likely to cause sags or drips even in properly applied paint. Some surface dirt will even bleed through, causing staining. Use a trisodium phosphate cleaner and carefully follow the manufacturer's instructions.

Many kitchens are painted with high gloss paint. You may need to de-gloss the old paint surface to ensure proper adhesion of the new paint. This can be done with a chemical paint de-glosser or by sanding. The de-glosser must be used with sufficient ventilation and you should wear a respirator.

Move the stove and refrigerator if they are not built in and paint behind them. This prevents paint from dripping or spattering onto cooling fins or into vent areas.

For professional results, check your walls for damage and repair the wallboard or plaster as needed. Carefully mask and tape all trim and cabinets, and cover countertops and the floor with drop cloths.

Tools and Materials

Tools: putty knife, paint scraper.

Materials: trisodium phospate, sandpaper, spackle, masking tape.

How to Patch Peeling Paint

1 Scrape away loose paint with a putty knife or paint scraper.

2 Apply spackle to the edges of chipped paint with a putty knife or flexible wallboard knife.

3 Sand the patch area with 150-grit production sandpaper. The patch area should feel smooth to the touch.

How to Mask Trim

Masking and draping materials include (clockwise from top left): plastic and canvas drop cloths, self-adhesive plastic, masking tape and pregummed masking papers.

1 Use pregummed paper or wide masking tape to protect wood moldings from paint splatters. Leave the outside edge of masking tape loose.

2 After applying the tape, run the tip of a putty knife along the inside edge of the tape to seal against seeping paint. After painting, remove the tape as soon as the paint is too dry to run.

How to Use a Paintbrush

1 Dip the brush, loading one-third of its bristle length. Tap the bristles against the side of the can. Dipping deeper overloads the brush. Dragging the brush against the lip of the can causes the bristles to wear.

2 Cut in the edges using the narrow edge of the brush, pressing just enough to flex the bristles. Keep an eye on the paint edge, and paint with long, slow strokes. Always paint from a dry area back into wet paint to avoid lap marks.

3 Brush wall corners using the wide edge of the brush. Paint open areas with a brush or roller before the brushed paint dries.

How to Paint With a Paint Roller

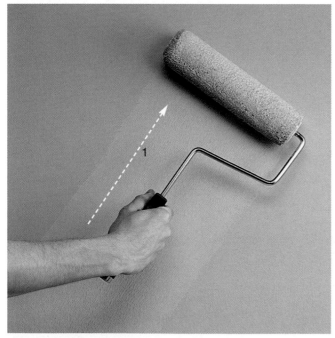 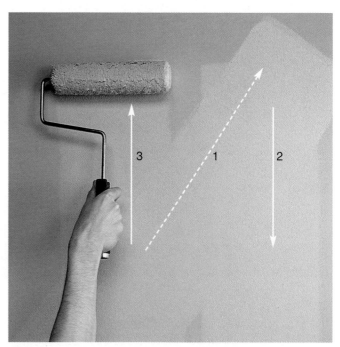

1 With the loaded roller, make a diagonal sweep (1) about 4 feet long on the surface. On walls, roll upward on the first stroke to avoid spilling paint. Use slow roller strokes to avoid splattering.

2 Draw the roller straight down (2) from top of the diagonal sweep. Shift the roller to the beginning of the diagonal and roll up (3) to complete the unloading of the roller. Distribute paint over the rest of the section with horizontal back-and-forth strokes.

How to Paint Ceilings

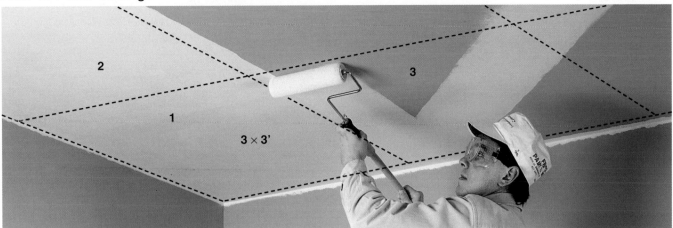

Paint ceilings with a roller handle extension. Use eye protection while painting overhead. Start at the corner farthest from the entry door. Cut in the edges with a brush, then paint the ceiling along the narrow end in 3-ft. × 3-ft. sections. Apply the paint with a diagonal stroke. Distribute the paint evenly with back-and-forth strokes. For the final smoothing strokes, roll each section toward the wall containing the entry door, lifting the roller at the end of each sweep.

How to Paint Walls

Paint walls in 2-ft. × 4-ft. sections. Start in an upper corner, cutting in the ceiling and wall corners with a brush, then rolling the section. Make the initial diagonal roller stroke from the bottom of the section upward, to avoid dripping paint. Distribute the paint evenly with horizontal strokes, then finish with downward sweeps of the roller. Next, cut in and roll the section directly underneath. Continue with adjacent areas, cutting in and rolling the top sections before the bottom sections. Roll all finish strokes toward the floor.

Hanging Wallcovering Borders

To determine the placement of a border, cut a strip of border several feet long. Tape the strip to the wall in different locations to help you visualize how the placement will affect the proportions of your kitchen.

Tools and Materials

Tools: pencil, carpenter's level, smoothing brush, paint tray and roller, wallboard knife, razor knife, seam roller, straightedge.

Materials: border, border adhesive, seam adhesive, sponge.

How to Hang Wallcovering Borders

1 If you are positioning the border on the wall other than along the ceiling or baseboard, draw a light pencil line around the room at the desired height, using a carpenter's level. Cut the first border strip. Prepare the strip, using border adhesive. Lay the strip pattern-side down on a flat surface. Apply adhesive evenly to the strip, using a paint roller.

2 Begin at the least conspicuous corner, overlapping the border onto the adjacent wall by ½". Have a helper hold the border while you apply it and smooth it with a smoothing brush.

3 At the inside corner, create a ¼" tuck from the overhang. Apply the adjoining border strip, trimming it with a razor knife.

4 Peel back the tucked strip, and smooth the strip around the corner, overlapping the border on the adjacent wall. Press the border flat. Apply seam adhesive to the lapped seam, if necessary.

5 If seams fall in the middle of a wall, overlap the border strips so the patterns match. Cut through both layers, using a razor knife with the back of a wallboard knife as a guide. Peel back the borders and remove the cut ends. Press the strips flat. Roll the seam after ½ hour, and wipe with a damp sponge.

6 Trim the border at door or window casings by holding the border against the outer edge of the casing with a wallboard knife and trimming the excess with a sharp razor knife. Wipe the border and casing, using a damp sponge.

How to Miter Border Corners

1 Apply the horizontal border strips, extending them past the corners a distance greater than the width of the border. Apply the vertical border strips, overlapping the horizontal strips.

2 Hold a straightedge along the points where the border strips intersect, and cut through both layers, using a razor knife. Peel back the strips and remove the cut ends.

3 Press the border back in place. Lightly roll the seam after ½ hour. Wipe any adhesive from the border, using a damp sponge.

Making & Using Stencils

Use stenciled motifs to highlight an area of your kitchen or to simulate architectural details. Pre-cut stencils are available, or you can create your own as shown here.

How to Make a Custom Stencil

1 Draw or trace the design onto a sheet of paper. Repeat the design, if necessary, so it is 13" to 18" long, making sure the spacing between repeats is consistent. Color the design, using colored pencils. Mark placement lines to help you position the stencil on the wall.

2 Position a Mylar sheet over the design so the edges of the sheet extend beyond the top and bottom of the design by at least 1". Secure the sheet with masking tape. Trace the areas that will be stenciled in the first color, using a marking pen. Transfer the placement lines to the Mylar.

3 Trace the design areas for each additional color onto a separate Mylar sheet. To help you align the stencil, outline the areas for previous colors with dotted lines. Layer all of the Mylar sheets, and check for accuracy. Using a mat knife and straightedge, trim the outer edges of the stencil plates, leaving a 1" to 3" border around the design.

4 Separate the Mylar sheets. Cut out the traced areas on each sheet, using a mat knife. Cut the smallest shapes first, then cut the larger ones. Pull the knife toward you as you cut, turning the Mylar sheet, rather than the knife, to change the cutting direction.

How to Stencil on Hard Surfaces

Tools and Materials

Tools: carpenter's level, stencil brushes, artist's brush.

Materials: pencil, precut or custom stencil, masking tape, spray adhesive, craft acrylic paints, or liquid or solid oil-based stencil paints, disposable plates, paper towels.

1 Mark the placement for the stencil on the surface with masking tape. Or, draw a light reference line, using a carpenter's level and a pencil. Position the stencil plate for the first color, aligning the placement line with the tape or pencil line. Secure the stencil in place, using masking tape or spray adhesive.

2 Place 1 to 2 tsp. of acrylic or oil-based paint on a disposable plate. Dip the tip of a stencil brush into the paint. Blot the brush onto a folded paper towel, using a circular motion, until the bristles are almost dry.

3 Hold the brush perpendicular to the surface. Apply the paint within the cut areas of the stencil, using a circular motion. Allow to dry and repeat with the second stencil plate.

221

KITCHEN REMODELING

*I*n this final section of *The Complete Guide to Kitchens*, you'll learn about the process of doing a major kitchen remodeling project, including structural and framing work, installing new plumbing and installing all-new wiring.

Such a project isn't for the timid, but plenty of do-it-yourselfers have done this kind of major project successfully. If you tackle it, though, we recommend that you be confident of your own abilities.

Many people hire contractors for some or all of the work, and if you follow this path, you'll find plenty of information on the following pages to help you plan and supervise the creation of an all-new kitchen.

The first part of this section covers guidelines for kitchen design and construction. Here you will get baseline information on accepted spacing and layouts for kitchens, as well as general information on codes for plumbing, electrical, lighting and structural elements. Remember that local Code requirements may be quite specific, and may differ from those mentioned here.

The remainder of this section contains step-by-step how-to photographs for removing wall surfaces, framing new walls, plumbing kitchen sinks, and creating and wiring kitchen electrical circuits.

Creating Plans

Whether you are doing the work yourself or hiring others, once you have a good idea of the features you want in your new kitchen, it's time to create detailed plan drawings. Good plan drawings will help you in several phases of the planning process:

• Selecting cabinets and appliances to fit your kitchen layout.

• Soliciting accurate work bids when negotiating with plumbers, electricians and other subcontractors.

• Obtaining a building permit at your local Building Inspections office.

• Scheduling the stages of a remodeling project.

• Evaluating the work of contractors. If a carpenter or cabinetmaker fails to meet your expectations, your plan drawings serve as proof that the contractor did not complete the work as agreed.

Codes & Standards

Creating plans for a kitchen can seem like an overwhelming challenge, but fortunately there are guidelines available to help you. Some of these guidelines are legal regulations specified by your local Building Code and must be followed exactly. Most codes have very specific rules for basic construction, as well as for plumbing and electrical installations.

Another set of guidelines, known as standards, are informal recommendations developed over time by kitchen designers, cabinetmakers and appliance manufacturers. These design standards suggest parameters for good kitchen layout, and following them helps ensure that your kitchen is comfortable and convenient to use.

Guidelines for Layout

The goal of any kitchen layout is to make the cook's work easier and, where possible, to allow other people to enjoy the same space without getting in the way. Understanding the accepted design standards can help you determine whether your present layout is sufficient or if your kitchen needs a more radical layout change or expansion.

Work triangle & traffic patterns. A classic kitchen design concept, the work triangle theory proposes that the sink, range and refrigerator be arranged in a triangular layout according to the following guidelines:

• Position of the triangle should be such that traffic flow will not disrupt the main functions of the kitchen.

• Total distance between the corners of the triangle should be no more than 26 ft. and no less than 12 ft.

• Each side of the triangle should be between 4 and 9 ft. in length.

If two people frequently work in the kitchen simultaneously, the layout should include two work triangles. In a two-triangle kitchen, the triangles may share one side, but they should not cross one another.

Don't fret too much if you can't make the triangle layout work perfectly. Some kitchens, for example, may have four work stations instead of three, and others may not have enough space to accommodate the classic triangle.

For general traffic design, it is recommended to leave 4-ft. "corridors" between all stationary items for walking comfort. Some designers will allow this standard to be reduced to 3 feet in smaller kitchens.

Countertop space. Lack of kitchen countertop space is one of the biggest complaints heard from homeowners and, in some cases, is the primary reason for remodeling the kitchen. Tables 1 and 2 on pages 226 and 227 outline the minimum standards for countertop space. Also make sure your kitchen has at least one food preparation area with an uninterrupted length of countertop that is at least 36" long.

Appliances. Table 1 shows standard dimensions for common kitchen appliances—information you can use when planning your layout. These dimensions are standard from manufacturer to manufacturer, although larger and smaller models may also be available.

Some things to keep in mind when planning the location of appliances in your kitchen layout:

• *Appliance* doors should open away from traffic areas and other appliances.

• *Proper spacing* around appliances is crucial. Leave an open space at least 30" × 48" in front of each appliance.

Cabinets. Table 2 on page 227 shows the minimum standards for cabinet storage in small and large kitchens. The blind, unusable portion of a corner cabinet should not be included when calculating linear footage for either wall or base cabinets.

The sizes of base cabinets and wall cabinets are fairly uniform among manufacturers, and unless you have them custom-built in unusual sizes, they will conform to the following standards:

• **Base cabinets:** height—34½"; depth—23" to 24"; width—9" to 48", in 3" increments.

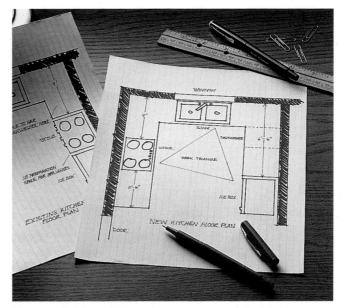

The work triangle is a layout concept that lets you develop a convenient arrangement of the range, sink and refrigerator in the kitchen.

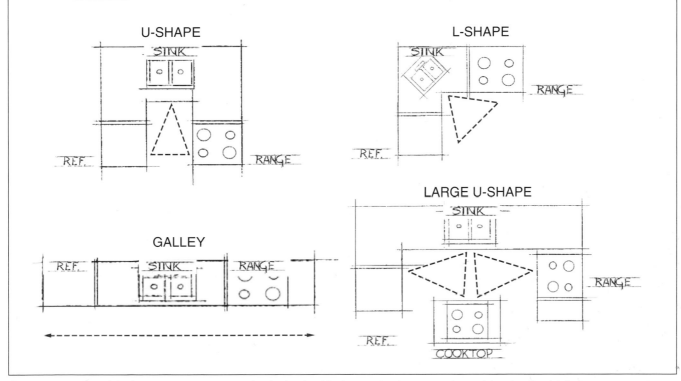

Some common kitchen arrangements include the U-shape, L-shape and corridor (galley) kitchen. Larger L- and U-shaped kitchens can often accommodate an island cabinet, which can shorten the legs of the kitchen triangle and make the cook's work easier.

- **Wall cabinets:** height—12", 15", 18", 24", 30", 33", 42"; depth—12"; width—24", 30", 33", 36", 42", 48".

- **Oven cabinets:** height—84", 96"; depth—24"; width—27", 30", 33".

- **Utility cabinets:** height—84"; depth—12", 24"; width—18", 24", 36".

Not every manufacturer will offer all these sizes and styles, so it's a good idea to obtain product catalogs when planning the layout of cabinets. Some other tips:

- *Use functional corner cabinets* rather than "blind" cabinets that provide no access to the corner area.

- *Include at least five storage/organizing units,* such as swing-out pantry units, appliance garages and specialized drawers or shelves.

Eating areas. Kitchen tabletops and countertops used for dining are generally positioned 30", 36", or 42" above the floor, and the recommended space for each person varies according to the height of the surface. Table 3 on page 227 shows the recommended per-person clearances for eating areas.

Islands. A kitchen island should be positioned so there is at least 36" of clear space between the edges of its countertop and surrounding walls or cabinets.

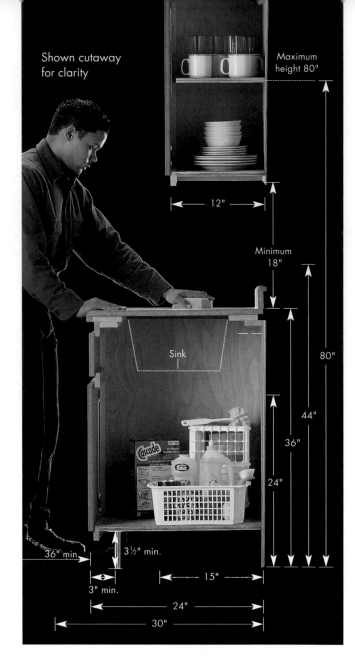

Table 1: Appliance Dimensions & Countertop Allowances

Appliance	Standard Dimension	Minimum Countertop Space	Comments
Refrigerator	36"	18" on latch side	12 cu. ft. for family of four; 2 cu. ft. for each additional person.
Sink	27" single 36" double	24" on one side 18" on other side	Minimum of 3" of countertop space between sink and edge of base cabinet.
Range	36"	15" on one side 9" on other side	If a window is positioned above a cooking appliance, the bottom edge of the window casing must be at least 24" above the cooking surface.
Cooktop	36"	15" on one side 9" on other side	
Wall oven	30"	15" on either side	Bottom edge should be between 24" and 48" above the floor.
Microwave	24"	15" on either side	

Table 2: Cabinet Standards

Recommended Minimums	Kitchen Size	
	Less than 150 sq. ft.	More than 150 sq. ft.
Countertops	132 lin. inches	198 lin. inches
Base cabinets	156 lin. inches	192 lin. inches
Wall cabinets	144 lin. inches	186 lin. inches
Roll-out shelving	120 lin. inches	165 lin. inches

Table 3: Eating Surface Standards

	Height of Eating Surface		
	30"	36"	42"
Min. width for each seated diner	30"	24"	24"
Min. depth for each seated diner	19"	15"	12"
Minimum knee space	19"	15"	12"

Recommended minimum spacing standards (tables 1, 2 and 3) are set by the National Kitchen & Bath Association. Following these guidelines helps ensure maximum convenience.

Guidelines for Basic Construction

Plans for a major remodeling project that involves moving or adding walls, or building a new room addition must accurately show the locations and dimensions of the new walls and all doors and windows. This will allow the construction carpenter to give you an accurate bid on the work and will allow him to obtain the necessary building permits. If you will be moving walls or adding windows or doors, you must identify load-bearing walls and provide appropriate support during removal and rebuilding.

Windows. Most Building Codes require that kitchens have at least one window, with at least 10 sq. ft. of glass area. Some local Building Codes, however, will allow windowless kitchens, so long as they have proper venting. Kitchen designers recommend that kitchens have windows, doors or skylights that together have a total glass surface area equal to at least 25% of the total floor area.

Doors. Exterior entry doors should be at least 3 ft. wide and 6½ ft. high. Interior passage doors between rooms must be at least 2½ ft. wide. A kitchen must have at least two points of entry, arranged so traffic patterns don't intrude on work areas.

Major structural work may include adding windows, doors or skylights, or moving walls. Your plan drawings should show the location and dimensions of all windows and doors in your new kitchen.

Examine your circuit breaker panel, usually located in the basement of your home or in an attached garage. It may have an index that identifies circuits serving the kitchen. If your service panel has open slots, an electrician can add additional kitchen circuits relatively easily. If your service panel is full, he may have to install a new service panel at additional cost.

Guidelines for Electrical Service & Lighting

Nearly any kitchen remodeling project will require some upgrading of the electrical service. While your old kitchen may be served by a single 120-volt circuit, it's not uncommon for a large modern kitchen to require as many as seven individual circuits. And in a few cases, the extra demands of the new kitchen may require that the main electrical service for your entire house be upgraded by an electrician. By comparing the electrical service in your present kitchen with the requirements described below, you'll get an idea of how extensive your electrical service improvements will need to be. Your plan drawings should indicate the locations of all the outlets, lighting fixtures and electrical appliances in your new kitchen.

The National Electric Code requires the following for kitchens:

• *Two small-appliance circuits* (120-volt, 20-amp) to supply power for the refrigerator and plug-in countertop appliances.

• *Wall outlets* spaced no more than 12 ft. apart.

• *Countertop outlets* spaced no more than 4 ft. apart.

• *GFCI* (ground-fault circuit interrupter), protected receptacles installed in any general use outlet, whether above counter or at floor level.

• *Dedicated circuits* for each major appliance. Install a 20-amp, 120-volt circuit for a built-in microwave, a 15-amp circuit for the dishwasher and food disposer. An electrical range, cooktop or wall oven requires a dedicated 50-amp, 240-volt circuit.

The Electric Code only requires that a kitchen have some form of lighting controlled by a wall switch, but kitchen designers have additional recommendations:

• *A general lighting circuit* (120-volt, 15-amp) that operates independently from plug-in outlets.

• *Plentiful task lighting,* usually mounted under wall cabinets or soffits, to illuminate each work area.

• *Decorative lighting fixtures* to highlight attractive cabinets or other features of the kitchen.

Guidelines for Plumbing

If your new kitchen layout changes the location of the sink, or if you are planning to add an additional sink or dishwasher, the water supply and drain pipes will need to be upgraded. Your plan drawings should indicate these intended changes.

Extending plumbing lines for a new kitchen is often fairly easy and surprisingly inexpensive, but there are some exceptions you should note:

Old pipes. If your present plumbing is more than 25 years old, there is a good chance the plumber will recommend replacing these pipes before installing the kitchen fixtures. Depending on circumstances, this can be an expensive proposition, but if you're faced with this decision, we strongly urge you to take a deep breath and do what the plumber suggests. Those corroded old pipes will need to be replaced someday, and this work is easier and cheaper if you're already in the process of remodeling the kitchen.

Outdated systems. Older plumbing systems may have drain trap and vent arrangements that violate modern Code requirements. If your plumber needs to run all-new vent pipes, this will increase the costs.

Island sinks. If your new kitchen will include an island sink, your plumber will need to run vent pipes beneath the floor. For this reason, plumbing an island sink is more expensive than plumbing a wall sink.

Guidelines for Heating, Ventilation & Air-conditioning

Your plan drawings should also show the locations of heating/air-conditioning registers or fixtures in your proposed kitchen. If you're planning a cosmetic make-over or a simple layout change, there is a pretty good chance you can get by with the same registers, radiators or heaters found in your present kitchen. But if your new kitchen will be substantially larger than it is now, or if the ratio of wall space filled by glass windows and doors will be greater, it's possible that you'll need to expand its heating and cooling capacity.

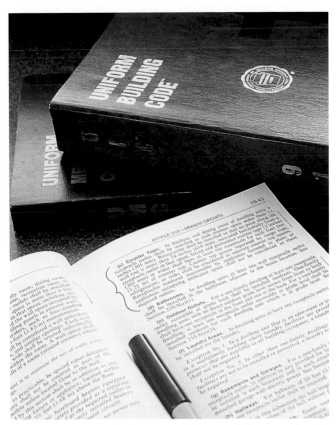

Code books can help you understand the structural, electrical and plumbing requirements for kitchens. In addition to the formal Code books, which are written for professional tradesmen, there are many Code handbooks available that are written for homeowners. Bookstores and libraries carry both the formal Code books and Code handbooks.

Increasing your kitchen's heating and cooling can be as simple as extending ducts by a few feet, or as complicated as installing a new furnace. When installing a large room addition, for instance, you may learn that the present furnace is too small to adequately heat the increased floor space of your home.

How do you determine what your kitchen needs in the way of expanded heating and cooling? Unless you happen to be a mechanical engineer, you'll need to consult a professional to evaluate your heating/ventilation/air-conditioning (HVAC) system. The Code requirements for room heating are quite simple, but the methods used to calculate required energy needs of a room are fairly complex.

The Building Code requires simply that a room must be able to sustain a temperature of 70°F, measured at a point 3 ft. above the floor. HVAC contractors use a complicated formula to calculate the most efficient way to meet this Code requirement. You can make this estimation more accurate by providing the following information:

Vent hoods are required by Code on all ranges and cooktops. The vent fan exhausts cooking fumes and moisture to the outdoors.

- *The exact dimensions* of your kitchen.

- *The thickness and amount of insulation* in the walls.

- *The number of doors and windows,* including their size and their energy ratings.

- *The total square footage* of your house.

- *The heating and cooling capacity* of your furnace and central air-conditioner, measured in BTUs. This information, usually printed on the unit's access panel, will help the HVAC contractor determine if the system can adequately serve your new kitchen.

Finally, your cooktop should be equipped with an electric vent hood to exhaust cooking fumes and moisture from the kitchen. The volume of air moved by a vent fan is restricted by Code, so you should always check with a Building Inspector before selecting a vent hood.

Metal ductwork for the vent hood must be run through an exterior wall or through the ceiling. If your cooktop is located in an island cabinet, a special island vent fan is necessary.

Drawing Plans

Now the fun starts. Armed with a vision of the features you want to include in your new kitchen and equipped with an understanding of the Code requirements and design standards, you're ready to put pencil to paper and begin to develop plan drawings—the next important step in transforming your dream kitchen into reality.

The key to success when developing plan drawings is to take as much time as you need and to remain flexible. A professional kitchen designer might take 30 to 80 hours to come up with precise floor plans and elevation drawings, so it's not unreasonable to allow yourself several weeks if you're doing this work yourself. You will almost certainly revise your plans several times before you settle on a layout that feels right to you. And it's not uncommon for kitchen plans to undergo changes as you make decisions about appliances and other materials. As you begin to research the price of cabinets and appliances and receive bids from contractors, you may well decide that it's prudent to scale back for the sake of your bank account, and these changes may require you to revise your plan drawings.

Developed plans for a kitchen remodeling

Finished plans for a kitchen remodeling project should include a floor plan—a scale drawing made from an overhead perspective, showing exact room dimensions, as well as the location of windows, doors, cabinets and appliances.

project should include both floor plans and elevation drawings.

A floor plan is a scaled drawing made from an overhead perspective, showing the exact room dimensions, as well as the location of windows, doors, cabinets, appliances, electrical and plumbing fixtures. Elevation drawings are plans depicting a wall surface as if viewed from the side. For clarity, use an architectural template to show the position of appliances and fixtures in your kitchen plans. These templates are available at drafting and office supply stores. Carpenters, electricians, plumbers and other contractors will understand exactly what you want if your plan drawings speak their language.

Wrapping Up

Once you've completed floor plans and elevation drawings of your kitchen-to-be, you're ready to begin choosing the appliances, cabinets and other materials for your new kitchen. Create a detailed shopping list that includes dimensions and specifications for each item you'll be buying.

Now would be a good time to enlist the aid of an interior designer to help you select colors and patterns for flooring, countertops and wall materials. Many installation contractors can also help you with design decisions.

231

Creating Floor Plans & Elevation Drawings

The process of creating finished plans for a kitchen project takes time and is done in three phases. First, you'll be drawing a floor plan of your present kitchen, providing a reference on which to base your new design. Next, you'll be experimenting with various layout options to find a design that best suits your needs, a process that can take several days, or even weeks. Finally, you'll be creating precise, finished floor plans and elevation drawings, which you will use when you begin interviewing contractors to do the work.

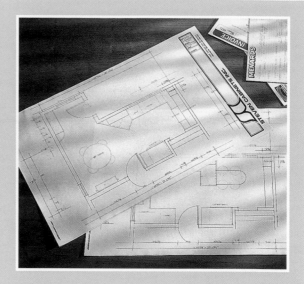

Tip: Creating Kitchen Plans

Although some homeowners have the artist's eye needed to draw accurate plans, others find this difficult if not impossible. If you fall into the latter category, don't be afraid to seek help. Home centers and cabinet manufacturers often have designers on staff who can help you draw up plans if you agree to buy materials from them. In addition, there are computer software programs that can help you develop accurate plans that can be printed out. And, of course, there are professional kitchen designers and architects who specialize in creating kitchen plans.

How to Create Floor Plans & Elevation Drawings

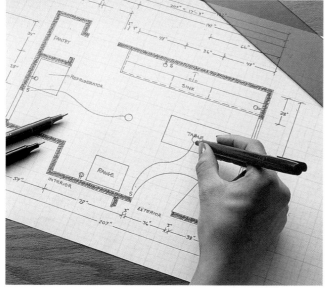

1 Measure each wall in your kitchen as it now exists. Take accurate measurements of the position and size of every feature, including doors, windows, cabinets, countertops and appliances. Also note the locations of all light fixtures and electrical outlets. Using graph paper, create a scaled floor plan of your present kitchen, using a scale of ½" equals 1 ft. Indicate doors, windows, interior and exterior walls. Add the cabinets, appliances and countertops, electrical outlets and lights, plumbing fixtures and HVAC registers and fixtures. In the margins, mark the exact dimensions of all elements.

2 Using tracing paper overlayed on your kitchen drawing, begin sketching possible layouts for your new kitchen, again using a scale of ½" equals 1 ft. As you develop your kitchen plan, refer often to your wish list of kitchen features and the kitchen standards and Code requirements listed earlier in this section. The goal is to create a kitchen that meets all your needs with the minimum possible impact on the present kitchen, because this will reduce the overall cost of your project.

3 If simple rearrangement of kitchen elements doesn't do the trick, explore the possibility of expanding your kitchen, either by enlarging the kitchen into an adjoining room, or by building a room addition. A kitchen designer or architect can help with this task.

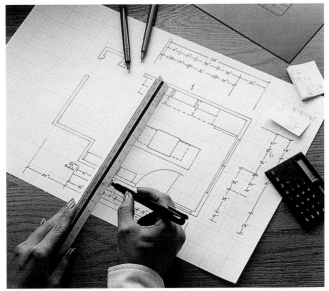

4 Once you settle on a layout, use graph paper to draw a very detailed floor plan of your new kitchen. Use dotted lines to fill in the base cabinets and appliances, and solid lines to show the wall cabinets and countertops. (For straight runs of cabinets, leave a margin of about 3" to allow for adjustments during cabinet installation.) In the margins around the wall outline, indicate dimensions of kitchen elements and the distances between them.

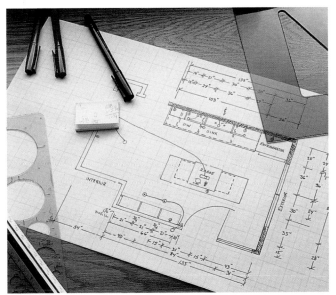

5 Use colored pencils to mark the locations of plumbing fixtures, electrical outlets and lighting fixtures and the heating registers, radiators or fixtures.

6 Draw a detailed, precise front elevation for each wall of your kitchen, using a scale of ½" equals 1 ft. Mark the vertical and horizontal measurements of all features, including doors, windows, wood moldings, cabinets, countertops, appliances and soffits. Draw a side elevation of each wall of the kitchen, complete with all measurements. When satisfied with the elevation drawings, add the locations for plumbing pipes, electrical outlets and lighting fixtures. Create close-up detail drawings of problem spots, such as the areas where appliances butt against window frames.

Use 2 × 6 lumber to build new plumbing walls that contain drain and supply pipes, called "wet walls." The extra thickness allows you to cut notches or drill holes for drain pipes without weakening the weight-bearing capacity of the wall.

Framing Kitchens

Adding new partition walls or moving existing walls will require framing work. Complete all framing work before you install new fixtures and surface materials.

Because of the presence of plumbing, some structural elements of floors and walls may have been subjected to water damage. Inspect the framing members and subfloors carefully, especially if wall or floor surfaces show signs of discoloration, cracking or peeling. Locate the source of any damage, such as a leaky pipe, and correct the problem before you replace or reinforce damaged wood.

If several framing members are warped, bowed or deteriorated, your house may have a serious structural problem. Have a building inspector or a licensed building contractor evaluate the damage.

If you're removing a loadbearing wall or creating a new or enlarged opening in one, use temporary supports to support the ceiling while the work is being done (see photo, below). All exterior walls are loadbearing. Temporary supports are not necessary for removing non-loadbearing walls. For in-depth information on framing and removing external wall surfaces, see *The Complete Guide to Windows and Doors,* or *The Complete Guide to Home Carpentry.*

Temporary supports are necessary when you create or enlarge a wall opening in a platform-framed house. Make sure the temporary supports run perpendicular to the ceiling joists, so they relieve the load on the wall studs while work is underway. Platform framing can be identified by the sole plate to which the wall studs are nailed.

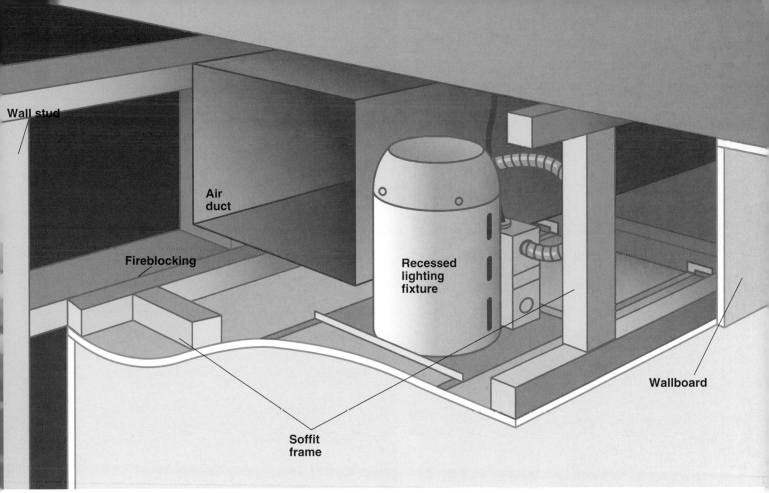

Wall stud

Air duct

Fireblocking

Recessed lighting fixture

Soffit frame

Wallboard

A soffit built from dimension lumber and covered with wallboard or other finish material can conceal ventilation ductwork (illustration, above) or finish the space above cabinets (illustration, below). An extra-wide soffit is also a great place to install recessed lighting fixtures.

Framing Soffits

Soffits are used to conceal ductwork and plumbing, to house light fixtures or to finish above-cabinet areas. Soffits also make large areas seem smaller and more intimate, a nice feature for eating areas. A soffit is usually constructed with 2 × 2 lumber, which is easy to work with and inexpensive. You can use 1 × 3s to keep the frame as small as possible and 2 × 4s for large soffits that will house other elements, such as lighting fixtures.

You may want to shape your soffits for a decorative effect. Just make sure the framing conforms to local Building Codes. There may be Code restrictions about the types of mechanicals that can be grouped together, as well as minimum clearances between the framing and what it encloses. And most Codes specify that soffits and other framed structures have fireblocking every 10 ft. and at the intersections between soffits and neighboring walls.

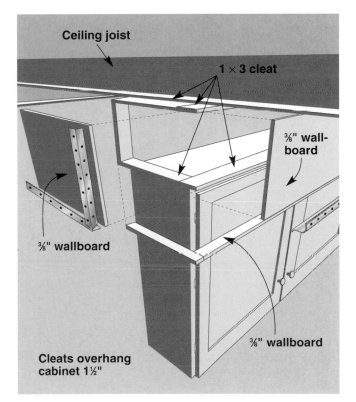

Ceiling joist

1 × 3 cleat

⅜" wallboard

⅜" wallboard

⅜" wallboard

Cleats overhang cabinet 1½"

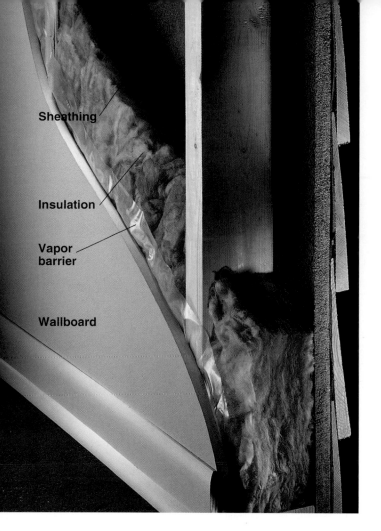

Sheathing

Insulation

Vapor barrier

Wallboard

Removing Wall Surfaces

You may have to remove and replace interior wall surfaces as part of your kitchen project. Most often, the material you'll be removing is wallboard, but if you live in an older home you may be removing plaster. Removing wall surfaces is a messy job, but it is not difficult. Before you begin, shut off the power and inspect the wall for wiring and plumbing.

Make sure you wear appropriate safety gear— glasses and dust masks—since you will be generating dust and small pieces of debris. Use plastic sheeting to close off doorways and air vents to prevent dust from spreading throughout the house. Protect floor surfaces with rosin paper securely taped down. Dust will find its way under drop cloths and quickly scratch your floor.

Tools and Materials

Tools: utility knife, pry bar, circular saw, straight-edge, reciprocating saw with bimetal blade, hammer.

Materials: masking tape, heavy tarp, rosin paper, protective eyewear, dust mask.

Removing Wallboard

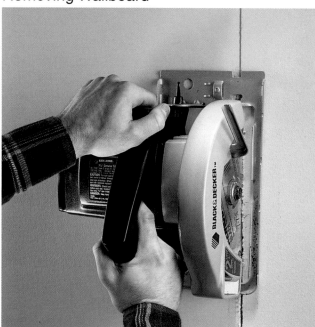

1 Remove baseboards and other trim, and prepare the work area. Make a ½"-deep cut from floor to ceiling, using a circular saw. Use a utility knife to finish the cuts at the top and bottom and to cut through the taped horizontal seam where the wall meets the ceiling surface.

2 Insert the end of a pry bar into the cut near one corner of the opening. Pull the pry bar until the wallboard breaks, then tear away the broken pieces. Take care to avoid damaging the wallboard outside the project area.

Removing Plaster

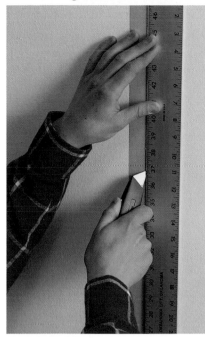

1 Remove baseboards and other trim and prepare the work area. Score the cutting line several times with a utility knife, using a straightedge as a guide. The line should be at least ⅛" deep.

2 Break the plaster along the edge by holding a scrap piece of 2 × 4 on edge just inside the scored line, and rapping it with a hammer. Use a pry bar to remove the remaining plaster.

3 Cut through the lath along the edges of the plaster, using a reciprocating saw or jig saw.

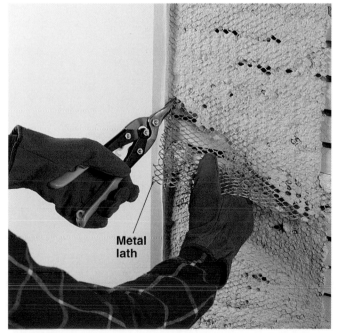

Metal lath

Variation: If the wall has metal lath laid over the wood lath, use aviation snips to clip the edges of the metal lath. Press the jagged edges of the lath flat against the stud. The cut edges of metal lath are very sharp; be sure to wear work gloves.

4 Remove the lath from the studs, using a pry bar. Pry away any remaining nails, and remove any vapor barrier and insulation.

A typical partition wall consists of top and bottom plates and 2 × 4 studs spaced 16" on center. Use 2 × 6 lumber for walls that will hold large plumbing pipes (inset).

Framing Partition Walls

Non-loadbearing, or partition, walls are typically built with 2 × 4 lumber and are supported by ceiling or floor joists or by blocking between the joists.

In remodeling projects it is generally much easier to build a wall in place, rather than to build a complete wall on the floor and tilt it upright, as in new construction. The build-in-place method allows for variations in floor and ceiling levels.

If the wall will include a door or other opening, see pages 242 to 245 before laying out the wall.

NOTE: After the walls are framed and the mechanical rough-ins are completed, be sure to install metal protector plates where pipes and wires run through framing members.

Tools and Materials

Tools: tape measure, hammer, combination square, chalk line, circular saw, framing square, plumb bob, T-bevel.

Materials: 2 × 4 lumber, blocking lumber, common nails (8d, 16d).

Variations for Fastening Top Plates to Joists

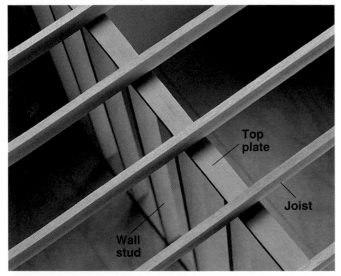

When a new wall is perpendicular to the ceiling or floor joists above, attach the top plate directly to the joists, using 16d nails.

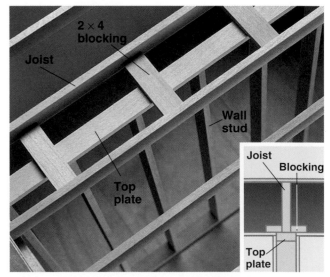

When a new wall falls between parallel joists, install 2 × 4 blocking between the joists every 24". The blocking supports the new wall's top plate and provides backing for the ceiling wallboard. If the new wall is aligned with a parallel joist, install blocks on both sides of the wall, and attach the top plate to the joist (inset).

Variations for Fastening Bottom Plates to Joists

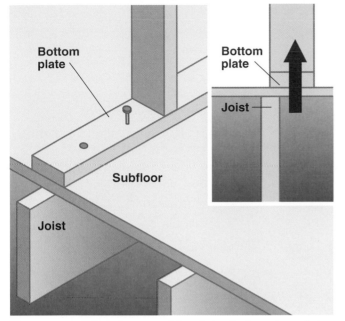

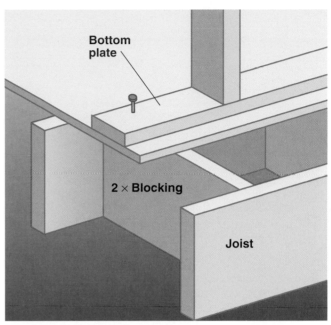

If a new wall is aligned with a joist below, install the bottom plate directly over the joist or off-center over the joist (inset). Off-center placement allows you to nail into the joist but provides room underneath the plate for pipes or wiring to go up into the wall.

If a new wall falls between parallel joists, install 2 × 6 or larger blocking between the two joists below, spaced 24" on center. Nail the bottom plate through the subfloor and into the blocking.

How to Frame a Partition Wall

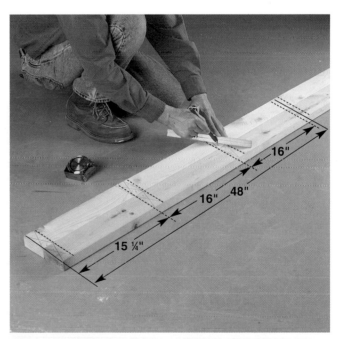

1 Mark the location of the leading edge of the new wall's top plate, then snap a chalk line through the marks across the joists or blocks. Use a framing square, or take measurements, to make sure the line is perpendicular to any intersecting walls. Cut the top and bottom plates to length.

2 Set the plates together with their ends flush. Measure from the end of one plate, and make marks for the location of each stud. The first stud should fall 15¼" from the end; every stud thereafter should fall 16" on center. Thus, the first 4 × 8-ft. wallboard panel will cover the first stud and "break" in the center of the fourth stud. Use a square to extend the marks across both plates. Draw an "X" at each stud location.

(continued next page)

3 Position the top plate against the joists, aligning its leading edge with the chalk line. Attach the plate with two 16d nails driven into each joist. Start at one end, and adjust the plate as you go to keep the leading edge flush with the chalk line.

4 To position the bottom plate, hang a plumb bob from the side edge of the top plate so the point nearly touches the floor. When it hangs motionless, mark the point's location on the floor. Make plumb markings at each end of the top plate, then snap a chalk line between the marks. Position the bottom plate along the chalk line, and use the plumb bob to align the stud markings between the two plates.

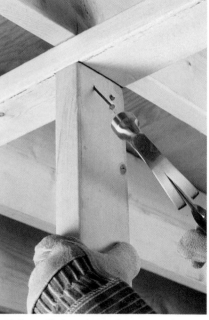

5 Fasten the bottom plate to the floor. On concrete, use a powder-actuated nailer or masonry screws, driving a pin or screw every 16". On wood floors, use 16d nails driven into the joists or sleepers below.

6 Measure between the plates for the length of each stud. Cut each stud so it fits snugly in place but is not so tight that it bows the joists above. If you cut a stud too short, see if it will fit somewhere else down the wall.

7 Install the studs by toenailing them at a 60° angle through the sides of the studs and into the plates. At each end, drive two 8d nails through one side of the stud and one more through the center on the other side.

How to Frame Corners (shown cut away)

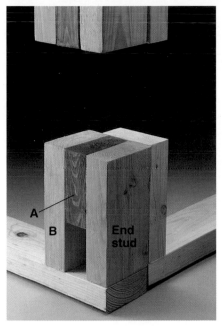

L-corners: Nail 2 × 4 spacers (A) to the inside of the end stud. Nail an extra stud (B) to the spacers. The extra stud provides a surface to attach wallboard at the inside corner.

T-corner meets stud: Fasten 2 × 2 backers (A) to each side of the side-wall stud (B). The backers provide an attaching surface for wallboard.

T-corner between studs: Fasten a 1 × 6 backer (A) to the end stud (B) with wallboard screws. The backer provides an attaching surface for wallboard.

The Steel Framing Alternative

Lumber is not the only material available for framing walls. Metal studs and tracks are also a choice for new construction and remodeling. Steel-framed walls can be installed faster than wood stud walls—the parts are attached by crimping and screwing the flanges—and the channels are precut to accommodate electrical and plumbing lines. Steel framing is also lighter in weight, easy to recycle, fireproof and comparable in price to lumber. If you are interested in using steel framing for a new wall in a kitchen remodel, consult a professional for information about electrical, plumbing and loadbearing safety precautions. Steel framing is available at most home centers.

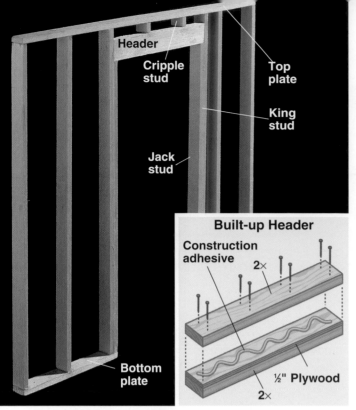

Framing Doors & Windows

Door frames for prehung doors start with king studs that attach to the top and bottom plates. Inside the king studs, jack studs support the header at the top of the opening. Cripple studs continue the wall-stud layout above the opening. In non-loadbearing walls, the header may be a 2 × 4 laid flat or a built-up header (inset). The dimensions of the framed opening are referred to as the rough opening.

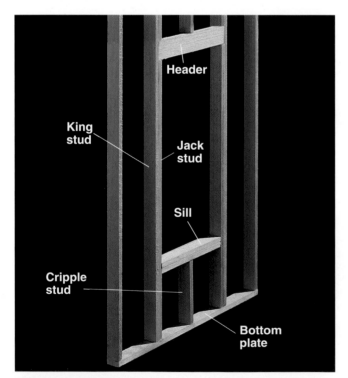

Window frames, like door frames, have full-length king studs, as well as jack studs that support the header. They also have a sill that defines the bottom of the rough opening.

In the following few pages you'll learn how to frame openings in walls. The projects presented are framing for an interior door, framing an exterior door and installing a patio door, but the same techniques are used for installing other types of exterior doors as well as windows. To lay out and build a door or window frame, you'll need the actual dimensions of the door or window unit you will be installing. Follow the manufacturer's specifications for rough opening size.

In new walls, build the door frames along with the rest of the wall. The project shown on pages 243 to 244 demonstrates framing a rough opening for an interior prehung door in a new, non-load-bearing partition wall.

Because exterior walls are loadbearing, exterior doors and window frames are required by Code to have built-up headers to carry the weight from above. The required size for the header is set by local Building Codes and varies according to the width of the rough opening.

When framing a rough opening in a finished wall, remove enough of the wall material so there is one additional stud bay on either side of the opening. (This provides you with space to work.) Also leave at least 6" of wall material at the ceiling to provide a surface for taping the joint between the new wall material and the existing surface.

All loadbearing walls must be supported until the header is in place. If you will be removing more than one wall stud when framing a rough opening in a non-loadbearing wall, make temporary supports to carry the structural load until the header is installed (see page 234).

Tools and Materials

Tools: tape measure, hammer, framing square, circular saw, handsaw, 4-ft. level, pry bar, nippers, plumb bob, combination square, reciprocating saw, staple gun, caulk gun.

Materials: door or window unit, 2× lumber, common nails (8d, 10d, 16d), ½"-thick plywood, construction adhesive, building paper, drip edge, silicone caulk.

How to Frame a Rough Opening for an Interior Prehung Door

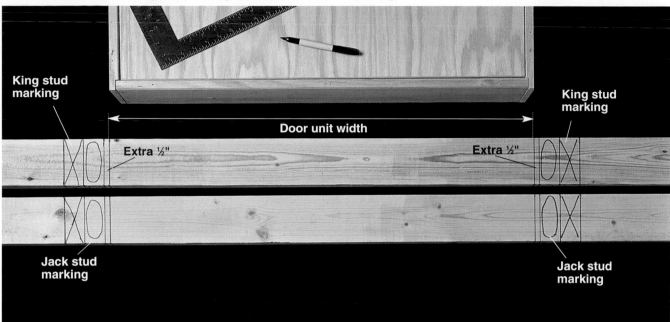

King stud marking

King stud marking

Door unit width

Extra ½"

Extra ½"

Jack stud marking

Jack stud marking

1 To mark the layout for the studs that make up the door frame, measure the width of the door unit along the bottom. Add 1" to this dimension to calculate the width of the rough opening (the distance between the jack studs). This gives you a ½" gap on each side for adjusting the door frame during installation. Mark the top and bottom plates for the jack and king studs.

2 After you've installed the top and bottom plates (pages 238 to 241), cut the king studs. Check for plumb, then toenail them in place at the appropriate markings, using 8d nails.

3 Measure the full length of the door unit, then add ½" to the height of the rough opening. Using that dimension, measure up from the floor and mark the king studs. Cut a 2 × 4 header to fit between the king studs. Position the header flat, with its bottom face at the marks, and secure it to the king studs with 16d nails.

4 Cut and install a cripple stud above the header, centered between the king studs. Install any additional cripples required to maintain the 16"-on-center layout of the standard studs in the rest of the wall.

(continued next page)

How to Frame a Rough Opening for an Interior Prehung Door (continued)

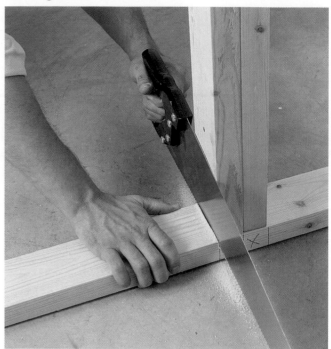

5 Cut the jack studs to fit snugly under the header. Fasten them in place by nailing down through the header, then drive 10d nails through the faces of the jack studs and into the king studs, spaced 16" apart.

6 Saw through the bottom plate so it's flush with the inside faces of the jack studs. Remove the cut-out portion of the plate. NOTE: If the wall will be finished with wallboard, hang the door after the wallboard is installed.

How to Frame a Window Opening

1 Prepare the project site, and remove the interior wall surfaces (pages 236 to 237). Measure and mark the rough opening width on the bottom plate, then mark the locations of the jack studs and king studs on the bottom plate. Where practical, use the existing studs as king studs.

2 Measure and cut king studs, as needed, to fit between the bottom plate and the top plate. Position the king studs and toenail them to the bottom plate with 10d nails. Check the king studs with a level to make sure they are plumb, then toenail them to the top plate with 10d nails.

3 Measuring from the floor, mark the rough opening height on one of the king studs. This line marks the bottom of the window header. For most windows, the recommended rough opening is ½" taller than the height of the window unit.

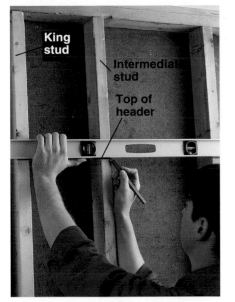

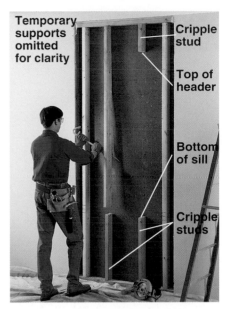

4 Measure and mark where the top of the window header will fit against the king stud. The header size depends on the distance between the king studs. Use a level to extend the lines across the intermediate studs to the opposite king stud.

5 Measure down from the bottom header line, and outline the rough double sill on the king stud. Use a level to extend the lines across the intermediate studs to the opposite king stud. Use a circular saw to cut through the intermediate studs along the lines that mark both the bottom of the rough sill and the top of the header. (Do not cut the king studs.)

6 On each stud, make a cut about 3" above the sill cut. Knock out the 3" pieces, then tear out the intermediate studs inside the rough opening, using a pry bar. Use nippers to clip away any exposed nails. Cut two jack studs to reach from the bottom plate to the bottom header lines on the king studs, then nail them to the king studs with 10d nails driven every 1".

7 Build a header to fit between the king studs on top of the jack studs, using two pieces of 2x lumber sandwiched around ½" plywood (page 242).

8 Position the header on the jack studs, using a hammer if necessary. Attach the header to the king studs, jack studs and cripple studs, using 10d nails.

9 Build the rough sill to reach between the jack studs by nailing together a pair of 2 × 4s. Position the rough sill on the cripple studs, and nail it to the jack studs and cripple studs with 10d nails. When you're ready to install the window, remove the exterior wall surface.

How to Frame an Exterior Door Opening (Platform Framing)

1 Measure and mark the rough opening width on the sole plate. Mark the locations of the jack studs and king studs on the sole plate. (Where practical, use existing studs as king studs.)

2 If new king studs are needed, cut them to fit between the sole plate and top plate. Position the king studs and toenail them to the sole plate with 10d nails. Check for plumb and toenail to top plate.

3 Measuring from the floor, mark the rough opening height on one king stud. For most doors, the recommended rough opening is ½" taller than the height of the door unit. This line marks the bottom of the door header.

4 Determine the size of the header needed and measure and mark where the top of it will fit against a king stud. Use a level to extend the lines across the intermediate studs to the opposite king stud. (The recommended header size for a 3-ft. to 5-ft. opening is ½" plywood sandwiched between two 2 × 6s.)

5 Cut two jack studs to reach from the top of the sole plate to the rough opening marks on the king studs. Nail the jack studs to the king studs with 10d nails driven every 12". Make temporary supports (page 234) if you are removing more than one stud.

6 Use a circular saw set to maximum blade depth to cut through the old studs that will be removed. The remaining stud sections will be used as cripple studs for the door frame. NOTE: Do not cut king studs. Make additional cuts 3" below the first cuts, then finish the cuts with a handsaw.

7 Knock out the 3" stud sections, then tear out the rest of the studs with a pry bar. Clip away any exposed nails, using nippers.

8 Build a header to fit between the king studs on top of the jack studs. Use two pieces of 2× lumber sandwiched around ½" plywood (page 242). Attach header to the jack studs, king studs and cripple studs, using 10d nails.

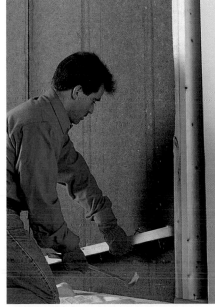

9 Use a reciprocating saw to cut through the sole plate next to each jack stud, then remove the sole plate with a pry bar. Cut off any exposed nails or anchors, using nippers.

10 From inside the home, drill through wall at corners of the framed opening. Push casing nails through the holes to mark their location. For round-top windows, drill holes around the curved outline.

11 Measure the distance between the nails on outside to make sure the dimensions are accurate. Mark cutting lines with a chalk line stretched between nails. Push nails back through the wall. Use a circular saw to cut through the wall suface.

How to Install a Patio Door

1 Prepare the work area and remove the interior wall surfaces (pages 236 to 237). Frame the rough opening for the patio door and remove the exterior surfaces inside the framed opening (pages 246 to 247). For metal or vinyl siding, remove the siding.

2 Test-fit the door unit, centering it in the rough opening. Check to make sure door is plumb. If necessary, shim under the lower side jamb until the door is plumb and level. Have a helper hold the door in place while you adjust it.

3 Trace the outline of the brick molding onto the siding, then remove the door unit.

4 Cut the siding along the outline, just down to the sheathing, using a circular saw. Stop just short of the corners to prevent damage to the remaining siding. Finish the cuts at the corners with a sharp wood chisel.

5 To provide an added moisture barrier, cut a piece of drip edge to fit the width of the rough opening, then slide it between the siding and the existing building paper at the top of the opening. Do not nail the drip edge.

6 Cut 8"-wide strips of building paper and slide them between siding and sheathing. Bend paper around framing members and staple it in place. Each piece overlaps the piece below it.

7 Apply several thick beads of silicone caulk to the subfloor at the bottom of the door opening.

8 Apply silicone caulk around the front edge of the framing members, where the siding meets the building paper.

9 Center the patio door unit in the rough opening so the brick molding is tight against the sheathing. Have a helper hold the door unit from outside until it is shimmed and nailed in place.

10 Check the door threshold to make sure it is level. If necessary, shim under the lower side jamb until the patio door unit is level.

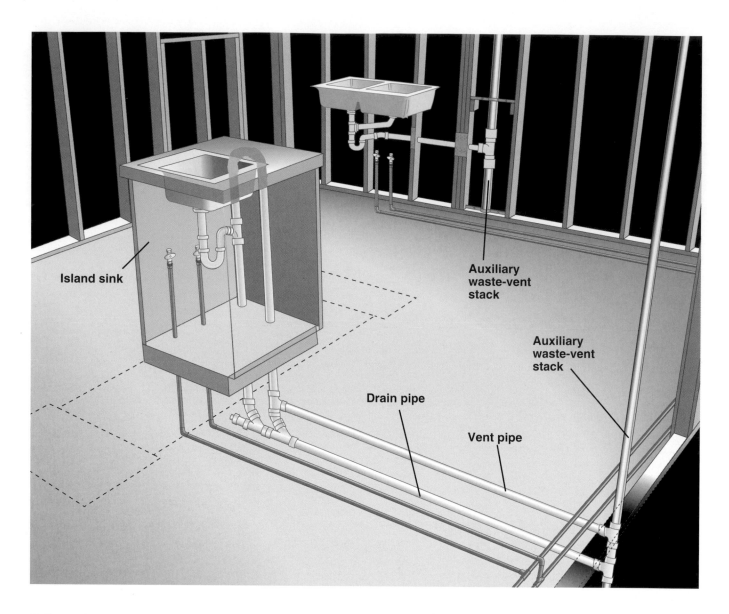

Island sink

**Auxiliary
waste-vent
stack**

**Auxiliary
waste-vent
stack**

Drain pipe

Vent pipe

Plumbing a Kitchen

Remodeling a kitchen often involves moving or adding sinks, which in turn involves adding new supply lines and drain-waste-vent (DWV) pipes. This is a relatively easy job if the sink is a wall sink. A common kitchen addition is the island sink, which is somewhat more complicated.

In most cases you will be able to extend or branch existing supply lines. Existing drain lines can often be used as well, but care must be taken to ensure that proper venting is present. Venting is necessary to allow air into the drain system which allows waste water to flow freely down drain pipes. The diagrams and chart on page 256 give guidelines regarding venting.

Also covered in this section is a brief overview of plumbing materials and the basic plumbing skills of sweating copper pipes and cementing PVC pipes. A section on plumbing guidelines gives general information on applying for a permit, venting requirements, and other plumbing areas. Step-by-step directions for installing DWV pipes and supply lines for a wall sink and simple island sink are also included.

This section does not include advanced information such as installing main vent stacks. For more detailed plumbing information, please refer to *The Complete Guide to Home Plumbing* or other plumbing reference book.

Plumbing Materials

Recognizing the different types of piping used in plumbing systems is important for trouble-shooting and crucial when purchasing supplies or making repairs. The materials used in home plumbing systems are closely regulated by Building Codes, so look for product standard Codes and check local plumbing regulations prior to making purchases.

Cast iron is commonly used for drain-waste-vent (DWV) purposes. Though it is the strongest piping, it's very heavy and somewhat difficult to join and install. Its thickness helps contain the noise inherent in drain systems.

Plastic piping is often used for water supply pipes where permitted by local Code. It's inexpensive, easy to handle, doesn't corrode or rust and has insulating properties. Plastic pipe is available in four types: acrylonitrile butadiene (ABS) and polyvinyl chloride (PVC) are used exclusively in DWV systems; chlorinated polyvinyl chloride (CPVC) is suitable for water supply lines; and polyethylene (PE) is used for outdoor water supply pipes.

Brass, and the more expensive but attractive chromed brass, are durable plumbing materials used for drains, valves and shutoffs.

Copper is considered the best choice for water supply lines and parts of some DWV systems. It resists scale deposits, maintains water flow and pressure, is lightweight and is easily installed. Copper is more expensive than plastic.

Fittings come in many sizes, but the basic shapes are standard to all metal and plastic pipes. In general, fittings used to connect DWV pipes have gradual bends for a smooth flow of waste water from drains. Because water in supply lines moves under pressure, the bends in water supply fittings can be sharper, conserving space.

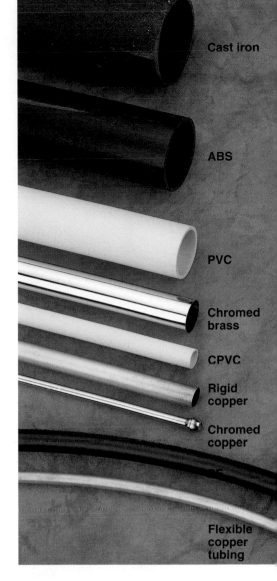

Cast iron

ABS

PVC

Chromed brass

CPVC

Rigid copper

Chromed copper

Flexible copper tubing

Standard Fittings

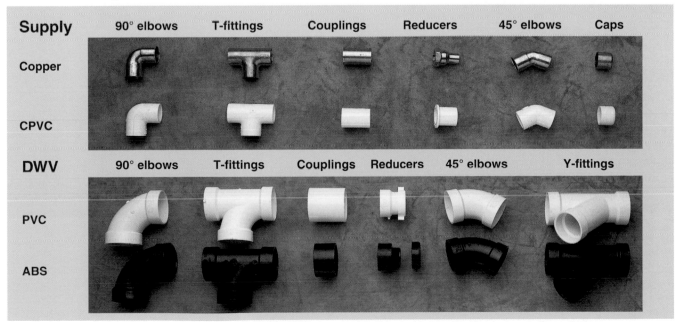

Supply	90° elbows	T-fittings	Couplings	Reducers	45° elbows	Caps
Copper						
CPVC						

DWV	90° elbows	T-fittings	Couplings	Reducers	45° elbows	Y-fittings
PVC						
ABS						

Cutting & Soldering Copper Pipe

Protect wood from the heat of the torch flame while soldering, using a double layer (two 18" × 18" pieces) of 26-gauge sheet metal available at hardware stores or home centers.

Tools and Materials

Tools: tubing cutter with reaming tip (or hacksaw and round file), wire brush, flux brush, propane torch, spark lighter.

Materials: copper pipe, copper fittings (or brass valve), emery cloth, soldering paste (flux), lead-free solder, dry rag.

The best way to cut rigid and flexible copper pipe is with a tubing cutter. A tubing cutter makes a smooth, straight cut—an important first step toward making a watertight joint. Remove any metal burrs on the cut edges with a reaming tool or round file.

Copper also can be cut with a hacksaw, which is useful in tight areas where a tubing cutter won't fit. Since it is more difficult to be accurate with a hacksaw, take care to make smooth, straight cuts.

To form a watertight seal, start with copper pipes and fittings that are clean and dry. Practice soldering scrap pipe before starting your project. Protect flammable surfaces with a double layer of 26-gauge sheet metal or a heat-absorbent pad (photo, left).

A soldered pipe joint, also called a sweated joint, is made by heating a copper or brass fitting with a propane torch until the fitting is just hot enough to melt metal solder. The heat draws the solder into the gap between the fitting and the pipe to form a watertight seal. A fitting that is overheated or unevenly heated will not draw in solder. The tip of the torch's inner flame produces the most heat.

How to Cut & Solder Copper Pipe

1 Place a tubing cutter over the pipe, then tighten the handle so the pipe rests on both rollers, and the cutting wheel is on the marked line. Turn the tubing cutter one rotation to score a continuous straight line around the pipe.

2 Rotate the tubing cutter in the opposite direction, tightening the handle slightly after every two rotations, until the cut is complete.

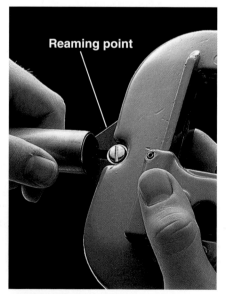

3 Remove sharp metal burrs from the inside edge of the cut pipe, using the reaming point on the tubing cutter or a round file.

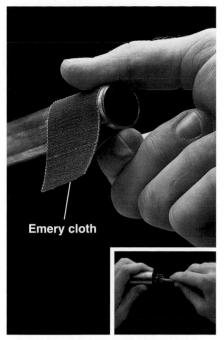

Emery cloth

4 Clean the end of each pipe by sanding it with emery cloth. The ends must be free of dirt and grease to ensure that the solder forms a good seal. Also clean inside each fitting with a wire brush or emery cloth (inset).

Flux brush

Plumbcraft® **soldering paste** NON CORROS. CAUTION: EYE IRRITA HARMFUL IF SWALL. READ PRECAUTION MEASURE ON BACK NET WT. 2. 71-00

5 Apply a thin layer of soldering paste (flux) to the end of each pipe, using a flux brush. Cover about 1" of the end of the pipe with the paste.

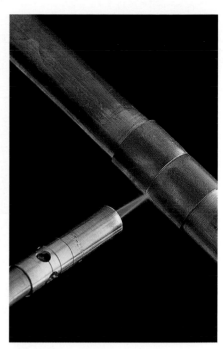

6 Hold the flame tip against the middle of the fitting for 4 to 5 seconds, until the soldering paste begins to sizzle.

7 Heat the other side of the copper fitting to ensure that the heat is distributed evenly. Touch the solder to the pipe. If the solder melts, the joint is ready to be soldered.

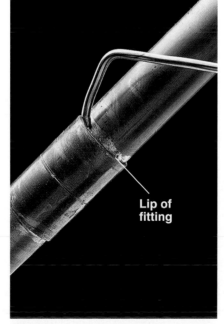

Lip of fitting

8 Remove the torch and quickly push ½" to ¾" of solder into each joint. Capillary action fills the joint with liquid solder. A correctly soldered joint shows a thin bead of solder around the lip of the fitting.

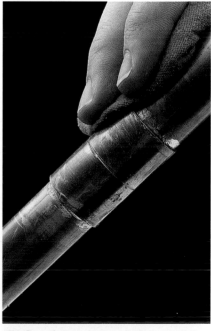

9 Carefully wipe away excess solder with a dry rag. (The pipes will be hot.) When all the joints have cooled, turn on the water and check for leaks. If a joint leaks, drain the pipes, disassemble and clean the pipe and fittings, then resolder the joint.

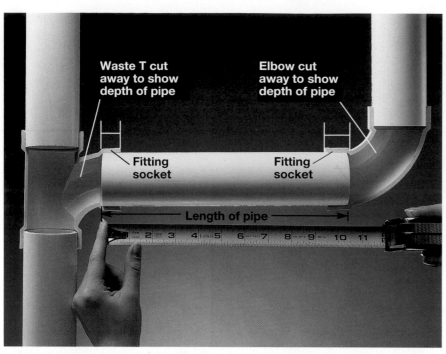

Fitting & Installing Plastic Pipe

Rigid ABS, PVC, or CPVC pipes can be cut with a tubing cutter or saw. Make sure all cuts are level and straight to ensure watertight joints.

CPVC pipes are joined using compression fittings. Rigid ABS and PVC plastics are joined using plastic fittings and primer and solvent glue specifically made for the pipe material being joined. All-purpose or universal solvents may be used on all types of rigid plastic pipe. Solvent glue hardens in about 30 seconds, so test-fit all plastic pipe and fittings before gluing the first joint. For best results, the pipe and fittings should be dulled with an emery cloth and liquid primer before being joined.

Liquid solvent glues and primers are toxic and flammable. Always provide adequate ventilation when fitting plastics, and store the products away from heat.

Find the length of plastic pipe needed by measuring between the bottoms of the fitting sockets (fittings shown here cut away). Mark the length on the pipe with a felt-tipped pen.

Tools and Materials

Tools: tubing cutter (or saw), felt-tipped pen, utility knife, jig saw or hole saw, drill, hammer.

Materials: plastic pipe and fittings, emery cloth, petroleum jelly, plastic-pipe primer, solvent glue, rag, masking tape, 1 × 4 lumber, pipe straps, metal protecter plates.

Cutting Rigid Plastic Pipe

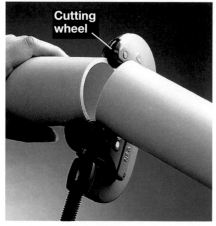

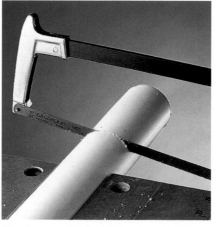

Tubing cutter: Tighten the tool around the pipe so the cutting wheel is on the marked line. Rotate the tool around the pipe, tightening the screw every two rotations, until the pipe snaps.

Hacksaw: Clamp the plastic pipe in a gripping bench or a vise. Keep the hacksaw blade straight while sawing. **Tip:** To draw a straight cutting line, wrap a sheet of paper around the circumference of the pipe and trace along the edge.

Miter saw: Make straight cuts on all types of plastic pipe with a power miter saw or hand miter box. With a hand miter box, use a hacksaw rather than a backsaw.

How to Fit Rigid Plastic Pipe with Solvent Glue

1 Measure and cut the pipe to length. Remove rough burrs on the cut ends, using a utility knife.

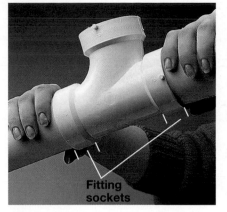

2 Test-fit all pipes and fittings. The pipes should fit tightly against the bottom of the fitting sockets.

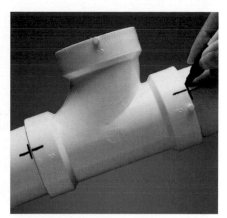

3 Make alignment and depth marks across each pipe joint, using a felt-tipped pen. Disassemble the pipes.

4 Clean the ends of the pipes and the fitting sockets, using an emery cloth.

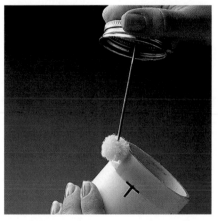

5 Apply plastic-pipe primer to one end of a pipe.

6 Apply plastic-pipe primer inside the fitting socket.

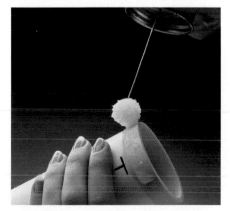

7 Apply a thick coat of solvent glue to the end of the pipe, and a thin coat to the inside surface of the fitting socket. Work quickly—solvent glue hardens in about 30 seconds.

8 Quickly position the pipe and fitting so the alignment marks are offset by about 2" and the end of the pipe fits flush against the bottom of the socket.

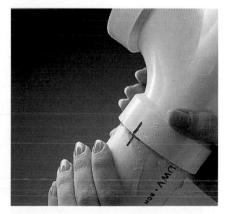

9 Twist the pipe until the marks are aligned. Hold the pipe in place for about 20 seconds, then wipe away any excess glue with a rag. Let the joint dry undisturbed for 30 minutes.

Wet Venting

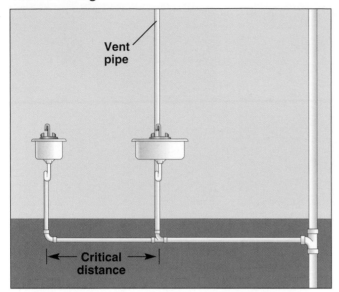

Vent pipe

Critical distance

Wet vents are pipes that serve as a vent for one fixture and a drain for another. The sizing of a wet vent is based on the total fixture units it supports: a 3" wet vent can serve up to 12 fixture units; a 2" wet vent is rated for 4 fixture units; a 1½" wet vent, for only 1 fixture unit. NOTE: The distance between the wet-vented fixture and the wet vent itself must be no more than the maximum critical distance.

Auxiliary Venting

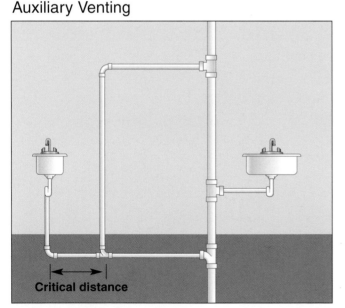

Critical distance

Fixtures must have auxiliary vents if the distance to the main waste-vent stack exceeds the critical distance. A bar sink, for example, should have a separate vent pipe if it is located more than 3½ ft. from the main waste-vent stack. This secondary vent pipe should connect to the stack or an existing vent pipe at a point at least 6" above the highest fixture on the system.

Plumbing Guidelines

In most communities, moving or adding a sink requires a permit from the local building department. When you apply for a permit, the building department will want a site plan, a water supply diagram and a DWV diagram to ensure your plans meet local plumbing Codes. If your project meets Code requirements, you will be issued a plumbing permit, which is your legal permission to begin work. As your project nears completion, the inspector will visit your home to check your work.

Local plumbing Codes are based on the National Uniform Plumbing Code. Handbooks that present the Code using diagrams and photographs are available at bookstores and libraries. Your local building inspector can be a valuable source of information and may provide you with a summary sheet of the regulations that apply to your project.

Vent Pipe Sizes, Critical Distances

Size of fixture drain	Minimum vent pipe size	Maximum trap-to-vent distance
1½"	1¼"	3½ ft.
2"	1½"	5 ft.
3"	2"	6 ft.
4"	3"	10 ft.

Vent pipes are usually one pipe size smaller than the drain pipes they serve. Code requires that the distance between the drain trap and the vent pipe fall within a maximum "critical distance," a measurement that is determined by the size of the fixture drain. Use this chart to determine both the minimum size for the vent pipe and the maximum critical distance.

Maximum Hole & Notch Sizes

Framing member	Maximum hole size	Maximum notch size
2 × 4 loadbearing stud	1 7/16" diameter	7/8" deep
2 × 4 non-loadbearing stud	2 1/2" diameter	1 7/16" deep
2 × 6 loadbearing stud	2 1/4" diameter	1 3/8" deep
2 × 6 non-loadbearing stud	3 5/16" diameter	2 3/16" deep
2 × 6 joists	1 1/2" diameter	7/8" deep
2 × 8 joists	2 3/8" diameter	1 1/4" deep
2 × 10 joists	3 1/16" diameter	1 1/2" deep
2 × 12 joists	3 3/4" diameter	1 7/8" deep

The maximum hole and notch sizes that can be cut into framing members for running pipes is shown above. Where possible, use notches rather than bored holes to ease pipe installation. When boring holes, there must be at least 5/8" of wood between the edge of a stud and the hole, and at least 2" between the edge of a joist and the hole. Joists can be notched only in the end one-third of the overall span; never in the middle one-third of the joist. When two pipes are run through a stud, the pipes should be stacked one over the other, never side by side.

Pipe Support Intervals

Type of pipe	Vertical support interval	Horizontal support interval
Copper	6 ft.	10 ft.
ABS	4 ft.	4 ft.
CPVC	3 ft.	3 ft.
PVC	4 ft.	4 ft.
Cast Iron	5 ft.	15 ft.

Minimum intervals for supporting pipes are determined by the type of pipe and its orientation in the system. Use only brackets and supports made of the same (or compatible) materials as the pipes. Remember that the measurements shown above are minimum requirements; many plumbers install pipe supports at closer intervals.

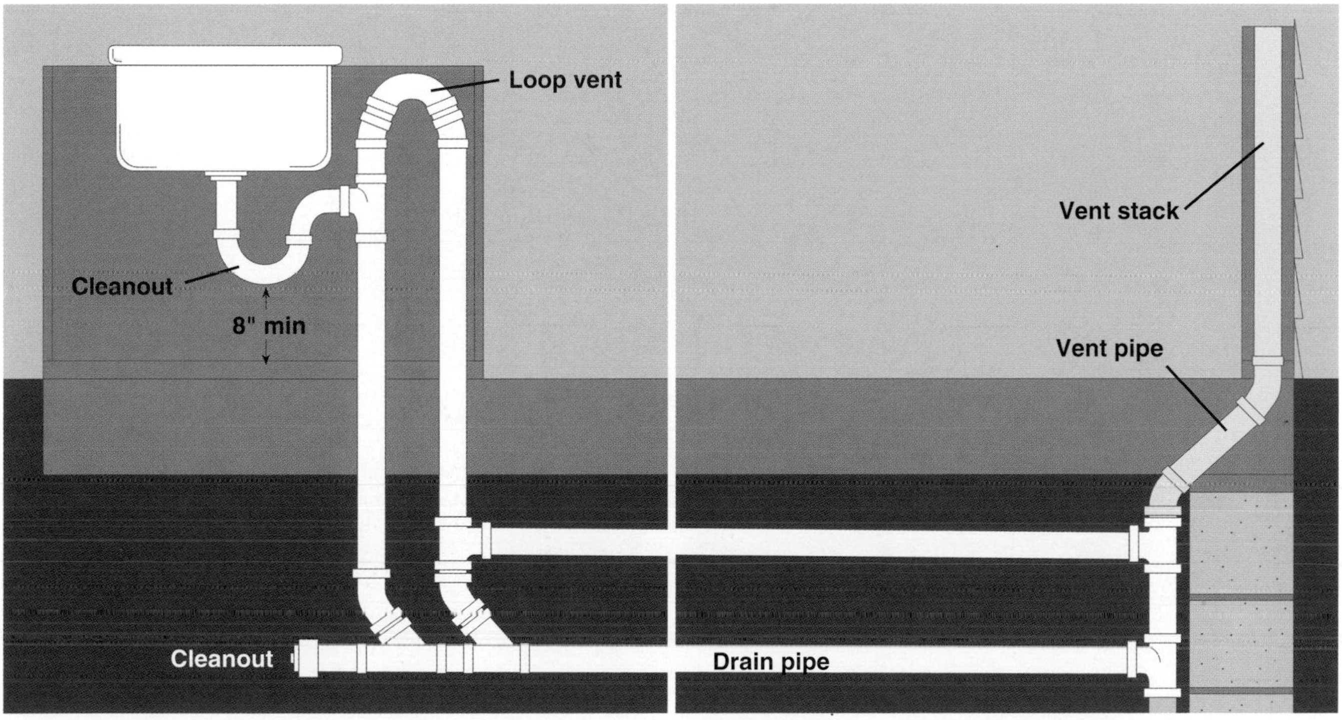

A loop vent makes it possible to vent a sink when there is no adjacent wall to house the vent pipe. The drain is vented with a loop of pipe that arches up against the countertop and away from the drain before dropping through the floor. The vent pipe then runs horizontally to an existing vent pipe. In our project, we have tied the island vent to a vent pipe extending up from a basement utility sink. NOTE: Loop vents are subject to local Code restrictions. Always consult your building inspector for guidelines on venting an island sink.

Installing DWV & Supply Pipes

The following projects show how to install a new wall sink using an existing DWV pipe, how to install a new island sink, and how to install new supply pipes.

The wall sink project is relatively easy because existing DWV pipes are used, but an island sink poses problems because there is no adjacent wall in which to run a vent pipe. For an island sink, you need to use a special plumbing configuration known as a loop vent. A diagram on page 257 shows the components of the island sink with loop vent project.

Tools and Materials

Tools: carpenter's level, right-angle drill, hole saw, reciprocating saw, hacksaw, tubing cutter, utility knife, propane torch.

Materials: riser clamps, 2 × 4 lumber, banded couplings, PVC pipe and fittings, solvent glue, copper pipe and fittings, flux, solder.

How to Install DWV Pipes for a Wall Sink

1 Determine the location of the sink drain by marking the position of the sink and base cabinet on the floor. Mark a point on the floor indicating the position of the sink drain opening. This point will serve as a reference for aligning the sink drain stub-out.

2 Mark a route for the new drain pipe through the studs behind the wall sink cabinet. The drain pipe should angle ¼" per foot down toward the waste-vent stack.

3 Use a right-angle drill and hole saw to bore holes for the drain pipe. On non-loadbearing studs, such as the cripple studs beneath a window, you can notch the studs with a reciprocating saw to simplify the installation of the drain pipe. If the studs are load-bearing, however, you must thread the run though bored holes, using couplings to join short lengths of pipe as you create the run.

258

4 Measure, cut and dry-fit a horizontal drain pipe to run from the waste-vent stack to the sink drain stub-out. Create the stub-out with a 45° elbow and 6" length of 1½" pipe. NOTE: If the sink trap in your instal-lation will be more than 3½ ft. from the waste-vent pipe, you will need to install a waste T and run a vent pipe up the wall, connecting it to the vent stack at a point at least 6" above the lip of the sink.

5 Remove the neoprene sleeve from a banded cou-pling, then roll the lip back and measure the thick-ness of the separator ring.

6 Attach two lengths of 2" pipe, at least 4" long, to the top and bottom openings on a 2" × 2" × 1½" waste T. Hold the fitting alongside the waste-vent stack, then mark the stack for cutting, allowing space for the separator rings on the banded couplings.

(continued next page)

7 Use riser clamps and 2 × 4 blocking to support the waste-vent stack above and below the new drain pipe, then cut out the waste-vent stack along the marked lines, using a reciprocating saw and metal-cutting blade.

8 Slide banded couplings onto the cut ends of the waste-vent stack, and roll back the lips of the neoprene sleeves. Position the waste T assembly, then roll the sleeves into place over the plastic pipes.

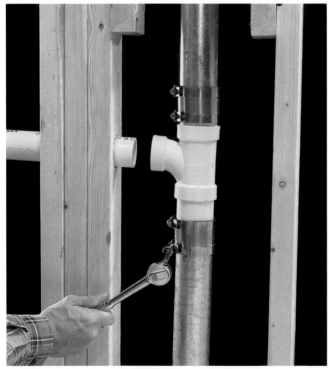

9 Slide the metal bands into place over the neoprene sleeves, and tighten the clamps with a ratchet wrench or screwdriver.

10 Solvent-glue the drain pipe, beginning at the waste-vent stack. Use a 90° elbow and a short length of pipe to create a drain stub-out extending about 4" out from the wall.

How to Install DWV Pipes for an Island Sink

1 Position the base cabinet for the island sink, according to your kitchen plans. Mark the cabinet position on the floor with tape, then move the cabinet out of the way.

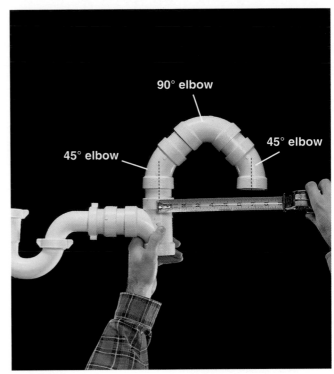

90° elbow

45° elbow

45° elbow

2 Create the beginning of the drain and loop vent by test-fitting a drain trap, waste T, two 45° elbows and a 90° elbow, linking them with 2" lengths of pipe. Measure the width of the loop between the centerpoints of the fittings.

3 Draw a reference line perpendicular to the wall to use as a guide when positioning the drain pipes. A cardboard template of the sink can help you position the loop vent inside the outline of the cabinet.

4 Position the loop assembly on the floor, and use it as a guide for marking hole locations. Make sure to position the vent loop so the holes are not over joists.

(continued next page)

How to Install DWV Pipes for an Island Sink (continued)

5 Use a hole saw with a diameter slightly larger than the vent pipes to bore holes in the subfloor at the marked locations. Note the positions of the holes by carefully measuring from the edges of the taped cabinet outline; these measurements will make it easier to position matching holes in the floor of the base cabinet.

6 Reposition the base cabinet, and mark the floor of the cabinet where the drain and vent pipes will run. (Make sure to allow for the thickness of the cabinet sides when measuring.) Use the hole saw to bore holes in the floor of the cabinet, directly above the holes in the subfloor.

7 Measure, cut and assemble the drain and loop vent assembly. Tape the top of the loop in place against a brace laid across the top of the cabinet, then extend the drain and vent pipes through the holes in the floor of the cabinet. The waste T should be about 18" above the floor, and the drain and vent pipes should extend about 2 ft. through the floor.

8 In the basement, establish a route from the island vent pipe to an existing vent pipe. (In our project, we are using the auxiliary waste-vent stack near a utility sink.) Hold a long length of pipe between the pipes, and mark for T-fittings. Cut off the plastic vent pipe at the mark, then dry-fit a waste T-fitting to the end of the pipe.

9 Hold a waste T against the vent stack, and mark the horizontal vent pipe at the correct length. Fit the horizontal pipe into the waste T, then tape the assembly in place against the vent stack. The vent pipe should angle ¼" per foot down toward the drain.

10 Fit a 3" length of pipe in the bottom opening on the T-fitting attached to the vent pipe, then mark both the vent pipe and the drain pipe for 45° elbows. Cut off the drain and vent pipes at the marks, then dry-fit the elbows onto the pipes.

11 Extend both the vent pipe and drain pipe by dry-fitting 3" lengths of pipe and Y-fittings to the elbows. Using a carpenter's level, make sure the horizontal drain pipe will slope toward the waste-vent at a pitch of ¼" per ft. Measure and cut a short length of pipe to fit between the Y-fittings.

(continued next page)

12 Cut a horizontal drain pipe to reach from the vent Y-fitting to the auxiliary waste-vent stack. Attach a waste T to the end of the drain pipe, then position it against the drain stack, maintaining a downward slope of ¼" per ft. Mark the auxiliary stack for cutting above and below the fittings.

13 Cut out the auxiliary stack at the marks. Use the T-fittings and short lengths of pipe to assemble an insert piece to fit between the cutoff ends of the auxiliary stack. The insert assembly should be about ½" shorter than the removed section of stack.

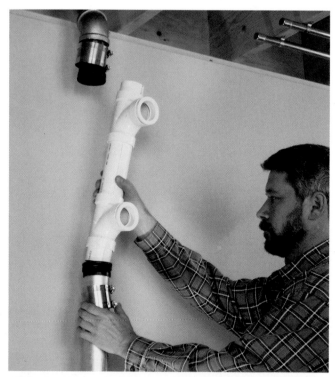

14 Slide banded couplings onto the cut ends of the auxiliary stack, then insert the plastic pipe assembly and loosely tighten the clamps.

15 At the open inlet on the drain pipe Y-fitting, insert a cleanout fitting.

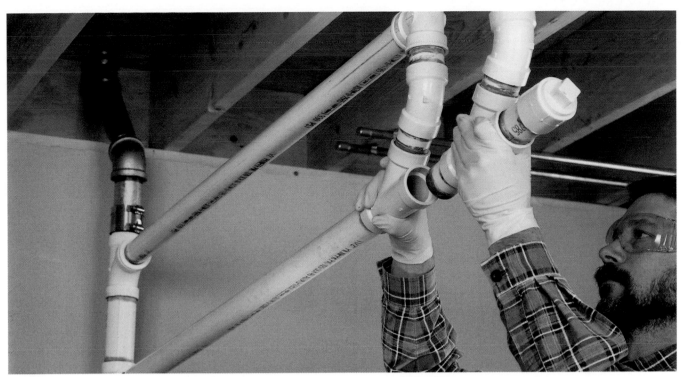

16 Solvent-glue all pipes and fittings found in the basement, beginning with the assembly inserted into the existing waste-vent stack, but do not glue the vertical drain and vent pipes running up into the cabinet. Tighten the banded couplings at the auxiliary stack. Support the horizontal pipes every 4 ft. with strapping nailed to the joists, then detach the vertical pipes extending up into the island cabinet. The final connection for the drain and vent loop will be completed as other phases of the kitchen remodeling project are finished.

17 After installing flooring and attaching cleats for the island base cabinet, cut away the flooring covering the holes for the drain and vent pipes.

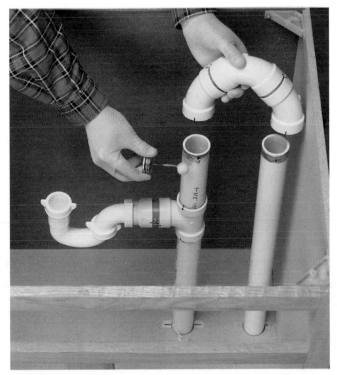

18 Install the base cabinet, then insert the drain and vent pipes through the holes in the cabinet floor and solvent-glue the pieces together.

1 Drill two 1"-diameter holes, spaced about 6" apart, through the floor of the island base cabinet and the underlying subfloor. Position the holes so they are not over floor joists. Drill similar holes in the floor of the base cabinet for the wall sink.

2 Turn off the water at the main shutoff, and drain the pipes. Cut out any old water supply pipes that obstruct new pipe runs, using a tubing cutter or hacksaw. In our project, we are removing the old pipe back to a point where it is convenient to begin the new branch lines.

3 Dry-fit T-fittings on each supply pipe (we used ¾" × ½" × ½" reducing T-fittings). Use elbows and lengths of copper pipe to begin the new branch lines running to the island sink and the wall sink. The parallel pipes should be routed so they are between 3" and 6" apart.

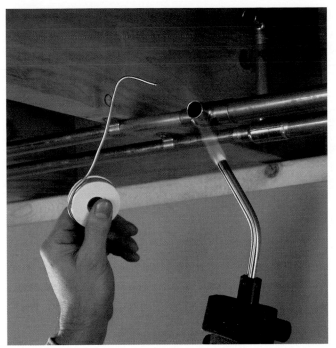

4 Solder the pipes and fittings together, beginning at the T-fittings. Support the horizontal pipe runs every 6 ft. with strapping attached to joists.

5 Extend the branch lines to points directly below the holes leading up into the base cabinets. Use elbows and lengths of pipe to form vertical risers extending at least 12" into the base cabinets. Use a small level to position the risers so they are plumb, then mark the pipe for cutting.

6 Fit the horizontal pipes and risers together, and solder them in place. Install blocking between joists, and anchor the risers to the blocking with pipe straps.

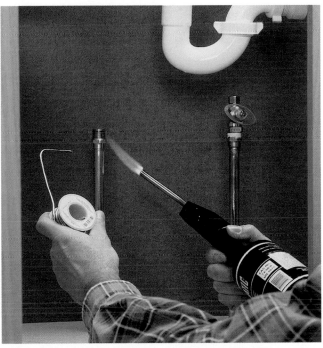

7 Solder male threaded adapters to the tops of the risers, then screw threaded shutoff valves onto the fittings.

6/3 cable

6/3 cable

6/3 cable

6/3 cable

6/3 cable

Learn How to Install These Circuits

■ **#1 & #2: Small-appliance circuits.** Two 20-amp, 120-volt circuits supply power to countertop and eating areas for small appliances. All general-use receptacles must be on these circuits. One 12/3 cable, fed by a 20-amp double-pole breaker, wires both circuits. These circuits share one electrical box with the disposer circuit (#5), and another with the basic lighting circuit (#7).

■ **#3: Range circuit.** A 50-amp, 120/240-volt dedicated circuit supplies power to the range/oven appliance. It is wired with 6/3 cable.

■ **#4: Microwave circuit.** A dedicated 20-amp, 120-volt circuit supplies power to the microwave. It is wired with 12/2 cable. Microwaves that use less than 300 watts can be installed on a 15-amp circuit, or plugged into the small-appliance circuits.

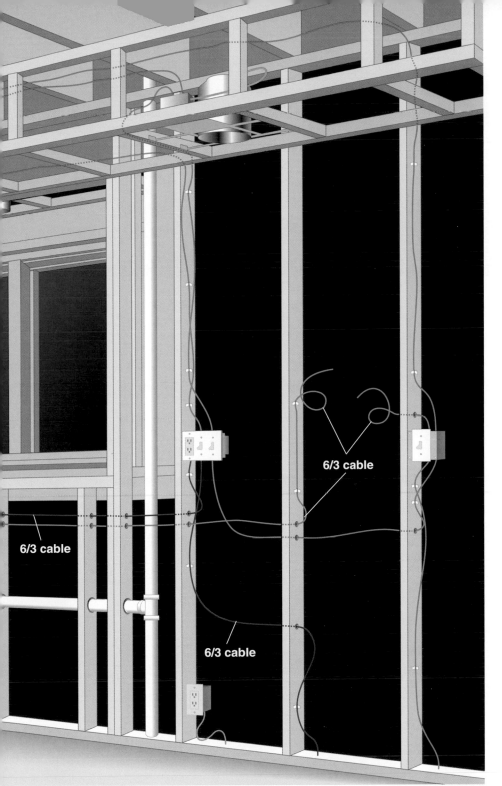

6/3 cable

6/3 cable

6/3 cable

Wiring a Remodeled Kitchen

This section gives information on complete wiring installation in a major kitchen remodeling project. It includes seven all-new circuits. Four of these are dedicated circuits: a 50-amp circuit supplying the range, a 20-amp circuit powering the microwave, and two 15-amp circuits supplying the dishwasher and food disposer. In addition, two 20-amp circuits for small appliances supply power to all receptacles above the countertops and in the eating area. Finally, a 15-amp basic lighting circuit controls the ceiling fixture, all of the recessed fixtures and the under-cabinet task lights.

All rough construction and plumbing work should be finished and inspected before beginning the electrical work. Divide the project into steps and complete each step before beginning the next.

The wiring information on the following pages concerns a kitchen project. If you are not familiar with basic wiring methods, see *The Complete Guide to Home Wiring.*

This section contains information on planning circuits, installing electrical boxes and cables, and making final connections.

■ **#5: Food disposer circuit.** A dedicated 15-amp, 120-volt circuit supplies power to the disposer. It is wired with 14/2 cable. Some local Codes allow the disposer to be on the same circuit as the dishwasher.

■ **#6: Dishwasher circuit.** A dedicated 15-amp, 120-volt circuit supplies power to the dishwasher. It is wired with 14/2 cable. Some local Codes allow the dishwasher to be on the same circuit as the disposer.

■ **#7: Basic lighting circuit.** A dedicated 15-amp, 120-volt circuit powers the ceiling fixture, recessed fixtures, and under-cabinet task lights. 14/2 and 14/3 cables connect the fixtures and switches in the circuit. Each task light has a self-contained switch.

Code requires receptacles above countertops to be no more than 4 ft. apart. Put receptacles closer together in areas where many appliances will be used. Any section of countertop that is wider than 12" must have a receptacle located above it. (Countertop spaces separated by items such as range tops, sinks and refrigerators are considered separate sections.) Every accessible receptacle in kitchens (and bathrooms) must be a GFCI. On walls without countertops, receptacles should be no more than 12 ft. apart.

Planning the Circuits

A kitchen generally uses more power than other rooms because it contains many light fixtures and appliances. Where you locate these items depends upon your needs. Make sure the main work areas of your kitchen have plenty of light and enough receptacles. Try to anticipate future needs: for example, install a range receptacle when remodeling, even if you currently have a gas range. It is difficult and expensive to make changes later.

Contact your local Building and Electrical Code offices before you begin planning. They may have requirements that differ from the National Electrical Code. Remember that the Code contains minimum requirements primarily concerning safety, not convenience or need. Work with the inspectors to create a safe plan that also meets your needs.

To help locate receptacles, plan carefully where cabinets and appliances will be in the finished project. Appliances installed within cabinets, such as microwaves or food disposers, must have their receptacles positioned according to manufacturer's instructions. Put at least one receptacle at table height in the dining areas for convenience in operating a small appliance.

The ceiling fixture should be centered in the kitchen ceiling. Or, if your kitchen contains a dining area or breakfast nook, you may want to center the light fixture over the table. Locate recessed light fixtures and under-cabinet task lights where they will best illuminate main work areas.

Before drawing diagrams and applying for a permit, evaluate your existing service and make sure it provides enough power to supply the new circuits you are planning to add. If you find that it will not, contact a licensed electrician to upgrade your service before beginning your work.

Bring the wiring plan and materials list to the inspector's office when applying for the permit. If the inspector suggests improvements to your plan, such as using switches with grounding screws, follow his advice. He can save you time and money.

A switch with a grounding screw is required when metal coverplates are used with plastic boxes.

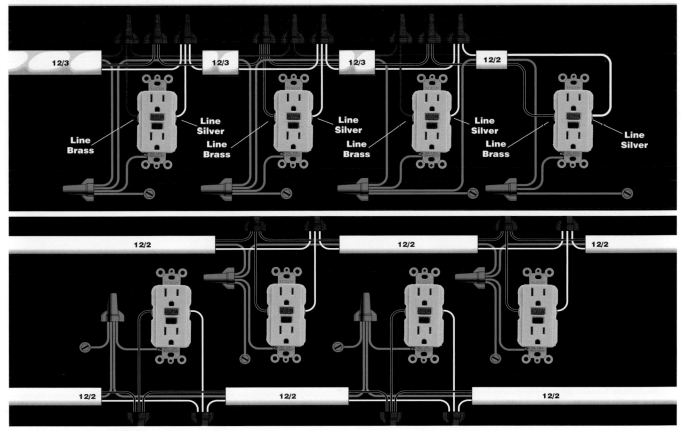

Two 20-amp small-appliance circuits can be wired with one 12/3 cable supplying power to both circuits (top), rather than using separate 12/2 cables for each circuit (bottom), to save time and money. Because these circuits must be GFCI protected, either place a GFCI receptacle first in each circuit (the remaining 20-amp duplex units are connected through the LOAD terminals on the GFCI) or use a GFCI receptacle at each location. In 12/3 cable, the black wire supplies power to one circuit for alternate receptacles (the first, third, etc.), the red wire supplies power for the second circuit to the remaining recep-tacles. The white wire is the neutral for both circuits. For safety, it must be attached with a pig-tail to each receptacle, instead of being connected directly to the terminal. These circuits must contain all general-use receptacles in the kitchen, pantry, break-fast area or dining room. No lighting outlets or recepta-cles from any other rooms can be connected to them.

Work areas at sink and range should be well lighted for convenience and safety. Install switch-controlled lights over these areas.

Ranges require a dedicated 40- or 50-amp 120/240-volt circuit (or two circuits for separate oven and coun-tertop units). Even if you do not have an electric range, it is a good idea to install the circuit when remodeling.

Dishwashers and food disposers require dedicated 15-amp, 120-volt circuits in most local Codes. Some inspectors will allow these appliances to share one circuit.

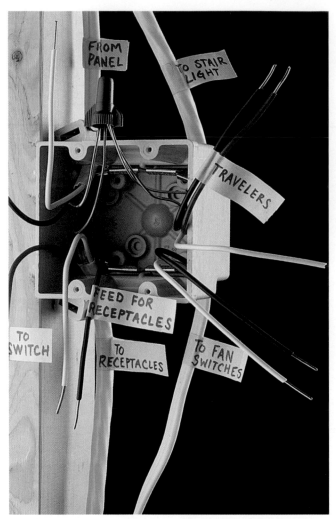

Label the cables entering each box to indicate their destinations. In boxes with complex wiring configurations, also tag the individual wires to simplify the final hookups. After all cables are installed, your rough-in work is ready to be reviewed by an electrical inspector.

Installing Electrical Boxes & Cables

Install electrical boxes for all devices only after your wiring plan has been approved by an inspector. Use your plan as a guide and follow electrical Code guidelines when laying out box positions. Some electrical fixtures, like recessed lights and exhaust fans, have their own wire connection boxes; install these along with the other electrical boxes.

After your boxes are installed, run all of the non-metallic (NM) cables. Start each new circuit near the service panel or subpanel, and run them to the first boxes in the circuit. Also run any branch cables between boxes on the same circuit. Schedule a rough-in inspection after the cables are run. When the rough-in wiring has been approved, you can close up the walls and install the electrical devices. Finally, make cable connections at the service panel or subpanel yourself, or hire an electrician to complete the task.

Tools and Materials

Tools: screwdrivers, drill, ⅝" and 1" bits, bit extender, needlenose pliers, fish tape, cable ripper, combination tool.

Materials: electrical boxes, NM cable, cable clamps and staples, cable lubricant, masking and electrical tape, grounding pigtails, wire connectors.

Tips for Installing Electrical Boxes

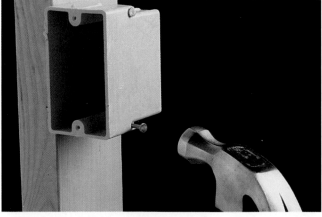

Position each box against a stud so the front face will be flush with the finished wall. For example, if you will be installing ½" drywall, position the box so it extends ½" past the front edge of the stud. Anchor the box by driving the mounting nails into the stud.

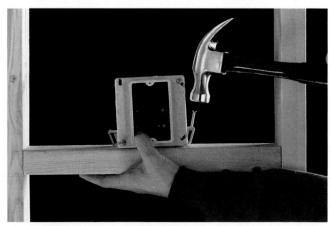

To install a switch box between studs, first install a cross block between the studs, with the top edge 46" above the floor. Position the box on the cross block so the front face will be flush with the finished wall, and drive the mounting nails into the cross block.

How to Install the Feeder Cable

1 Drill access holes through the sill plate where the feeder cables will enter from the circuit breaker panel. Choose spots that offer easy access to the circuit breaker panel as well as to the first electrical box on the circuit.

2 Drill ⅝" holes through framing members to allow cables to pass from the circuit breaker panel to access holes. Front edge of hole should be at least 1¼" from front edge of framing member.

3 For each circuit, measure and cut enough cable to run from circuit breaker panel, through access hole into the kitchen, to the first electrical box in the circuit. Add at least 2 ft. for the panel and 1 ft. for the box.

4 Anchor the cable with a cable staple within 12" of the panel. Extend cable through and along joists to access hole into kitchen, stapling every 4 ft. where necessary. Keep cable at least 1¼" from front edge of framing members. Thread cable through access hole into kitchen, and on to the first box in the circuit. Continue circuit to rest of boxes.

How to Install NM Cable in New Framing

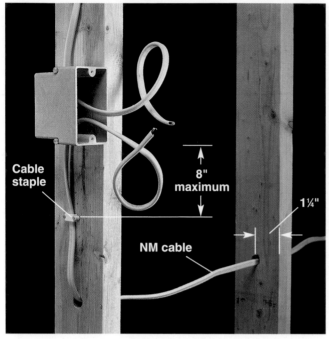

1 Anchor NM sheathed cable to framing members with cable staples driven no more than 4 ft. apart, and within 8" of electrical boxes. Run cable through the framing members by drilling ⅝" holes, set back at least 1¼" from the front of the framing members.

2 Open one knockout for each cable that will enter the box. You can open the knockouts as you install the boxes or wait until you run cable to each box. Open a knockout by striking inside the scored lines of the knockout with a screwdriver and hammer. Then, use the screwdriver to break off any sharp edges that might damage the vinyl sheathing of the cable.

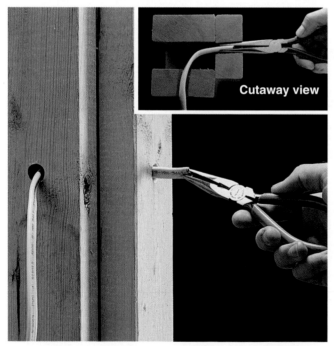

At corners, drill intersecting holes in adjoining faces of studs. Form a slight L-shaped bend in the end of the cable at corners and insert it into one hole. Retrieve the cable through the other hole, using needlenose pliers (inset).

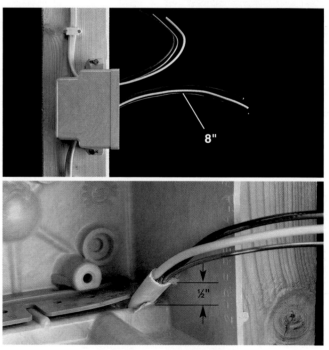

3 Extend wire at least 8" beyond the front face of electrical boxes (top photo). Cables should have at least ½" of outer sheathing extending intact into the box (bottom photo). The sheathing protects the cable wires from possible damage caused by the clamp.

274

How to Install NM Cable in Finished Walls

1 Position a retrofit electrical box at the box location, then outline it with a pencil. Drill a pilot hole at one corner of the outline, then complete the cutout with a drywall saw or jig saw.

2 Plan a route for running cable between electrical boxes. Where cable must cross framing members, cut an access opening in the wall or ceiling surface, then cut a notch into the framing member with a wood chisel.

3 Insert a fish tape (a semi-rigid wire used to pull cables) through the access hole (top photo), and extend it until it pokes out of the cutout for the new electrical box (bottom photo).

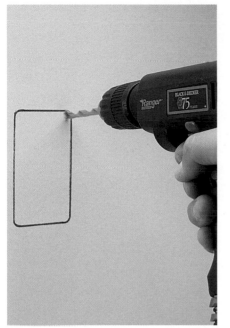

Variation: If there is access to ceiling joists above the cutout area, drill a 1" hole down through the top plate and into the wall cavity, using a spade bit. Extend a fish tape through the hole and to the nearest wall cutout.

4 Trim back 2" of outer insulation from the end of the NM cable, then insert the wires through the loop at the tip of the fish tape.

5 Bend the wires against the cable, then use electrical tape to bind them tightly. Apply cable-pulling lubricant to the taped end of the fish tape.

(continued next page)

275

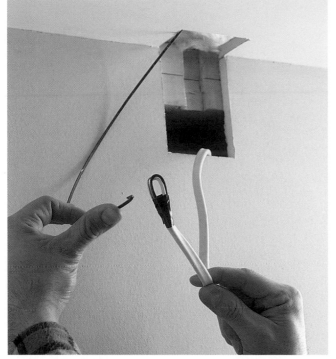

6 Use the fish tape to pull the cable through the remaining access openings until the entire cable run has been completed.

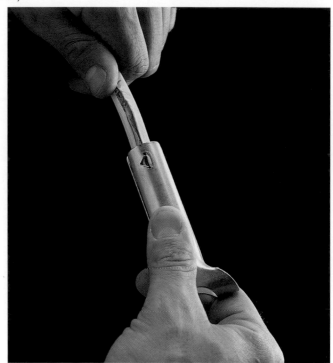

7 Cut cable so at least 18" remain at each end of the cable run, then use a cable ripper to strip back 12" of sheathing from each end.

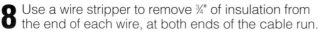

8 Use a wire stripper to remove ¾" of insulation from the end of each wire, at both ends of the cable run.

9 Insert cables into the retrofit box, then tighten the cable clamp. Insert the retrofit box into the cutout, flush against the wall surface. Tighten the mounting screw in the rear of the box. This causes the bracket on the back side of the box to draw the "plaster ears" of the mounting flange tight against the wall surface. Patch any access opening in the wall.

Making Final Connections

Make the final connections for switches, receptacles and fixtures after the rough-in inspection. First, make final connections on recessed fixtures (it is easier to do this before wallboard is installed). Then, finish the work on walls and ceiling, install the cabinets, and make the rest of the final connections. Use the photos on the following pages as a guide for making the final connections. The last step is to connect the circuits at the breaker panel. After all connections are made, your work is ready for the final inspection.

Tools and Materials

Tools: screwdriver, combination tool.

Materials: pigtail wires, wire connectors, tape.

■ Circuits #1 & #2

Two 20-amp, 120-volt small appliance circuits.

- 7 GFCI receptacles

- 20-amp double-pole circuit breaker

Note: In this project, two of the GFCI receptacles are installed in boxes that also contain switches from other circuits.

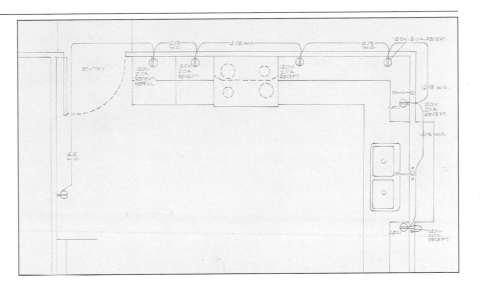

How to Connect Small-appliance Receptacles (two 20-amp circuits fed by one 12/3 cable)

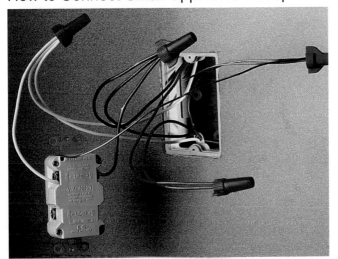

1 At alternate receptacles in the cable run (first, third, etc.), attach a black pigtail to brass screw terminal marked LINE on the receptacle and to black wire from both cables. Connect a white pigtail to a silver screw (LINE) and to both white wires. Connect a grounding pigtail to the grounding screw and to both grounding wires. Connect both red wires together. Tuck wires into box, then attach the receptacle and coverplate.

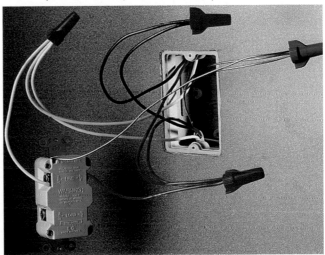

2 At remaining receptacles in the run, attach a red pigtail to a brass screw terminal (LINE) and to red wires from the cables. Attach a white pigtail to a silver screw terminal (LINE) and to both white wires. Connect a grounding pigtail to the grounding screw and to both grounding wires. Connect both black wires together. Tuck wires into box, attach receptacle and coverplate.

How to Install a GFCI & a Disposer Switch

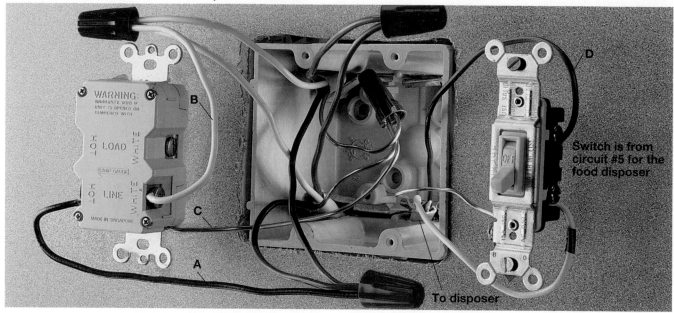

Connect black pigtail (A) to GFCI brass terminal marked LINE, and to black wires from three-wire cables. Attach white pigtail (B) to silver terminal marked LINE, and to white wires from three-wire cables. Attach grounding pigtail (C) to GFCI grounding screw and to grounding wires from three-wire cables. Connect both red wires together. Connect black wire from two-wire cable (D) to one switch terminal. Attach white wire to other terminal, and tag it black indicating it is hot. Attach grounding wire to switch grounding screw. Tuck wires into box; attach switch, receptacle and coverplate.

How to Install a GFCI & Two Switches for Recessed Lights

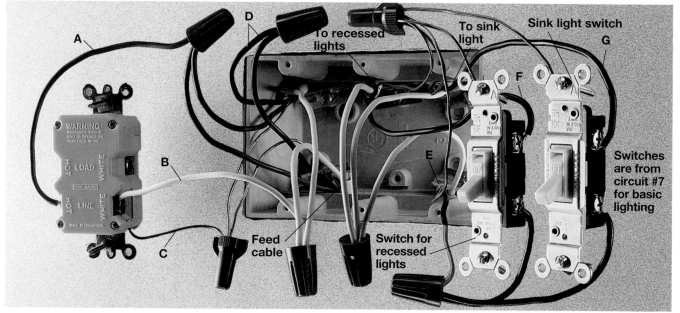

Connect red pigtail (A) to GFCI brass terminal labeled LINE, and to red wires from three-wire cables. Connect white pigtail (B) to silver LINE terminal and to white wires from three-wire cables. Attach grounding pigtail (C) to grounding screw and to grounding wires from three-wire cables. Connect black wires from three-wire cables (D) together. Attach a black pigtail to one screw on each switch and to black wire from two-wire feed cable (E). Connect black wire (F) from the two-wire cable leading to recessed lights to remaining screw on the switch for the recessed lights. Connect black wire (G) from two-wire cable leading to sink light to remaining screw on sink light switch. Connect white wires from all two-wire cables together. Connect pigtails to switch grounding screws and to all grounding wires from two-wire cables. Tuck wires into box; attach switches, receptacle and coverplate.

■ Circuit #3

A 50-amp, 120/240-volt circuit serving the range.

- 50-amp receptacle for range
- 50-amp double-pole circuit breaker

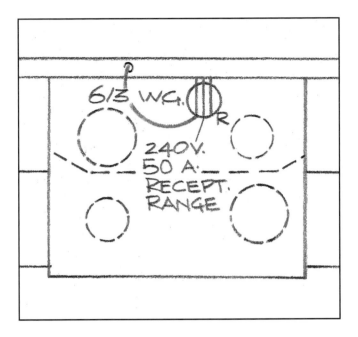

How to Install 120/240 Range Receptacle

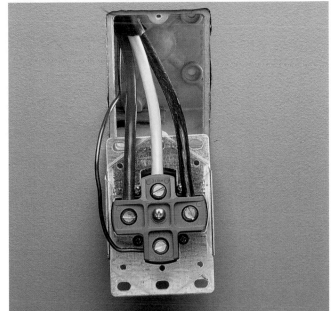

Attach the white wire to the neutral terminal, and the black and red wires to the remaining terminals. Attach the bare copper grounding wire to the grounding screw on the receptacle. Attach receptacle and coverplate.

■ Circuit #4

A 20-amp, 120-volt circuit for the microwave.

- 20-amp duplex receptacle
- 20-amp single-pole circuit breaker

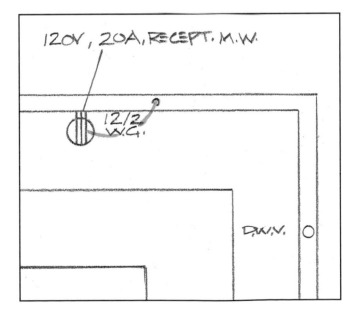

How to Connect Microwave Receptacle

Connect black wire from the cable to a brass screw terminal on the receptacle. Attach the white wire to a silver screw terminal and the grounding wire to the receptacle's grounding screw. Tuck wires into box, then attach the receptacle and the coverplate.

■ Circuit #5

A 15-amp, 120-volt circuit for the food disposer.

- 15-amp duplex receptacle
- Single-pole switch
- 15-amp single-pole circuit breaker

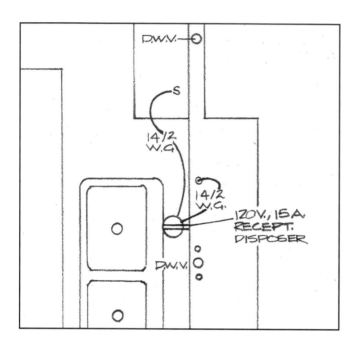

How to Connect Disposer Receptacle

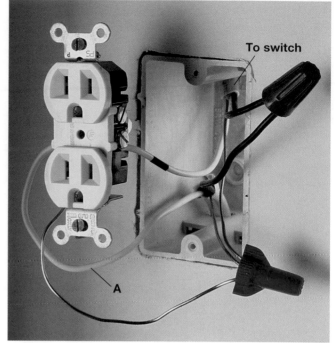

Connect black wires together. Connect white wire from feed cable (A) to silver screw on receptacle. Connect white wire from cable going to the switch to a brass screw terminal on the receptacle, and tag the wire with black indicating it is hot. Attach a grounding pigtail to grounding screw and to both cable grounding wires. Tuck wires into box, then attach receptacle and coverplate.

■ Circuit #6

A 15-amp, 120-volt circuit for the dishwasher.

- 15-amp duplex receptacle
- 15-amp single-pole circuit breaker

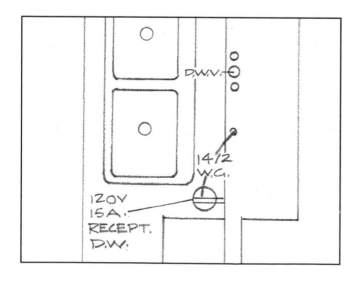

How to Connect Dishwasher Receptacle

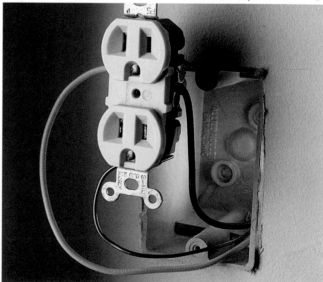

Connect the black wire to a brass screw terminal. Attach the white wire to a silver screw terminal. Connect the grounding wire to the grounding screw. Tuck wires into box, then attach receptacle and coverplate.

▉ Circuit #7

A 15-amp basic lighting circuit serving the kitchen.

- 2 three-way switches with grounding screws
- 2 single-pole switches with grounding screws
- Ceiling light fixture
- 6 recessed light fixtures
- 4 fluorescent under-cabinet fixtures
- 15-amp single-pole circuit breaker

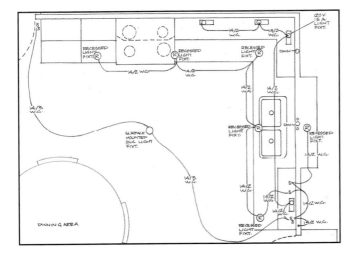

How to Connect First Three-way Switch

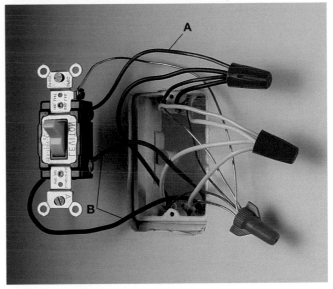

Connect a black pigtail to the common screw on the switch (A) and to the black wires from the two-wire cable. Connect black and red wires from the three-wire cable to traveler terminals (B) on the switch. Connect white wires from all cables entering box together. Attach a grounding pigtail to switch grounding screw and to all grounding wires in box. Tuck wires into box, then attach switch and coverplate.

How to Connect Surface-mounted Ceiling Fixture

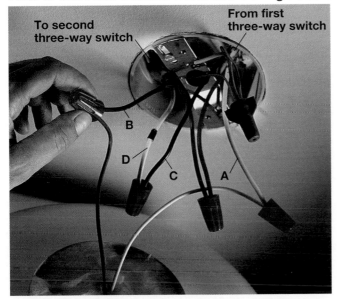

Connect white fixture lead to white wire (A) from first three-way switch. Connect black fixture lead to black wire (B) from second three-way switch. Connect black wire (C) from first switch to white wire (D) from second switch, and tag this white wire with black. Connect red wires from both switches together. Connect all grounding wires together. Mount fixture following manufacturer's instructions.

How to Connect Second Three-way Switch

Connect black wire from the cable to the common screw terminal (A). Connect red wire to one traveler screw terminal. Attach the white wire to the other traveler screw terminal, and tag it with black indicating it is hot. Attach the grounding wire to the grounding screw on the switch. Tuck wires in box, then attach switch and coverplate.

281

Contributors

A special thank you to Mill's Pride for their generosity in providing cabinets for our photography. You can find Mill's Pride cabinets at Home Depot®.

Mill's Pride
800-441-0337
www.millspride.com

Amana Appliances
800-843-0304
www.amana.com

Appliance Outlet Center
952-975-6090

Armstrong World Industries, Inc.
800-233-3823
www.armstrong.com

AM Appliance Group-Asko
800-898-1879
www.askousa.com

Buddy Rhodes Studio, Inc.
877-706-5303
www.buddyrhodes.com

Dal-Tile
214-398-1411
www.daltileproducts.com

DuPont Corian
800-426-7426
www.corian.com

Dura Supreme®
888-711-3872
www.durasupreme.com

Elkay
630-574-8484
www.elkay.com

Expanko, Inc.
800-345-6202
www.expanko.com

Fireclay Tile, Inc.
408-275-1182
www.fireclaytile.com

GE Consumer Products
800-626-2000
www.geappliances.com

Green Mountain Soapstone Corporation, Castleton, VT
800-585-5636
greenmountainsoapstone.com

Hi-Ho Industries, Inc.
Mosaic-Tile Arts
St. Paul, MN
651-649-0992

Hubbardton Forge
802-468-5515
www.vtforge.com

IKEA Home Furnishings
800-434-4532
www.IKEA.com

Jenn-air
800-688-1100
www.jennair.com

John Boos & Co.
217-347-7710
www.johnboos.com

Kitchenaid
800-422-1230
www.kitchenaid.com

Kohler Co.
800-4-Kohler
www.kohler.com

Koechel Peterson & Associates
612-721-5017
www.koechelpeterson.com

Lutron Electronics Company, Inc.
800-523-9466
www.lutron.com

Maytag Appliances
1-888-4-MAYTAG
www.maytag.com

MIRAGE Prefinished hardwood floors
418-227-1181
www.boa-franc.com

Plain & Fancy Custom Cabinetry
800-447-9006
www.plainfancycabinets.com

Plato Woodwork, Inc.
800-328-5924
www.platowoodwork.com

Poggenpohl U.S., Inc.
www.poggenpohl.com

Progress Lighting
864.599.6000
www.progresslighting.com

SieMatic Corporation
800-765-5266
www.siematic.com

Silestone by Cosentino
800-291-1311
www.silestone.com

Sub-Zero Freezer Co., Inc.
800-222-7820
www.subzero.com

Wilsonart International
800-710-8846
www.wilsonart.com

Wolf Appliance Co., LLC.
800-332-9513
www.wolfappliance.com

Photographers

Beateworks, Inc.
LosAngeles, CA
www.beateworks.com
©Micheal Anuad/Beateworks.com: p. 8 (bottom); ©Brad Simmons/Beateworks.com pp. 15 (left), 20 (top); ©Andrea Rugg/Beateworks.com p. 34; Tim-Street Porter/Beateworks.com: pp. 69, 210-11.

Balthazar Korab, Ltd.
Troy, MI
©Balthazar Korab: p. 192

Northlight Photography
Roger Turk
Southworth, WA
www.nlpinc.com
©Northlight Photography: pp. 67 (bottom right), 71 (bottom), 195 (top)

Karen Melvin
Architectural Stock Images, Inc.
Minneapolis, MN
©Karen Melvin: p. 19 (left), and for the following designers: YA Architecture: p4; Rottlund Homes Minnesota: pp 24, 212

Andrea Rugg Photography
Minneapolis, MN
©Andrea Rugg: p. 204 (top)

Pat Sudmeier
©Pat Sudmeier for Plato Woodwork, Inc.: p. 12

Additional Resources

Air-Conditioning and Refrigeration
  Institute
703-524-8800
www.ari.org

American Institute of Architects
800-242-3837
www.aia.org

American Lighting Association
800-274-4484
www.americanlightingassoc.com

American Society of Interior
  Designers
202-546-3480
www.asid.org

Association of Home Appliance
  Manufacturers
202-872-5955
www.aham.org

Center for Inclusive Design &
  Environmental Access
  School of Architecture and
  Planning University of Buffalo
716-829-3485
www.ap.buffalo.edu

Center for Universal Design
  NC State University
919-515-3082
www.dcsign.ncsu.edu

Construction Materials Recycling
  Association
630-548-4510
www.cdrecycling.org

Energy & Environmental Building
  Association
952-881-1098
www.eeba.com

Energy Star
888-762-7937
www.energystar.gov

International Associatioon of
  Lighting Designers
312-527-3677
www.iald.org

International Residential Code
  Book International Conference
  of Building Officials
800-284-4406
www.icbo.com

Kitchen Cabinet Manufacturers
  Association
703-264-1690
www.kcma.org

Lighting Design Lab
877-604-6592
www.lightingdesignlab.com

National Association ot Home
  Builders (NAHB) Research Center
800-638-8556
www.nahbrc.com

National Association of the
  Remodeling Industry (NARI)
847-298-9200
www.nari.org

National Kitchen & Bath Association
  (NKBA)
800-843-6522
www.nkba.org

National Wood Flooring Association
800-422-4556
www.woodfloors.org

Resilient Floor Covering Institute
301-340-8580
www.rfci.com

The Tile Council of America
864-646-8453
www.tileusa.com

U.S. Environmental Protection
  Agency-Indoor Air Quality
www.epa.gov

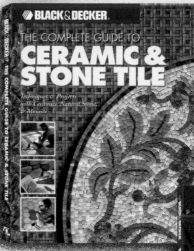
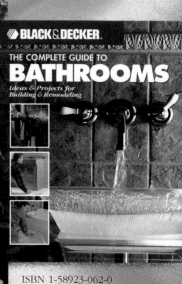